Formalising Natural Languages with Nooj 2014

Formalising Natural Languages with Nooj 2014

Edited by

Johanna Monti,
Max Silberztein,
Mario Monteleone
and Maria Pia di Buono

Selected papers from the NooJ 2014 International Conference
University of Sassari, 3-5 June 2014

Cambridge Scholars Publishing

Formalising Natural Languages with Nooj 2014

Edited by Johanna Monti, Max Silberztein, Mario Monteleone
and Maria Pia di Buono

This book first published 2015

Cambridge Scholars Publishing

Lady Stephenson Library, Newcastle upon Tyne, NE6 2PA, UK

British Library Cataloguing in Publication Data
A catalogue record for this book is available from the British Library

ISBN (10): 1-4438-7558-9
ISBN (13): 978-1-4438-7558-5

TABLE OF CONTENTS

EDITORS' PREFACE

NooJ is a linguistic development environment that provides tools for linguists to construct linguistic resources that formalise a large gamut of linguistic phenomena: typography, orthography, lexicons for simple words, multiword units and discontinuous expressions, inflectional and derivational morphology, local, structural and transformational syntax, and semantics.

For each resource that linguists create, NooJ provides parsers that can apply it to any corpus of texts in order to extract examples or counter-examples, to annotate matching sequences, to perform statistical analyses etc. NooJ also contains generators that can produce the texts that these linguistic resources describe, as well as serving as a rich toolbox that allows linguists to construct, maintain, test, debug, accumulate and reuse linguistic resources.

For each elementary linguistic phenomenon to be described, NooJ proposes a set of computational formalisms, the power of which ranges from very efficient finite-state automata to very powerful Turing machines. This makes NooJ's approach different from most other computational linguistic tools that typically offer a unique formalism to their users.

Since its first release in 2002, NooJ has been enhanced with new features every year. Linguists, researchers in Social Sciences and more generally all professionals who analyse texts have contributed to its development and participated in the annual NooJ conference. In 2013, a new version for NooJ was released, based on the JAVA technology and available to all as an open source GPL project. Moreover, several private companies are now using NooJ to construct business applications in several domains, from Business Intelligence to Opinion Analysis.

The present volume contains 22 articles selected from the 53 papers presented at the International NooJ 2014 Conference, which was held from June 2nd to 4th at the University of Sassari in Sardinia (Italy). These articles are organised in three parts: "Vocabulary and Morphology" containing seven articles; "Syntax and Semantics" containing seven articles; "NooJ Applications" containing eight articles.

The articles in the first part involve the construction of dictionaries for simple words, multiword units as well as the development of morphological grammars:

— Max Silberztein's article "The DEM and the LVF dictionaries for NooJ" gives a glimpse at how 'ideal' NooJ electronic dictionaries will look: he presents the recently released linguistic DEM and LVF dictionaries, and shows what work will have to be done in order to convert them into NooJ electronic dictionaries.
— Hajer Cheikhrouhou's article "The Formalization of Movement Verbs for Automatic Translation using NooJ Platform" shows the author's effort to add an Arabic translation to the movement verbs described in the LVF dictionary and the application of the resulting bilingual electronic dictionary to machine translation.
— Maximiliano Duran's article "Morphological and Syntactic Grammars for the Recognition of Verbal Lemmas in Quechua" presents an electronic dictionary for verbs in Quechua associated with a very powerful morphological engine.
— Serena Pelosi and Alessandro Maisto's article "A Lexicon-Based Approach to Sentiment Analysis. The Italian Module for NooJ" presents a set of specialised dictionaries aimed at the automatic recognition of sentiments expressed in Italian texts.
— Zoe Gavriilidou, Lena Papdopoulou and Elina Chatjipapa's article "<Material> Adjectives in Greek NooJ Module" describes the construction of a specialised electronic dictionary.
— Matea Srebacic, Krešimir Šojat and Božo Bekavac's article "Croatian Derivational Patterns in NooJ" shows how the authors have solved the problem of linking a lexical entry to a large number of morphological forms in Croatian.
— Mario Monteleone and Maria Pia Di Buono's article "The Inflection of Italian Pronominal Verbs" describes an elegant solution to the formalisation of the conjugation of pronominal verbs in Italian.

The articles in the second part involve the construction of syntactic and semantic grammars:

— Annibale Elia and Alberto Maria Langella's article "Semantic Role Labelling with NooJ: Communication Predicates in Italian" shows a set of linguistic lexical and syntactic resources that can be used to automatically annotate expressions of communication in Italian texts.
— Valerie Collec-Clerc's article "Recognition of Honorific Passive Verbal Form in Japanese with NooJ" shows a set of syntactic grammars capable of identifying Honorific Passive Forms in Japanese texts.

— Mourad Aouini's article "A NooJ Module for Named Entity Recognition in Middle French Texts" presents a set of grammars used to identify named entities in a corpus of Middle French texts.
— Azeddine Rhazi's article "Morpho-syntaxical based recognition of Arabic MWUs with NooJ" presents a set of grammars used to identify and extract Arabic multiword units from texts.
— Lena Papadopoulou's article "Local Grammars for Pragmatemes in NooJ" presents a set of syntactic grammars that recognise pragmatemes in Greek texts.
— Tatsiana Okrut, Yuras Hetsevich, Boris Lobanov and Yauheniya Yakubovich's article "Resources for Identification of Cues with Author's Text Insertions in Belarusian and Russian Electronic Texts" presents a set of linguistic resources that can be used to identify cues in Belarusian and in Russian texts.
— Simona Messina and Alberto Maria Langella's article "Paraphrases V↔N↔A in one Class of Psychological Predicates" presents a set of lexical and syntactic grammars that can be used to produce paraphrases of psychological predicates.

The articles in the third part describe various NLP applications based on the use of NooJ's linguistic engine:

— Božo Bekavac, Kristina Kocijan and Marko Tadić's article "Near Language Identification Using NooJ" shows how to automatise NooJ to automatically identify the language of a text.
— Hayet Ben Ali, Hela Fehri and Abdelmajid Ben Hamadou's article "Translating Arabic Relative Clauses into English using NooJ Platform" shows an interesting Machine Translation application for NooJ, and compares its results with the ones produced by Google Translate.
— Alena Skopinava, Yuras Hetsevich and Julia Borodina's article "Converting Quantitative Expressions with Measurement Units into an Orthographic Form, and Convenient Monitoring Methods for Belarusian" presents an automatic application for Belarusian texts that converts quantitative expressions into an orthographic form.
— Julia Frigière and Sandrine Fuentes' article "Pedagogical Use of NooJ dealing with French as a Foreign Language" shows how the authors use NooJ as a Lab tool to teach French at the Autonomous University of Barcelona.
— Kristina Kocijan and Marko Požega's article "Building Family Trees with NooJ" presents a series of complex grammars that can

automatically identify family relations of persons described in texts.

— Johanna Monti, Mario Monteleone and Maria Pia di Buono's article "A Knowledge-Based CLIR Model for Specific Domain Collections" presents the CLIR model and how it can be used to automatically collect and classify texts.

— Maria Pia di Buono and Mario Monteleone's article "Knowledge Management and Extraction from Cultural Heritage Repositories" presents an application that can mine texts on cultural heritage in order to automatically build a knowledge base of the domain.

— Slim Mesfar and Essia Bessaies' article "Automatic Document Classification and Event Extraction in Standard Arabic" shows a set of semantic grammars capable of identifying events in Arabic texts, and how this can be used to automatically classify documents.

This volume should be of interest to all users of the NooJ software because it presents the latest development of the software as well as its latest linguistic resources. To date, there are NooJ modules available for over 50 languages; more than 3,000 copies of NooJ are downloaded each year.

Linguists as well as Computational Linguists who work on Arabic, Belarusian, English, French, Greek, Italian, Japanese, Quechua, or Russian will find in advanced, up-to-the-minute linguistic studies for these languages this volume.

We think that the reader will appreciate the importance of this volume, both for the intrinsic value of each linguistic formalisation and the underlying methodology, as well as for the potential for developing NLP applications along with linguistic-based corpus processors in the Social Sciences.

The Editors

PART I:

VOCABULARY AND MORPHOLOGY

THE DEM AND LVF DICTIONARIES IN NOOJ

MAX SILBERZTEIN

Abstract

We have integrated Jean Dubois and Françoise Dubois-Charlier's DEM and LVF dictionaries into the NooJ linguistic software. We discuss their applications for Natural Language Processing applications.

Introduction

The NooJ project is aimed at constructing a large-coverage formalised description of natural languages. The project has two parts: (1) to represent the standard vocabulary of languages and (2) to describe how to combine the elements of the vocabulary in order to construct phrases, sentences and, more generally, to carry complex meaning. The vocabulary is a finite set of units called *Atomic Linguistic Units* (or ALUs) and is represented by an Electronic Dictionary.

Several Electronic Dictionaries exist for the vocabulary of French. For example, the Lexicon-Grammar of Verbs, developed at the LADL laboratory (*Laboratoire d'Automatique Documentaire et Linguistique*), describes the syntactic properties of over 12,000 verbs of standard French vocabulary. Entries that share a number of properties are grouped into tables; for instance, intransitive verbs (structure $\mathbf{N_0}$ **V**) are stored in Tables 31x, direct transitive verbs (structure $\mathbf{N_0}$ **V** $\mathbf{N_1}$) are stored in Tables 4, 6 and 32x, etc.[1] Following the same model, other elements of the vocabulary have been described: there are Lexicon-Grammar tables for adjectives, adverbs, conjunctions, support-verbs and frozen expressions, and there are also Lexicon-Grammar tables for languages other than French[2].

Lexicon-Grammars are exhaustive and very precise. However, they are not autonomous linguistic resources, so automatic parsers cannot use them to perform any type of linguistic analysis. In particular, Lexicon-Grammars do not contain the minimal orthographical or morphological

[1](Leclère 1990) presents the classification of the verbs in the Lexicon-Grammar.

[2](Leclère 1998) lists works on various lexicon-grammars.

information[3] necessary to perform even a basic lexical analysis of texts. The LADL also developed the DELA[4] system of Electronic Dictionaries, which has been used successfully to parse large corpora of texts[5]. The DELA covers the standard vocabulary, but it only contains morphological information, more precisely, inflectional morphology[6].

The DELA system of dictionaries

The DELA has been designed to list all the elements of standard French vocabulary and describe their inflectional morphology. Its main components are:

— the DELAS dictionary which describes the inflection of simple words
— the DELAC dictionary which describes the inflection of multiword units

In these two electronic dictionaries, each lexical entry is associated with a series of codes that represent its morpho-syntactic properties. For instance, the following is a typical lexical entry from the DELAS[7] (cf. Courtois, 1990):

abaisser,V3+tr+z1

The lexical entry *abaisser* (to lower something) is a verb (code **V**) that conjugates according to paradigm **V3** (the same paradigm as *aimer*); it is a transitive verb (**+tr**) and it belongs to basic French vocabulary (**+z1**). The DELAS dictionary contains approximately 130,000 entries. Following is a lexical entry from the DELAC (cf. Silberztein 1990):

---

[3]Several tables of the lexicon-grammar contain verbs that are semantically similar, but they also contain verbs that have very different meanings. (Courtois, 1990) poses the problem of merging the DELAS and the lexicon-grammar; (Silberztein 1990) integrated in the DELAC dictionary a list of adverbs described in several lexicon-grammar tables, but these projects have not been pursued.
[4]Cf. (Courtois, Silberztein Ed. 1990).
[5]Cf. (Silberztein 1993).
[6]There are other electronic dictionaries that are similar to the DELA dictionary. In particular, the DM dictionary, included in NooJ, combines lexical entries from the DELAS and from the Morphalou dictionaries, cf. (Trouilleux 2012).
[7]Blandine Courtois constructed the DELAS dictionary (*Dictionnaire Electronique du LADL pour les mots Simples*), with some help from Jean Dubois.

pomme de terre,N+NDN+Conc+z1

The lexical entry *pomme de terre* (potato) is a noun (code **N)**; its structure is **NDN** (Noun *de* Noun). It represents a concrete noun (**+Conc**) and belongs to the basic French vocabulary (**+z1**). The DELAC dictionary contains over 300,000 lexical entries, most of which are compound nouns. Thanks to the description of the inflectional paradigm of each entry in the DELAS and the DELAC, the INTEX software[8] could automatically produce the list of all the corresponding forms for each entry of these two dictionaries: the DELAF contains the list of all the inflected forms that correspond to entries of the DELAS dictionary, whereas the DELACF contains the list of all the inflected forms that correspond to DELAC dictionary entries. The DELA system of electronic dictionaries still constitutes, over twenty years later, a reference among the electronic dictionaries used by NLP applications. However, it does not satisfy some of the requirements of the NooJ linguistic project.

From the DELA to NooJ

The first problem with the DELA is that it was not designed to be an autonomous linguistic resource, but rather to complement the Lexicon-Grammars. But these two databases cannot be merged, as they describe lexical entries and properties that are not comparable. For instance, in the DELAS dictionary, there are two lexical entries for the verb *voler*:

voler,V3
voler,V3U

The inflectional code **V3** is used to produce all the conjugated forms of the verb *voler*, including the four forms of the past participle *volé, volée, volés, volées* (eg in *Les fleurs que tu as volées*). The code **V3U** is used to produce only one form for the past participle: *volé* (eg *L'avion a volé au dessus de la Sibérie*). The lexical entry associated with the code **V3** corresponds to three entries of the Lexicon-Grammar:

Luc vole un cendrier à Marie. Le commerçant vole Luc de 10 euros.
Tu ne l'as pas volée !

[8]Cf. http://intex.univ-fcomte.fr. (Silberztein 1993) presents the DELA and the INTEX software. INTEX has been used as a linguistic tool as well as the linguistic engine of several Natural Linguistic Processing software applications, cf. for instance (Fairon Ed. 1999).

The lexical entry associated with the code **V3U** corresponds to two other entries of the Lexicon-Grammar:

L'avion vole vers Paris. La porte vole en éclats.

Two lexical entries in the DELAS correspond to five lexical entries in the Lexicon-Grammar. This situation is general for all levels of the linguistic description. For instance, the DELAS dictionary contains over 1,000 artefacts that are components of multiword units, which are listed independently in the DELAC dictionary (such as '*parce*' in *parce que*). Some entries of the DELAC are also listed in Lexicon-Grammar tables for adverbs as well as in the tables for conjunctions, but there is no way to know if they represent the same ALU, or if they represent different meanings ie different ALUs. There is no direct way to connect frozen expressions listed in the Lexicon-Grammar to their components listed in a DELA-type dictionary, etc.

The NooJ project requires a new type of electronic dictionary, the goal of which is to exhaustively formalise the vocabulary of the language. In order to formalise the vocabulary of a language, we need an electronic dictionary in which (1) all ALUs (simple words, multiword units and expressions) are described in a unified way, (2) there is an explicit link between all orthographical, morphological, syntactic and semantic properties for each lexical entry, and (3) there is an equivalence between ALUs and lexical entries such as one ALU = one lexical entry. NooJ provides linguists with the formal tools and methodology necessary for this formalisation. The dictionaries **DEM** (*Dictionnaire Electronique des Mots*)[9] and **LVF** (*Les Verbes Français*)[10] from Dubois & Dubois-Charlier could become the basis of an ideal electronic dictionary for NooJ.[11]

The DEM dictionary

The DEM dictionary (*Dictionnaire Électronique des Mots*) contains 145,135 entries in all morpho-syntactic categories.

[9]Cf. (Dubois 2010).
[10]Cf. (Dubois 1997).
[11]Cf. (Sabatier 2013).

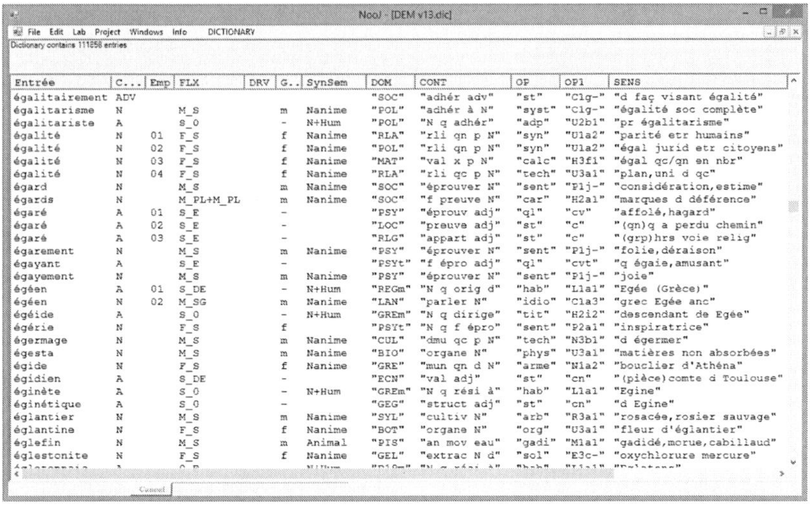

Entrée	C...	Emp	FLX	DRV	G..	SynSem	DOM	CONT	OP	OP1	SENS
égalitairement	ADV						"SOC"	"adhér adv"	"st"	"C1g-"	"d faç visant égalité"
égalitarisme	N		M_S		m	Nanime	"POL"	"adhér à N"	"syst"	"C1g-"	"égalité soc complète"
égalitariste	A		S_0		-	N+Hum	"POL"	"N q adhér"	"adp"	"U2b1"	"pr égalitarisme"
égalité	N	01	F_S		f	Nanime	"RLA"	"rli qn p N"	"syn"	"U1a2"	"parité etr humains"
égalité	N	02	F_S		f	Nanime	"POL"	"rli qn p N"	"syn"	"U1a2"	"égal jurid etr citoyens"
égalité	N	03	F_S		f	Nanime	"MAT"	"val x p N"	"calc"	"H3f1"	"égal qc/qn en nbr"
égalité	N	04	F_S		f	Nanime	"RLA"	"rli qc p N"	"tech"	"U3a1"	"plan,uni d qc"
égard	N		M_S		m	Nanime	"SOC"	"éprouver N"	"sent"	"P1j-"	"considération,estime"
égards	N		M_PL+M_PL		m	Nanime	"SOC"	"f preuve N"	"car"	"H2a1"	"marques d déférence"
égaré	A	01	S_E		-		"PSY"	"éprouv adj"	"ql"	"cv"	"affolé,hagard"
égaré	A	02	S_E		-		"LOC"	"preuve adj"	"st"	"c"	"(qn)q a perdu chemin"
égaré	A	03	S_E		-		"RLG"	"appart adj"	"st"	"c"	"(grp)hrs voie relig"
égarement	N		M_S		m	Nanime	"PSY"	"éprouver N"	"sent"	"P1j-"	"folie,déraison"
égayant	A		S_E		-		"PSYt"	"f épro adj"	"ql"	"cvt"	"q égaie,amusant"
égayement	N		M_S		m	Nanime	"PSY"	"éprouver N"	"sent"	"P1j-"	"joie"
égéen	A	01	S_DE		-	N+Hum	"REGm"	"N q orig d"	"hab"	"L1a1"	"Egée (Grèce)"
égéen	N	02	M_SG		m	Nanime	"LAN"	"parler N"	"idio"	"C1a3"	"grec Egée anc"
égéide	A		S_0		-	N+Hum	"GREm"	"N q dirige"	"tit"	"H2i2"	"descendant de Egée"
égérie	N		F_S		f		"PSYt"	"N q f épro"	"sent"	"P2a1"	"inspiratrice"
égermage	N		M_S		m	Nanime	"CUL"	"dmu qc p N"	"tech"	"N3b1"	"d égermer"
égesta	N		M_S		m	Nanime	"BIO"	"organe N"	"phys"	"U3a1"	"matières non absorbées"
égide	N		F_S		f	Nanime	"GRE"	"mun qn d N"	"arme"	"N1a2"	"bouclier d'Athéna"
égidien	A		S_DE		-		"ECN"	"val adj"	"st"	"cn"	"(pièce)comte d Toulouse"
éginète	A		S_0		-	N+Hum	"GREm"	"N q rési à"	"hab"	"L1a1"	"Egine"
éginétique	A		S_0		-		"GEG"	"struct adj"	"st"	"cn"	"d Egine"
églantier	N		M_S		m	Nanime	"SYL"	"cultiv N"	"arb"	"R3a1"	"rosacée,rosier sauvage"
églantine	N		F_S		f	Nanime	"BOT"	"organe N"	"org"	"U3a1"	"fleur d'églantier"
églefin	N		M_S		m	Animal	"PIS"	"an mov eau"	"gadi"	"M1a1"	"gadidé,morue,cabillaud"
églestonite	N		F_S		f	Nanime	"GEL"	"extrac N d"	"sol"	"E3c-"	"oxychlorure mercure"

Figure 1 – The DEM dictionary

Each lexical entry is associated with a dozen properties, including: [12]

CAT (syntactic category) for instance Adverb, Verb, etc.
SENSE: each meaning is represented as a different lexical entry
DOMAIN: semantic domain of the term.
OPER: Semantic prototypical scheme of the term.
SCLASS: semantic class of the term.

Note that, as opposed to the DELA or the Lexicon-Grammar dictionaries, CAT may have more than one value, for instance when one ALU can be used both as a Noun and as an Adjective, eg *artiste*. This possibility is crucial if we want to satisfy the constraint '1 ALU = 1 lexical entry'. The SENSE, DOMAIN and SCLASS properties ensure that we always have '1 ALU= 1 lexical entry'.

The LVF Dictionary

The LVF dictionary (*Les Verbes Français*) contains 25,609 verbal entries.

[12] I translate each property code into English for better clarity.

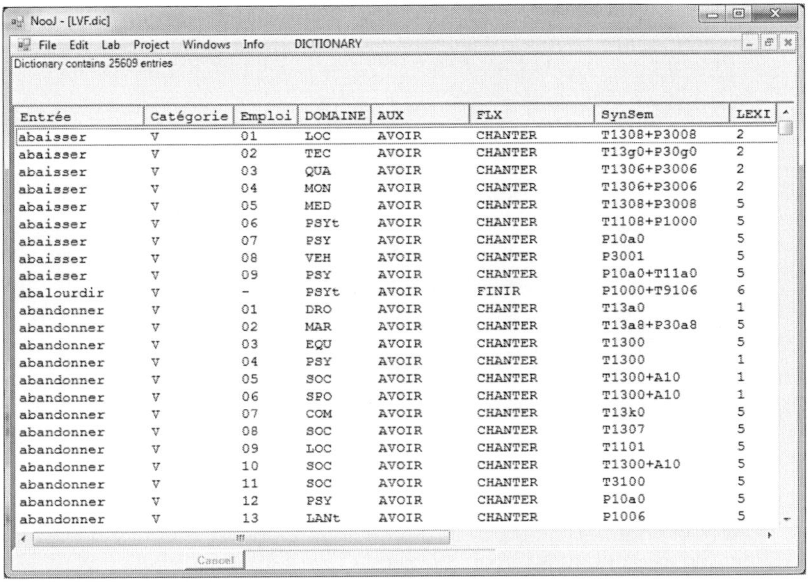

Entrée	Catégorie	Emploi	DOMAINE	AUX	FLX	SynSem	LEXI
abaisser	V	01	LOC	AVOIR	CHANTER	T1308+P3008	2
abaisser	V	02	TEC	AVOIR	CHANTER	T13g0+P30g0	2
abaisser	V	03	QUA	AVOIR	CHANTER	T1306+P3006	2
abaisser	V	04	MON	AVOIR	CHANTER	T1306+P3006	2
abaisser	V	05	MED	AVOIR	CHANTER	T1308+P3008	5
abaisser	V	06	PSYt	AVOIR	CHANTER	T1108+P1000	5
abaisser	V	07	PSY	AVOIR	CHANTER	P10a0	5
abaisser	V	08	VEH	AVOIR	CHANTER	P3001	5
abaisser	V	09	PSY	AVOIR	CHANTER	P10a0+T11a0	5
abalourdir	V	-	PSYt	AVOIR	FINIR	P1000+T9106	6
abandonner	V	01	DRO	AVOIR	CHANTER	T13a0	1
abandonner	V	02	MAR	AVOIR	CHANTER	T13a8+P30a8	5
abandonner	V	03	EQU	AVOIR	CHANTER	T1300	5
abandonner	V	04	PSY	AVOIR	CHANTER	T1300	1
abandonner	V	05	SOC	AVOIR	CHANTER	T1300+A10	1
abandonner	V	06	SPO	AVOIR	CHANTER	T1300+A10	1
abandonner	V	07	COM	AVOIR	CHANTER	T13k0	5
abandonner	V	08	SOC	AVOIR	CHANTER	T1307	5
abandonner	V	09	LOC	AVOIR	CHANTER	T1101	5
abandonner	V	10	SOC	AVOIR	CHANTER	T1300+A10	5
abandonner	V	11	SOC	AVOIR	CHANTER	T3100	5
abandonner	V	12	PSY	AVOIR	CHANTER	P10a0	5
abandonner	V	13	LANt	AVOIR	CHANTER	P1006	5

Figure 2 – The LVF dictionary

Each entry of the LVF dictionary is associated with 10 properties, including:

SENSE: each meaning is represented as a different lexical entry
DOMAIN: semantic domain for the verb.
OPER: semantic prototypical scheme of the verb.
SCLASS: semantic class of the verb.
CONJUGATION: the conjugation paradigm for the verb.
STRUCTURE: one or more syntactic structures for the verb.
DERIVATION: potential derivational paradigms for the verb.

The fact that each verbal entry is associated with inflectional, derivational, syntactic and semantic information imposes the use of various processing tools, which is compatible with the NooJ approach, but not with 'mono-formalism' approaches. Here is for instance a lexical entry for the NooJ dictionary based on the DEM and LVF dictionaries:

abaisser,
V+SENSE=01+DOMAIN=LOC+AUX=AVOIR+FLX=CHANTER
+SCLASS=T3c+T1308+P3008+LEVEL=2+DRV=BASE1
+DRV=ABLE+DRV=MENT+DRV=EUR+OPER='r/d bas qc'

abaisser is a verb (V); the lexical entry corresponds to sense #1 (SENSE=01); its semantic domain is 'Locative' (DOMAIN=LOC); its semantic class is 'T3c'; its semantic analysis is 'r/d bas qc' (make something low). The verb is conjugated according to the paradigm 'CHANTER' and is conjugated with auxiliary verb *avoir* (AUX=AVOIR). It accepts the two following syntactic structures: T3108 (Human Subject + Verb + Non-animated Object + Instrumental Complement) and P3008 (Non-animated Subject + Pronominal Verb + Instrumental Complement). The verb accepts three derivations: the adjective *abaissable* (DRV=ABLE), the noun *abaissement* (DRV=MENT) and the noun *abaisseur* (DRV=EUR). The verb is associated with the base noun *abaisse*. It belongs to the basic French vocabulary (LEXI=2).

The reader will appreciate the huge qualitative difference with the DELA dictionaries. As an example, I now present how I used the **STRUCTURE** syntactic property in the LVF[13] to construct a new type of search engine capable of finding specific meanings for a given verb.

The STRUCTURE property

Each of the lexical entries of the LVF dictionary is associated with one or more syntactic structures, among 318 different ones[14], that I have described using four generic grammars: A (intransitive structure), N (indirect transitive structure), P (pronominal structure), and T (direct transitive structure). Each of the A, N, P and T structures has been implemented by a corresponding NooJ grammar.

Remember that when a verb has more than one meaning, each of its meanings is listed as a separate entry, and is associated with its syntactic structures. For instance, consider the five senses for the verb *abriter* as described in the LVF dictionary:

[13](Silberztein 2010) presents a more detailed description of the process of adapting the LVF dictionary so that NooJ parsers can process its information.

[14](François, Le Pesant, Leeman 2007) present the semantic classification of the LVF dictionary in detail.

abriter #1 (T11b8, P10b8): *Luc abrite Léa de la pluie avec son parapluie*
 'Luc protects Lea from the rain with his umbrella'
abriter #2 (T1101, P1001): *Luc abrite des réfugiés chez lui*
 'Luc gives shelter to refugees'
abriter #3 (T3100): *Cet immeuble abrite les services du Ministère de l'éducation*
 'This building hosts the Minister of Education'
abriter #4 (P10b1): *Luc s'abrite des ennuis derrière Léa*
 'Luc hides from trouble behind Lea'
abriter #5 (T13b8): *Luc abrite le port des vagues avec des digues*
 'Luc shields the harbour from the waves with a seawall'

Thanks to the LVF dictionary as well as the four grammars A, N, P and T, NooJ can extract all the sentences from a corpus of texts that contain a specific structure for a given verb, and hence identify its specific meaning. For instance, by applying grammar T to a corpus constituted by over 7,000 articles of the newspaper *Le Monde diplomatique*, NooJ produces the following concordance:

centre de Pristina	, il abritait plusieurs partis politiques des minorités ethniques	. L'attentat visait
selon vous, Monsieur	, le bâtiment qui abrite la plus grande quantité de rêves	? L'école? Le
chimiques et bactériologiq...	Ce pays abrite le plus grand réseau mondial de drogue	, et ses banques
froideur presque menaçante	, il abrite des banques	et un inévitable
de produits nucléaires...	Chaque pays abrite ses milieux criminels	. Les principales orga
journée pour 5 livres (6)	: elle abrite un cirque	(sans animaux), un
Alexandra et Lenasia	, elle abrite deux millions cinq cent mille personnes	. Un grand bidonville
'Etat de droit.	Le Cambodge abrite une société structurée	non pas en
ses contradictions internes.	Ce pays montagneux abrite un grand nombre de groupes ethniques	, y compris parmi
terre de Flandre	. la ville qui abrite la Commission européenne	suscite bien des

Figure 3 – Occurrences of the verb *abriter* used in a direct transitive structure

We find occurrences of sense #3 of the verb *abriter*, whereas senses #1, #2 and #5 are excluded since they require prepositional complements that are not present in the sentences[15]. In the same way, if we apply grammar P, NooJ produces the following concordance:

[15]The N, P and T grammars contain the same reference to prepositional noun phrases. In the original LVF dictionary, the 'b' character in structure codes T11b8 and P10b8 represents the *de* preposition.

première fois aussi	, le premier ministre israélien ne s'abrita pas derrière les slogans traditionnels	- "Jérusalem ui
désarmé. En Europe	, il s'abrite derrière les pressions exercées	par le Luxemb(
la corruption endémique.	Les responsables politiques s'abritent derrière le carcan traditionnel	des "valeurs a
prend pas parti.	Il s'abrite derrière sa tâche d'homme	de théâtre qui
dissimuler le fond	, il s'abrite en général derrière des considérations de forme,	et remet tout
système financier international.	Il s'abrite derrière le contentieux colonial,	dont il exige
à visage découvert	, ils s'abritent derrière des notables traditionnels	qui les utilisent

Figure 4 – Occurrences of the verb *abriter* in a pronominal structure

Here, we find occurrences of sense #2, whereas senses #1 and senses 4 are excluded because there is no complement introduced by the preposition *de*. Therefore, NooJ can extract sentences from a corpus of texts that contain a specific meaning for a verb: no other search engine or linguistic corpus processor can perform this type of operation. This application constitutes qualitative progress in corpus linguistics.

Distribution Selection

The STRUCTURE code includes the distributional class of each verb argument. For instance, the two first digits correspond to the subject and to the object complement of the verb: '1' = Human; '3' = Thing. The last character corresponds to the specific adverbial complement (the '*circonstant*'): '0' = no complement, '1' = locative complement, '8' = instrumental complement. The distributional selection described in the LVF dictionary is useful in order to distinguish between different meanings of a given verb, and they can be used to link verbs to the nouns that are described in the DEM dictionary. For instance, in order to distinguish between sense #2 and sense #3 of the verb *abriter*, we can use the fact that sense #2 requires a Human subject, whereas sense #3 requires a locative subject. However, adding distribution selection constraints in the four generic grammars would stop NooJ from finding a number of occurrences for each meaning, for several reasons:

— Metonymies (which are frequent) would be systematically rejected. For instance, the French word ambassade (embassy) is described in the DEM dictionary as a non-human noun. In consequence, sentences such as 'The embassy invited the Prime Minister' would not be recognised, since the word 'embassy' here plays the role of a Human noun.

— More generally, a large number of noun phrases that are 'lexically non-human' in fact play the role of humans in certain contexts. For instance, the sentence Luc achète le silence du fonctionnaire (Luc buys the government employee's silence) is associated with the structure T1106 (object complement = Human); however the noun silence cannot be described as Human in the DEM dictionary.

Inversely, a number of human noun phrases can acquire the function of a thing, depending on their context. For instance, sense #1 of the verb *agacer* in *Ces nouvelles agacent Luc* (this news bothers Luc) is associated with the structure code T3100 (subject = thing). But it is totally possible to have a human noun as a subject in this sentence[16], eg in *Léa agace Luc* (Lea bothers Luc). In other words, it is possible to use the distribution selection information provided in the LVF dictionary, linked with the corresponding distributional class described in the DEM dictionary: the resulting concordance would be more precise, but at the expense of a much lower recall. I believe that this is still the right approach: sentences that have been 'rightfully' rejected by the NooJ grammars should be the objects of some linguistic computation capable of solving metonymies and metaphors.

Conclusion

Our first experiments show how rich the DEM and the LVF dictionaries are. Using the information stored in these two dictionaries can greatly enhance the precision of NLP software applications, by shifting from 'word-based' to 'sense-aware' search engines. Transforming and enriching these two dictionaries in order to construct the electronic dictionary that will formalise the French vocabulary would probably take several years for a small team of linguists:

— We will need to fully merge these two dictionaries. Most verbs described in the DEM are also described in the LVF; some verbs in DEM are not described in the LVF dictionary. A number of nouns and adjectives are represented both as independent entries in the DEM and as derived from a verbal entry in the LVF.
— The entries of the DEM dictionary have no inflectional or derivational description. We will have to add both descriptions.
— Several codes in the DEM and LVF dictionaries encode combinations of properties that must be properly untangled and formalised. For instance, property CAT in the DEM represents three types of information: the morpho-syntactic category (eg

[16](Gross 1975) uses the 'unrestricted' category to describe complements that can accept any noun, such as the subject of sentence: *(Luc | This country | The table | The dog | This event | The rain | The fact that she came) bothers Lea.*

Noun), the gender (eg Feminine) and the semantic class (eg Human)[17].

— We will need to add to these dictionaries multiword units, frozen expressions as well as Support Verb/Predicative Noun combinations[18].

References

Courtois, Blandine. 1990. Un système de dictionnaires électroniques pour les mots simples du français. In *Dictionnaires électroniques du français*, Courtois, Silberztein Eds. Langue française n° 87, pp. 5-10. Larousse : Paris.

Courtois, Blandine and Max Silberztein Éds. 1990. Les dictionnaires électroniques. Langue française n° 87. Paris : Larousse.

Dubois, Jean and Françoise Dubois-Charlier. 1997. Les verbes français.

—. 2010. La combinatoire lexico-syntaxique dans le Dictionnaire électronique des mots. In *Langages 179-180.* Armand Collin : Paris, pp. 31-56.

Fairon, Cédric éd. 1999. Analyse lexicale et syntaxique : le système INTEX. Lingvisticae Investigationes, tome XXII: 1998-1999. John Benjamins Publishing Company: Amsterdam.

François, Jacques, Denis Le Pesant, and Danielle Leeman Eds. 2007. Le classement syntactico-sémantique des verbes français. Langue française n° 153. Armand Colin : Paris.

Gross, Maurice. 1975. *Méthodes en syntaxe*. Hermann : Paris.

—. 1977. Grammaire transformationnelle du français, 2 : Syntaxe du nom. Larousse : Paris.

Leclère, Christian. 1990. Organisation du lexique-grammaire des verbes français. In *Dictionnaires électroniques du français*, Courtois, Silberztein Eds. Langue française no 87, pp. 104-111. Larousse : Paris.

[17]I have refined the inflectional description of the LVF dictionary because certain conjugation paradigms of LVF had to be separated into several different NooJ paradigms; conversely, several different conjugation paradigms could be unified thanks to the use of NooJ 'intelligent' morphological operators, cf. (Silberztein 2010b). Paradigms in LVF did not take defective or impersonal conjugations into account: I had to add the corresponding paradigms in NooJ.

[18]A large number of frozen expressions and Support verb/Predicative nouns combinations have been listed and described in Lexicon-Grammars, but, here too, we will need to add missing properties in order to import them into the NooJ platform.

—. 1998. Travaux récents en lexique-grammaire. Travaux de linguistique n°37. Rijksuniversiteit van Gent Ed. p 191

Sabatier, Paul and Denis Le Pesant. 2013. Les dictionnaires électroniques de Jean Dubois et Françoise Dubois-Charlier et leur exploitation en TAL. In *Ressources Lexicales, Linguisticae Investigationes Supplementa* 30. John Benjamins Publishing Company : Amsterdam.

Silberztein, Max. 1990. Le dictionnaire électronique des mots composés. In *Dictionnaires électroniques du français*, Courtois, Silberztein Eds. Langue française n° 87, pp. 11-22. Larousse : Paris.

—. 1993. Dictionnaires électroniques et analyse automatique de textes : le système INTEX. Masson : Paris.

—. 2004. Une description formalisée des déterminants français. In *Hommage à la mémoire de Maurice Gross*. Linguisticae Investigationes, E. Laporte, C. Leclère, M. Piot, M. Silberztein Eds. pp. 589-600.

—. 2005. NooJ Dictionaries. In *Proceedings of the 2nd Language and Technology Conference*. Poznan.

—. 2010. La formalisation du dictionnaire LVF avec NooJ et ses applications pour l'analyse automatique de corpus. In *Théorie, empirie, exploitation : l'exemple des travaux de Jean Dubois sur les verbes français*. Langages n° 179-180, Danielle Leeman, Paul Sabatier Eds.

Trouilleux, François. 2012. A New French Dictionary for NooJ : le DM. In *Selected papers from the 2011 International NooJ Conference*. Cambridge Scholar Publishing : Newcastle.

THE FORMALISATION OF MOVEMENT VERBS FOR AUTOMATIC TRANSLATION USING NOOJ PLATFORM

HAJER CHEIKHROUHOU

Abstract

This paper is concerned with French verbs and in particular, the movement verbs (entry/exit). In this paper, we will first propose a semantic and syntactic description of the movement verbs while relying on Dubois's dictionary. Second, we will show the linguistic characteristics of the Arabic verbs. Finally, we will try to use the platform NooJ to achieve an automatic translation of movement verbs.

Introduction

The mass of documents has become increasingly difficult to operate and manage. In fact, the user encounters many difficulties in finding the relevant information, especially if it is not written in the preferred language. As a result, a new need, regarding translation of this information to the desired language, has emerged.

Thus, the requirement for more reliable automatic translation systems is increasing. For this reason, we are interested, in this study, in devising a machine translation system for the French-Arabic language pair. We chose mainly to process and analyse the verb since it is a fundamental element in the structure of sentences in all natural languages. In this context, we will essentially study the movement verbs (entry/exit), which constitute the E class database of Jean and Françoise Dubois - Charlier (LVF).

In this paper, we will first propose a semantic and syntactic description of the movement verbs relying on Dubois's dictionary. Secondly, we will show the linguistic characteristics of the Arabic verbs. Finally, we will try to use the NooJ platform to achieve an automatic translation of movement verbs.

The Linguistic Description of the E Class

The French Verbs of Jean Dubois and Françoise Dubois-Charlier (LVF) is a thesaurus of syntactic-semantic classes. The LVF is composed of 25,610 entries for 12,310 different verbs. There are fourteen classes, including Class E which contains 2,444 entries representing the class of movement verbs. To accomplish this task, we will examine the semantic-syntactic classes, operators, syntactic constructions and, finally, the domain.

The semantic-syntactic classes

Class E contains four semantic-syntactic classes E1, E2, E3 and E4.

E1	-«sortir/venir de qp, aller/entrer qp», sujet humain ou animal propre (« leave/come from somewhere, go/enter into somewhere» human subject or animal subject) -«faire sortir, aller, entrer qnqp» (« let out, go, enter s.o somewhere»)	7 subclasses
E2	- figuré de E1 (figurative E1)	5 subclasses
E3	- «sortir/venir de qp, aller/entrer qp», sujet non-animé («leave/come from somewhere, go/enter somewhere» inanimate subject) -«faire sortir/entrer qc qp» («let out/in s.o somewhere»)	6 subclasses
E4	- figuré de E3 (figurative E3)	6 subclasses

Table 1 – Semantic and syntactic classes of Class E

The Syntactic subclasses

The four semantic-syntactic classes are divided into tewenty-four syntactic subclasses.

Class E1, 698 entries, «sortir/venir de qp ; aller/entrer qp», sujet humain ; «faire sortir, aller, entrer qn qp». (« leave/come from somewhere, go/enter into somewhere « human subject , « let out/in, go, enter s.o somewhere»)		
Syntactic sub-classes	**Entries**	**Example**
E1a-b-c-d-e-f-g	698entries	Aller15(Go), Attirer03(Attract)
Class E2, 440 entries, « figuré de E1 » humain figuré (« figurative E1 » human figurative)		
E2a-b-c-d-e	440entries	Avancer04(Advance),Balancer06(Sway)
Class E3, 984 entries, «(faire) sortir/venir de qp ; (faire) aller/entrer qp», sujet non-animé propre («leave/come from somewhere, go/enter somewhere» inanimate subject)		
E3a-b-c-d-e-f	984 entries	Vibrer03 (Vibrate), Courir03 (Run)
Class E4, (322 entries), «figuré de E3», sujet non-animé figuré («figurative E3 » inanimate figurative)		
E4a-b-c-d-e-f	322 entries	Sortir10 (Leave),Venir06 (Come)

Table 2 – The syntactic subclasses of E1

The operators

Each verb entry is defined with a syntactico-semantic diagram, encoded with a sequence of alphabetical characters called operator. Class E operators are:

ex = sortir de (leave)	**f.ex = faire sortir de (leave)**	**f.ire = faire aller qp (go to)**	**ire = aller qp go somewhere**

The syntactic constructions

The coding of syntactic constructions includes a combination of letters and numbers such as the coding [N3b] which means that the verb is transitive with an indirect complement introduced by the preposition «de». **Example:** *dériver* (06) (derive), *émigrer* (03) (migrate).

We notice that there are verbs that take two syntactic constructions like the word *débarquer* (disembark). The latter belongs to the subclass syntax E1b and can have two syntactic constructions A13 and T1130.

- A13 means that the verb is intransitive with a human subject and a locative complement.

- T1130 means that the verb is transitive with a human subject, a human direct object and a locative complement.

Operators that define this sub-syntactic classification are related to the operator f.ex which means *faire sortir* (leave).

The Domain

Dubois, in LVF, devotes a section to the field (DOM) which states:

- the pragmatic, technical and scientific verbal domains
- the levels of language and regionalism

Concerning the pragmatic domains to which the movement verbs belong, we essentially have:

- ***Locatif et lieux*** (locatives, places) coded by **LOC**. These verbs represent the majority of the verbs of movement. The verbs that belong to this domain can be at the familiar, popular, literary and old language level.

Examples:

— *Abattre*(09) (shoot) belongs to the domain LOC ie locative.
— *Balader*(01) (backpack) is a familiar register encoded by LOCf.
— *Carapater*(s) (carapate) is a popular register encoded by LOCp, the meaning of the verb is *s'enfuir (*to escape).
— *Cortéger* (accompany) is a literary register coded LOCt whose meaning is *accompagner, escorter (*to accompany, escort).
— *Ensauver*(s) is encoded by an old register Locv whose meaning is *s'enfuir, se débiner (*to flee, to run away).

— ***Elevage*** (Elevation) is coded by **ELV**.

Examples:

— *Chasser*(05) (hunt) = *pousser devant soi (*push ahead)
— *Traire*(02) (milk) = *tirer le lait de* (shoot milk)

•

— ***Bâtiment*** (building) encoded by **BAT**.

Examples:

— *Cloisonner01* (partition) = *comprtimenter* (compartmentalise)
— *Décoffrer* (stripping framework) = *ôter de son coffrage* (remove from its casing)

The linguistic characteristics of the Arabic verb

For grammarians of Arabic, the verb is an essential element in the construction of the sentence. Associated with the subject, it forms the core of the sentence. Around this core, other items are ordered. For this reason, it is classified as a basic component. In the most important dictionary of Arabic, *lisān al -'arab de Ibn Manẓū r*, we found the following definition of the verb (*fi'l*):

> 'al- fi'lu kināyatun 'an kulli 'amalin muta'addin 'aw ġayri muta'addin (…) maṣdar min fa'ala yaf'alu - fa'lan wa fi'lan '[1]. (The verb is the name of any do transitive or intransitive (...) it is a name of action fa'ala - yaf'alu)

In fact, in grammar, the oldest definition of the verb dates back to Sibawayhi. It distinguishes the concept of the verb and the name of the particle. He says in the chapter (bābu 'ilmi mā al- kalimu mina -l- 'arabiyya):

> ' … wa 'ammā al-fi'lu fa'amṯilatun 'uḫiḏ at min lafẓi 'aḥdāṯi al-'asmā'i wa buniyat limā maḍā wa limā yakūnu wa lam yaqa' wa mā huwa kā'inun lam yanqaṭi' (As for verbs, they are structures derived from the noun and built on what happened, what will happen or be and what did not happen, and what is and what is not interrupted).

This definition emphasises the two dimensions that comprise the verb, namely action and time.This implies that any verb is derived from the name of the action *''ismu al-ḥadaṯi'* which is nothing other than the (*maṣdar*). As for the concept of time, Sibawayhi did not merely detail it. He clarified that the verb (*fi'l*) is either past or present or future.

Like Hebrew and Syriac, Arabic is a Semitic language. In this family of languages, we give the term 'consonantal root' to the consonant clusters that occur in a fixed order. The number of consonants, called the radical consonants, is:

— **Three**: in this case we speak of a triconsonantal root.
eg: دخل (to enter)
— **Four**: in this case we speak of a quadriconsonantal root.
eg: دحرج (to budge)

[1]Ibn Manẓūr : Lisān 'al -'arab : terme (fa'ala) (1956 : XI, p. 568).

In addition to these two roots, there are monoconsonantal roots. They include, in particular, the roots of subject pronoun affixes to the verb as in those of gender and number eg: تَـفْعَلُـــــــونَ

In a conjugation of Arabic, there are two basic paradigms:

— the accomplished, الماضي
— the unaccomplished, المضارع

The value of these two paradigms is both:

1. aspectual: showing how the progress is considered as expressed by the verb, regardless of when we talk, eg: ذَهَبَ إلى السينما, '*Il est allé au cinéma'* (He went to the cinema) accomplished and completed processes.

2. Temporal**:** showing the relationship of the time progress of the past, present or future in relation to the time of speaking.

Example**:** - سأرجع '*je reviendrai*' (I will return) (future),

- رجعت '*je suis revenu*' (I returned) (past).

Indeed, the conjugation indicates the accomplished; this event is completed, which often involves the past. In unfinished or unaccomplished processes, it may involve the present or the future.

These two paradigms are characterised by:

— the suffixation, which marks the person, the gender, the number and the modes accomplished
— the prefixation and suffixation of the unaccomplished.

Translation of the verb «sortir» in Arabic

In LVF, the verb '*sortir*' (to leave) has twenty different inputs. In this section, we will discuss only the entry «sortir02».

A	B	C	D	E	F	G	H	I	K
sortir 02	LOC	E1a	ex D lc qp	s'en aller hors	On s~de son bureau,	3dA	A13	-1 -A— -	5

Figure 1 – «sortir02» in LVF

This use of the verb is of the locative domain. It belongs to the semantic-syntactic subclass E1a in which the semantic operator is '*sortir de quelque part*'. This verb follows the syntactic schema A13 that is to say, it is an intransitive verb with a human subject [+ Human] followed by an original locative supplement '*d'où on vient*' (where you come from) [+

Loc] introduced by the preposition '*de'* (from). This verb can have as a synonym the verb '*s'en aller*'.

Example: *Il sort de son bureau*.(He gets out of his office)

The verb '*sortir*' (get out) in this use, is translated into Arabic by the word '**خرج**' (*kharaja*).

Example: خرج من البيت *kharaja mina al-bayti* (*Il sort de la maison* He leaves the house). This verb is also a movement verb. The verb '*kharaja*' means the movement from an enclosed place to another place. It is also an intransitive verb followed by a preposition (من '*mina*') that specifies the place of origin, thus the use of a locative supplement is needed (البيت '*al-bayti*').

We can deduce that the use of the verb «sortir02» has not only the same syntactic-semantic pattern but also the same syntax as the corresponding Arabic word *'kharaja'*. Moreover, the two verbs are marked by the same semantic features of the subject and complement which are respectively [+ Hum], [+ Loc]. We also notice the presence of the preposition in both cases with the same syntactic and semantic significance.

The implementation of movement verbs in the NooJ platform

In this step of the implementation of verbs, we will firstly create derivational paradigms (.nof) that describe the specifics of movement verbs. Then, we will integrate the verbs in the French-Arabic bilingual dictionary. Finally, we will try to produce formal grammars to achieve the translation phase.

Creating derivational paradigms

The rubric (DER) in LVF represents the derivation codes. These codes are alphanumeric. For example lower 01 has the following derivation: 1-- -1 –RA- meaning that the verb can have the derivational forms *Abaissable/Abaissement/Abaisseur*.

NooJ as a software has its own tools, thus we have to create derivational paradigms (paraderivational.nof) suitable for NooJ. For the first form the following paradigm is used:

#abaisser=abaissable ; ***AV1=<B2>able/A;***
For the second form: *abaisser=abaissement*; ***DN5=<B2>ement/N;***
For the third form: *#abaisser= abaisseur*; ***DN14=<B2>eur/N.***

It is reported that there are derivatives that admit two verb forms such as:

*franchir*01 2-- -1 ---- --. These two forms are described by the paradigm AV1H.

#franchir=franchissable=infranchissable

AV1h=<B2>issable/A|<B2>issable<LW>in/A;

We also find that the majority of movement verbs are preceded by prefixes.

For example: *abaisser*, *désemprisonner*, *décontextualiser*, *déparquer…*

To generate the base word or deverbal, we used specific paradigms. For example:

#déparquer=parc ; ***Dev148=<B4>c<LW><R2><B2>/N;***
#décontextualiser=context; ***Dev142=<B7>e<LW><R2><B2>/N;***
#abaisser=baisse; ***Dev137=<B><LW><R><B>/N;***
#désemprisonner=prison; ***Dev155=<B3><LW><R5><B5>/N;***

These derivational paradigms will be used in the dictionary of verbs of movement to derive the appropriate verb forms.

The bilingual dictionary of movement verbs

In this step, we have integrated the movement verbs in a bilingual French-Arabic dictionary. In this dictionary, we studied only those verbs whose subject is human [+ Hum]. This dictionary contains 1,910 verbal entries:

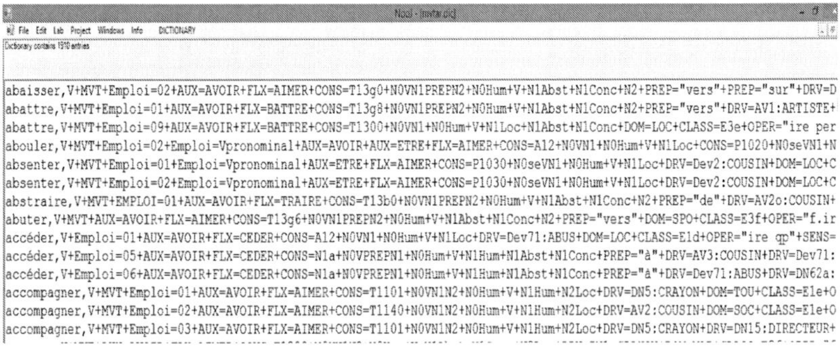

Figure 2 – Extract from the « mvtar » dictionary

Example:

```
   accompagner,V+MVT+Emploi=01+AUX=AVOIR+FLX=AIMER
   +CONS=T1101+N0VN1N2+N0Hum+V+N1Hum+N2Loc+DRV=DN5:CRAYON+D
OM=TOU+CLASS=E1e+OPER="f.ireqp qn avsoi"+SENS="guider
   ,cornaquer"+BASE=Dev131:TABLE+LEXI=1+AR="رَافَقَ"
```

This entry describes the verb '*accompagner*' (accompany) and notes that the verb is a movement verb « MVT » whose employment is 01.

This verb is conjugated with the auxiliary «AVOIR» and follows the inflectional paradigm «AIMER». It has the syntactic construction [T1101] which indicates that the verb is transitive, the subject is human [+ Hum], the direct object is human and it is followed by a locative supplement [+ Loc]. As regards the derivation, it is associated with the derivational paradigm DN5 giving the name '*abaissement*' inflected as the paradigm «CRAYON». This verb belongs to the domain TOU which means '*tourisme, loisirs*' (tourism, entertainment). 'Accompany 01' belongs to the subclass E1e that states '*faire aller qn qp, d'un lieu à l'autre, vers un lieu*'. The operator is '*f.ire qp qn av soi*' that is to say to take someone somewhere with you. As a synonym, it may have the verbs '*guider, cornaquer*' (to guide, to show around). To obtain the deverbal, we use the derivational paradigm Dev131 which will derive '*companion*', which flexes as the paradigm «TABLE ». For LEXI = 1 it notes that this entry is taken from the *dictionnaire fondamental* (basic dictionary). Finally, we indicate the Arabic translation of the word, which is ' رَافَقَ'.

In this bilingual dictionary we attempted to mention all of the linguistic properties of the verb: semantic- syntactic, syntactic structure, derivation, conjugation, lexicon and translation. To validate this dictionary, we will apply it to a journalistic text that represents a selection of articles extracted from the newspaper 'Le Monde'. This selection of articles deals with the subject of the Tunisian Revolution.

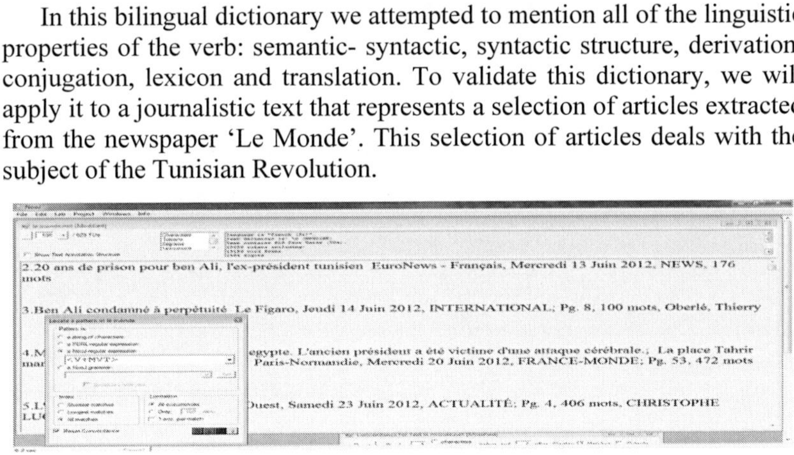

Figure 3 – Extract from the text « le monde »

If we apply the operation « Locate » in the text, we will get the following results:

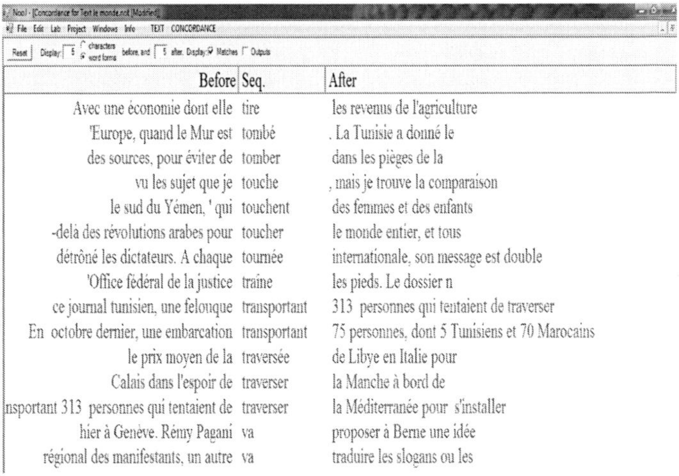

Figure 4 – Extract of the results <V+MVT>

We note that we obtained encouraging results that mention verbs of movement, for example: *tomber*, *transportant*, *traverser*, *va* (fall, carrying, cross, go). Following this phase of the creation of a bilingual dictionary, we will outline the second phase which is the production of formal grammars.

The creation of formal grammars

Verbs from Class E have a syntactic construction distinct from other classes. Indeed, the majority have a locative supplement [+Loc].

This supplement, in most cases, is introduced by a preposition. We already know that the change of the preposition must cause a change in meaning. The semantic nature of the complement ([+N1Hum], [+N1Loc], [+N1Anim], [+N1Conc]) is also within the meaning of the verb. This semantic and syntactic problem creates an obstacle for the automatic translation of verbs.

As an example, we will deal with the use 01, 07, 10 of the verb '*amener*', which has three different syntactic constructions:

— [T1120]+CONS=T1120+N0VN1N2+N0Hum+V+N1Hum+N2Lo c
— [T1302] +CONS=T1302+N0VN1N2+N0Hum+V+N1Abst+N1Conc+ N2Loc
— [T13g0]+CONS=T13g0+N0VN1PREPN2+N0Hum+V+N1Abst +N1Conc+N2+PREP=«vers»+PREP=«sur»

The first construction means '*conduire*, *mener*' (drive, conduct) which gives the Arabic verb ' اِصْطَحَبَ'. The second, '*porter à'*, (bring) is translated as 'أوصل'. The last construction means '*descendre les voiles*' (down the sails) and is translated as the Arabic verb 'أَنْزَلَ'.

In this phase, we will attempt to create formal grammars that can syntactically analyse and properly translate the verbs.

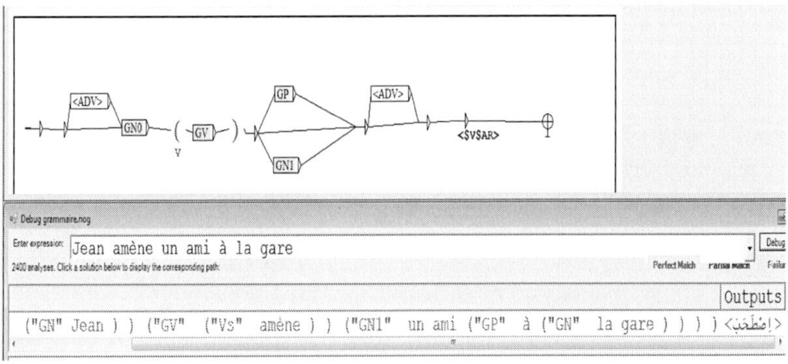

Figure 5 – Syntactic analysis of the construction [T1120]+ translation to « اِصْطَحَبَ»

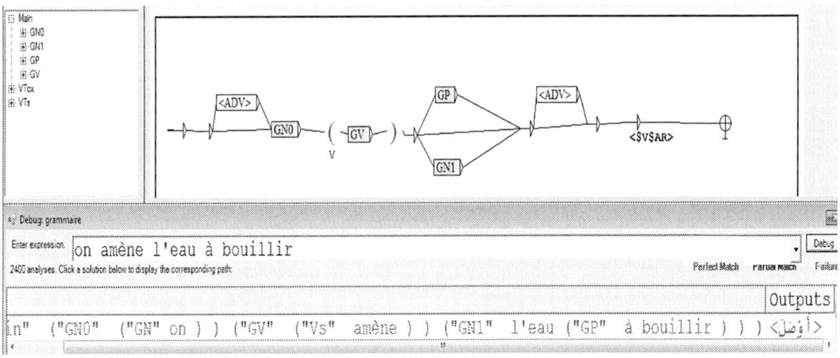

Figure 6 – Syntactic analysis of the construction [T1302]+ translation to «أَوْصَلَ»

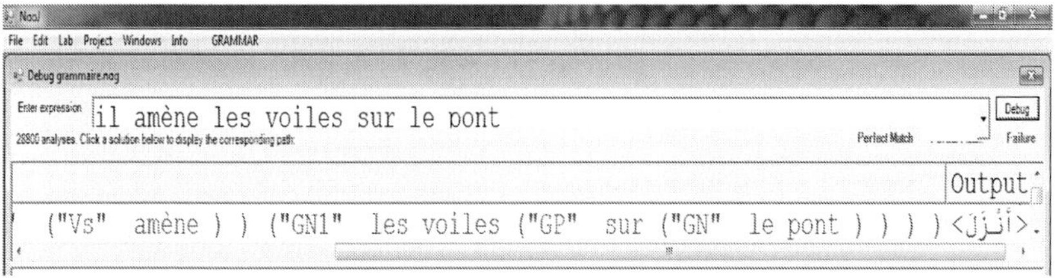

Figure 7 – Syntactic analysis of the construction [T13g0] + translation to «أَنْزَلَ »

As a result, we find that the formal grammars we created give an adequate translation and syntactic analysis.

Conclusions

In this study of movement verbs (entry/exit), we aimed to make a detailed linguistic analysis, taking into account syntactic structures, semantic and syntactic properties and pragmatic field. Subsequently, we defined the verb in Arabic. We also made a comparative study of the Arabic verb and the French verb. To reach the stage of machine translation, we implemented the Class E verbs in a French-Arabic bilingual dictionary. We also created formal grammars, aiming to perform not only a proper analysis of different syntactic constructions but also of translated verbs.

In a later work, we will consider treating other Base Data Jean Dubois and Françoise Dubois - Charlier (LVF) classes, such as the class of psychological verbs. We will also attempt to overcome the problems arising from the syntactic and semantic analysis of verbs, by trying to improve our formal grammars, in order to get a suitable translation.

References

Abi, Aad Albert. 2001. *Le système verbal de l'arabe comparé au français*. Maisonneuve et Larose, Paris.

Cheikhrouhou, Hajer. 2014. Recognition of Communication Verbs with NooJ.In *Formalising Natural Languages with NooJ 2013*. Edited by Svetla Koeva, Slim Mesfar and Max Silberztein. Cambridge Scholars Publishing, Newcastle, UK. pp 153-168.

Ibn, Manẓūr. 1956. *Lisān Al-'arab*. Volumes 9 et 11, Ed. Dār Ṣādir, Beyrouth.

Leeman, Danielle. 2010. Description, taxinomie, systémique : un modèle pour les emplois des verbes français. In *Langages N°179-180*, Armand Colin.

Salkoff, Morris. 1973. *Une grammaire en chaîne du Français, analyse distributionnelle*. Dunod éditeur, Paris.

Silberztein, Max. 2003. *NooJ Manual*. Available at: http://www.nooj4nlp.net.

—. 2003. Finite-State Description of the French Determiner System. In *Journal of French Language Studies,13*. Cambridge University Press, pp221-246.

—. 2010. La formalization du dictionnaire LVF avec NooJ et ses applications pour l'analyse automatique de corpus. In *Langages N°179- 180*. Armand Colin.

—. 2011. Variable Unification with NooJ v3. In *Automatic Processing of Various Levels of Linguistic Phenomena*. Kristina Vuckovic, Bozo Bekavac, Max Silberztein Eds. Cambridge Scholars Publishing : Cambridge, 2011.

Wu, Mei. 2010. Integrating a dictionary of psychological verbs into a French-Chinese MT system. In *Finite-State Language Engineering with NooJ*. Edited by Abdelmajid Ben Hamadou, Slim Mesfar and Max Silberztein. Centre de publication Universitaire Sfax, Tunisia. pp 315-324.

—. 2013. The Auxiliary Verbs in NooJ's French-Chinese MT System. In *Formalising Natural Languages with NooJ*. Edited by Anaïd Donabédian, Victoria Khurshudian and Max Silberztein. Cambridge Scholars Publishing, Newcastle, UK. pp 221-222.

Morphological and Syntactic Grammars for Recognition of Verbal Lemmas in Quechua

Maximiliano Duran

Abstract

This article presents the process of using the inflectional and derivational structures of Quechua verbs to recognise verbal forms in a corpus. With the aid of morphological and syntactic NooJ grammars, we show how to retrieve and to extract the hidden verbs.

Introduction

Existing Quechua dictionaries contain fewer than 1,500 verbs and yet ancient Quechua writings contain many unknown verbs. They appear in inflected forms. My motivation was to isolate these verbal lemmas to enhance the verb lexicon. First, I describe briefly how I formalised the corpus which includes some ancient documents. Then, I present the set of morphological and syntactic grammars that I constructed with NooJ. These grammars will serve to analyse the corpus for searching verbal forms. Once these forms are identified I apply an algorithm of NooJ operators to extract and list the verbs. We have identified nearly three hundred unknown verbs.

Motivation for the project

The Quechua language was the official language of the Inca civilisation. It originated in the central Andes of Peru around the first half of the first millennium of the present era. In 2009 UNESCO declared it an endangered language. We would like to contribute to its survival and its development.

Our long term project is to build a linguistic resources platform for automatic text processing of Quechua.

The first step is to build a French-Quechua electronic dictionary based on the 25,000 French verbs of Dubois & Dubois[1].

The Corpus

The following documents from the beginning of the 16th century contain a total of 67,900 tokens:

— Gonçalez Holguin, Diego, 1608, *Vocabulario de la Lengua General de todo el Perú llamada Lengua Qquichua o del Inca.*
— Santo Thomas, Domingo de, 1560, *Lexicon, o vocabulario de la lengua general del Peru.*
— Francisco de AVILA's, 1598? *Dioses y hombres de Huarochiri.* A Quechua narrative gathered by Francisco de Avila

I first standardised the orthography of these texts using the Ayacucho's Quechua alphabet.

Inflected verbal forms

A typical Quechua sentence has the following structure: IPS + PR ENDING + PPS where:

IPS[2] : Interposed suffix is a set of 31 suffixes, and
PPS[3] : Post-posed suffix containing 19 suffixes.
PR ENDING[4]: is the set of seven present tense endings (which behave as fixed points during the inflections).

We can note that Quechua is a polysynthetic language. For example the English sentence:

'We have to do the work leaving aside everything else' becomes *llamkananchikraqmi*

[1]Dubois & Dubois 2007
[2]IPS =(chi, chka, ikacha, ikachi, ikamu, ikapu, ikari, iku, isi, kamu, kapu, ku, lla, mu, na, naya, pa, paya, pti, pu, ra, raya, ri, rpari, rqa, rqu, ru, spa, sqa, tamu, wa)
[3]PPS=(ch, chaa, chiki, chui, chun, chusina, maa, man, mm, mmi, ña, pas, puni, qa, raq, ssi, sis, taq, yaa)
[4]PR ENDING= (-ni , -nki , -n , -nchik , -niku , -nkichik, nku)

A whole sentence in English represents a single verbal form in Quechua.

Let us see the behavior of some of these suffixes and their combinations in the following inflections of the verb *qallariy* 'to begin':

verb lemma : qallari-
*qallari-**nchik*** 'we begin'
-*nchik* is the ending of PR p +1
*qallari-chka-**nchik*** ' we are beginning'
*qallari-isi-chkak-**nchik*** 'we are helping someone to begin'
*qallari-isi-chka-**nchik**-ña* 'we are already helping someone to begin'
*qallari-isi-chka-**nchik**-ña- taq* 'and yet we are already helping him to begin'

The personal ending ***nchik*** remains fixed at the end of the IPS combinations or before the PPS combinations.

The morphology of Quechua is very much dominated by this kind of agglutination of suffixes placed after a verbal, nominal, adverbial or adjectival lemma.

Matrix approach to verbal suffix combinatorials

What we call the present tense is in fact an indefinite present. On the one hand it places the statement at the moment in which this statement takes place, but on the other hand it may also place it in a moment in which the statement has just taken place and is still not completed.

The conjugation for the three singular persons has the following structure:

ñoqa (I) root +***NI***
qam (you) root + ***NKI***
pay (he, she) root +***N***
For the future we have the scheme:
ñoqa (I) root +***SAQ***
qam (you) root + ***NKI***
pay, (he, she) root +***NQA***

The present tense form plays a crucial role in the conjugated Quechua verbal form of the other tenses. It is a kind of fixed point around which all the inflectional topology based on the combinatorial of the suffixes is constructed (tenses, modes, aspects, etc.)

For instance, the past preterit is obtained by taking this present structure and interposing the IPS suffix *-rqa-*, between the verbal root and the ending of the person. We then have:

Present		Past preterit	
taki-ni	I sing	*taki-**rqa**-ni*	I sang
taki-nki	you sing	*taki- **rqa**-nki*	you sang
taki-n	he sings	*taki- **rqa**-n*	he sang

According to the Quechua verb morphology, we can build combinations of 2, 3, or 4 of IPS and PPS suffixes which are very productive inflection wise.

To obtain the complete set of these combinations that are syntactically correct, we first manually constructed a two-entry matrix having as the first row and the first column all the inter-positional suffixes IPS in one case and the set of the PPS ones in the other case. We then filled the 961 cells with 0 or 1 for the IPS's and 261 cells for the PPS's. The value '1' means 'grammatically valid combination' and '0' means 'not valid'. For instance the cell corresponding to the point (*chi*, *chka*) as coordinates in this matrix bears '1', because the combination *-chichka* is compatible and may be agglutinated to the root of the verb 'to sing' *takiy* to get the verbal form *taki-chichka-ni* 'I am making him sing', or for the cell (*kacha, ku*), which bears '1' also, will have the combination *-kachaku*, *taki-kachaku-ni* 'I keep singing once and over again'. In all, we found 295 '1's for the IPS's case.

	CHI	CHKA	IKACHA	IKARI	IKU	ISI	KACHA	KAPU	KU	LLAV	MU	NAV
CHI	0	1	0	0	1	1	0	0	1	1	1	1
CHKA	0	0	0	0	0	1	0	0	0	0	0	0
IKACHA	1	1	0	0	0	1	0	0	1	1	1	0
IKARI	1	1	0	0	1	1	0	0	1	1	1	0
IKU	1	1	0	0	0	1	0	1	1	1	0	0
ISI	1	1	0	0	1	0	0	1	0	1	1	0
KACHA	1	1	0	0	1	0	0	1	1	1	1	1
KAPU	1	1	1	0	1	0	0	0	0	1	1	1
KU	0	1	0	0	1	0	0	1	0	1	0	1
LLAV	1	1	1	0	1	1	0	0	0	0	1	1
MU	0	1	0	0	0	0	0	0	0	1	0	1

Figure 1 – Matrix of bi-dimensional combinations of interposition suffixes

We then obtained the valid combinations of three IPS's. The corresponding matrix is one that has as the first row the set of 31 IPS's and as the first column the 295 valid binary combinations that we have just obtained. We found 57 valid or attested three-fold agglutinations. Here are some examples:

-ñachusinam -ñapaschá -ñapaschik -ñapaschu -ñapasmi -ñataqsi -punichusinam -puniñach -puniñachá - puniñachik -puniñachu? -puniñachu -puniñachusina -puniñamá -puniñam -puniñapas -puniñas

Postposition suffixes PPS

They are placed after the verbal ending, as in the following examples:

*rima-**nki** -man* you should talk
*rima-**nki** -man-pas* besides, you should talk
*rima-**nki** -man-pas-cha* you should perhaps talk
*rima-**n** - man-ña-taq* I fear that he speaks up

The binary PPS combinations matrix contains 56 compatible agglutinations as shown in Fig. 2.

	CHUN	CHUS	CHUSINA	MAA	MAN	MMI	ÑA	PAS	PUNI	QA	RAQ
CHUN	0	0	0	0	0	0	0	0	0	0	0
CHUS	0	0	0	0	0	0	0	0	0	0	0
CHUSINA	0	0	0	0	0	0	0	0	0	0	0
MAA	0	0	0	0	0	0	0	0	0	0	0
MAN	2	2	2	0	0	2	2	2	0	0	2
MMI	0	0	0	0	0	0	0	0	0	0	0
ÑA	1	1	1	1	0	1	0	1	0	0	0
PAS	1	0	0	0	0	0	0	0	0	0	0
PUNI	1	1	1	1	0	1	1	1	0	1	1
QA	0	0	0	0	0	0	0	0	0	0	0
RAQ	1	1	1	1	0	1	0	1	1	0	0
SSI	0	0	0	0	0	0	0	0	0	0	0
TAQ	0	0	0	0	0	0	0	0	0	0	0

Figure 2 – Compatibility binary matrix of post positioned suffixes

Here too, the '1' corresponding to the point (*ña, mmi*) indicates that the combination *–ñammi* is grammatically valid, thus we have:

rima-nchik-ña-m, which we have already mentioned (*m* alone if it follows a vowel). (The '2' stands for the modified PRM2 of the PR structure).

Créer Matrice	CH	CHAA	CHIKI	CHUI	CHUN	CHUS	CHUSINA	MAA	MAN	MMI
MANCHAA	0	0	0	0	0	0	0	0	0	0
MANMMI	0	0	0	0	0	0	0	0	0	0
MANÑA	ANÑAC	ANÑACHA	NÑACH	ANÑAC	ANÑACH	NÑACH	ÑACHU	ANÑAM	0	ANÑAMI
MANPAS	0	NPASCH	NPASCH	0	NPASCH	0	0	0	0	0
MANRAQ	0	NRAQCH	NRAQCH	NRAQCI	NRAQCH	NRAQCH	RAQCHU	NRAQM	0	NRAQM
MANTAQ	0	0	0	0	0	0	0	0	0	0
ÑAMMI	0	0	0	0	0	0	0	0	0	0
ÑAPAS	0	APASCH	APASCHI	0	APASCHI	0	0	0	0	0
ÑASSI	0	0	0	0	0	0	0	0	0	0
PUNIMMI	0	0	0	0	0	0	0	0	0	0
PUNIÑA	UNIÑAC	NIÑACH	NIÑACH	NIÑACH	NIÑACH	NIÑACH	IÑACHU	NIÑAM	0	NIÑAMI
PUNIPAS	0	NIPASCH	NIPASCH	0	NIPASCH	0	0	0	0	0
PUNIQA	0	0	0	0	0	0	0	0	0	0
PUNIRAQ	0	NIRAQCH	NIRAQCH	NIRAQC	NIRAQCH	NIRAQCH	RAQCHU	NIRAQM	0	NIRAQM

Figure 3 – Partial view of the matrix of compatible tertiary combinations of post-positioned suffixes

Similarly, we obtained the matrix of tertiary combinations having the 56 compatible binary combinations as the first column and the vector PPS as the first row. The result contains only 80 non null elements, as shown in Figure 3.

Following the same method, we obtained the matrix $MPPS_{3x1}$ of compatible combinations of four post- positioned suffixes. Some of the resulting valid combinations are listed below:

-manñapaschá, -puniraqpaschá, -puniraqpaschiki, puniraqpaschu -raqpuniñachu, -raqpuniñachus
-raqpuniñachusina, -manñapaschiki, -manñapaschun

We are working on the matrix of combinations of five suffixes and six PPS.

The Quechua morpho-syntax rules allow the mixing of both cases to obtain a large number of inflectional forms, of mixed agglutinations of inter and post-positioned suffixes as in the examples:

*rima-ri-**nki**-man* 'you should perhaps talk'
*rima-ri-lla-**nki**-man-raq* 'I think you should before etc'.

Here again we see that the endings behave as stable fixed points.

Programming the corresponding NooJ grammars

We applied these results to program the corresponding paradigms in NooJ. Here are some examples:

conjugVERBES = <E>/INF|:CHU |:progCHU |:pasCHU |:futCHU |:impeCHU |:iptiiCHU |:imanCHU |:nominITA|:GSTA;
VERBEAY = <E>/INF|:CHU |:PRESENT |:FUT |:RQA |:PREASS |:CHKAASS |:IMP |:COND |:PPL |:PTIC |:presenCHU |:progCHU|:impeCHU |:FUTCHU |:iptiiCHU |:imanCHU |:sqaCHU |:ptiiqaCHU |:GDYN |:STINCHU |:TA |:SQAIKI |:TRTS1 |:WANCHU |:TRDE1 |:DE1PCHU |:TRDE3 |:DE3PCHU |:TRTA2 |:accustfTA |:WANKICHU |:TRDE1CHU |:TRTS1CHU |:PIDF2 |:PIDF2CHU |:PIDF2 |:PICTR |:PICTRAC |:SPA |:GSPA |:IPI;

Using the verb dictionary, NooJ will generate the corresponding verbal forms. Below we have a small list of entries for the verb *takiy* 'to sing'.

takiychu,takiy,V+FR="chanter"+FLX=conjugVERBES+NEG
takichka**ni**kuchu,takiy,V+FR="chanter"+FLX=conjugVERBES+pex+1+NEG
takichka**n**kuchu,takiy,V+FR="chanter"+FLX=conjugVERBES+p+3+NEG

We have programmed more than 200 paradigms up to now. In the future, we will complete the study for the cases of combinations of more than three suffixes.

When we apply the program to a transitive verb like *mikuy* to eat, we obtain more than 7,500 inflected forms as shown in Figure 4.

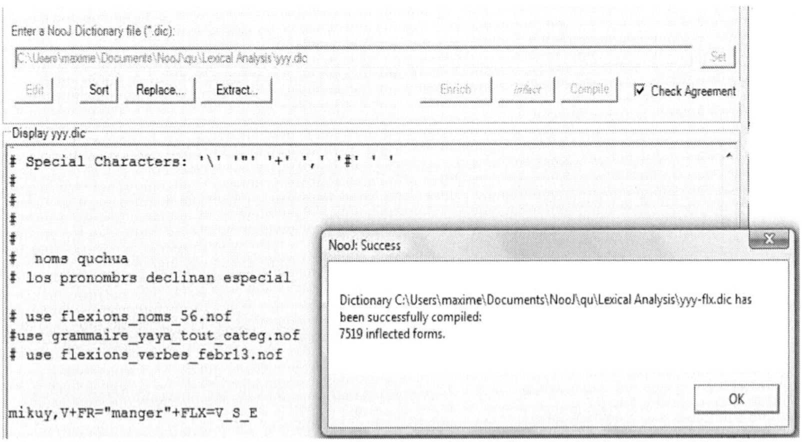

Figure 4 – Result of the flections of the verb *mikuy*

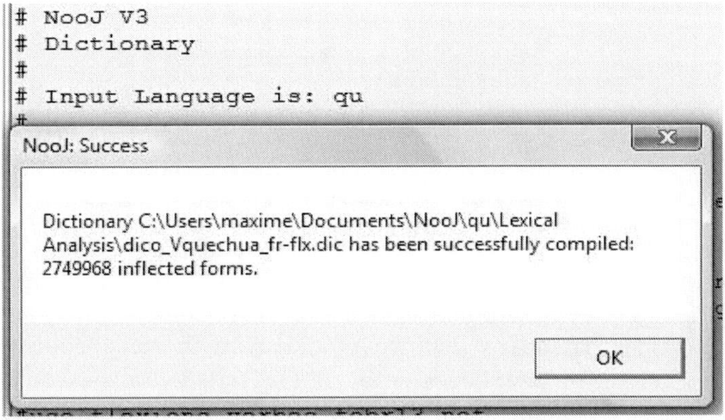

Figure 5 – Inflected forms for 400 transitive verbs

The same program, applied to a set of 400 transitive Quechua verbs generates 2,749,968 inflected forms as is shown I Fig. 5.

Recognition, extraction and recovery of lost verbs

We have applied several queries of concordances on our corpus using operators like

NI_q_extr == Find/ Replace (PERL pattern, ni$ | q$, extract lines)
VOC-ni_q == NI_q_extr (VOC-H_brut)
VOC-chay_rayay_nayay == *Find/ Replace (PERL pattern, chay$|, rayay$| nayay$|, extract lines)*

which gave us all of the verbal forms containing potential verbal lemmas (5.541 forms).

From here we can extract the verbal lemmas hidden in this set by applying some algorithms using NooJ operators. We have got a list of 298 verbs considered 'lost' verbs. The compilation of this catalogue of new verbs is an important step for the lexical preservation for the language. We present a sample of the obtained unknown verbs:

qalluykuy to cheat
aknay to exhibit
rampay to guide a blind person
tullpuy to dye

utiy to become mad
takuriy to revolutionise
tokapuy to decorate

Conclusion

We have conducted a comprehensive study of the way in which inter- and post-positioned suffixes combine to generate thousands of inflections out of a single verb. Our corpus contains many complex inflected verbs. The grammar paradigms that we programmed in NooJ allowed us to identify among these inflections all of the verbal forms in our corpus, which helped us to obtain 298 lost 'new' verbs for our verb lexicon.

References

Bogacki, Krzysztof. 2008. Polish module for NooJ. In the Procedings of the 2007 NooJ Conference. Autonomus University of Barcelona. Cambridge Scholars Publishing. Newcastle.

De Avila, Francisco. 1598?. *Dioses y hombres de Huarochiri. Narracion Quechua recogida por Francisco de Avila Traduccion J. M. Arguedas*. Lima. Peru 1966. Edicion bilingüe facsimilar 2012.

de Santo, Thomas Domingo. 1560. *Lexicon, o vocabulario de la lengua general del Peru*. Valladolid: Francisco Fernandez de Cordova.

Dubois, Jean and Françoise Dubois-Charlier, (D&D). 2007. *Le verbes français (le «dictionnaire électronique des verbes français* (DEV), 1992 Diffusé à partir de septembre 2007 par MoDyCo dans un format Excel.

Duran, Maximiliano. 2009. *Diccionario Quechua-Castellano*. Éditions HC. Paris.

Goncalez Holguin, Diego. 1608. *Vocabulario de la Lengua General de todo el Perú llamada Lengua Qquichua o del Inca*. Edición y Prólogo de Raúl Porras Barrenechea. Lima, Universidad Nacional Mayor de San Marcos 1952.

Itier, César. 2011. *Dictionnaire Quechua-Français*, Paris. L'Asiathèque. Paris.

Perroud, Pedro Clemente. 1970. *Diccionario Castellano - Kechwa Dialecto de Ayacucho*. Lima. Edición.

Silberztein, Max. 2003, *NooJ Manual*. htpp://www.nooj4nlp.net (220 pages updated regularly).

A LEXICON-BASED APPROACH TO SENTIMENT ANALYSIS: THE ITALIAN MODULE FOR NOOJ

SERENA PELOSI AND ALESSANDRO MAISTO

Abstract

In this paper we present a lexicon–based method for the automatic analysis of opinionated documents. We built a Sentiment Lexicon and a grammar network of Contextual Valence Shifters with NooJ and tested them on a dataset of multi-domain customer reviews, reaching an average Precision of 74% and Recall of 97% on the document-level classification task.

Introduction

In the last decade, the rise of online commerce, the growth of user-generated contents, the phenomenon of customer empowerment and the increasing impact of online word-of-mouth (Vollero, 2010) made it necessary for companies to automatically extract, analyse and summarise not only factual information, but also opinions expressing people's positive or negative judgements regarding any kind of product or service offered (Liu, 2010; Bloom, 2011). An opinion can be a positive or negative appraisal of a topic, stated by the opinion holder. It can be represented as a quintuple (o_j, f_{jk}, oo_{ijkl}, h_i, t_l), where o_j is the object, f_{jk} is the feature, oo_{ijkl} is the opinion orientation, h_i is the opinion holder and t_l is the time when the opinion is expressed. Undeniably, an appropriate management of the online corporate reputation requires a careful monitoring of the new digital environments which strengthen the stakeholders' influence and independence and give support during the decision-making process.

For these reasons, software capable of transforming unstructured texts written in natural language into structured data which can then be stored and queried in database tables is vitally necessary.

In the present paper we focus on the 'document-level sentiment polarity classification', which means classifying an opinionated document as expressing a positive or negative opinion on an object. The whole document is considered as the basic information unit and its Semantic Orientation (SO) is calculated on its basis. SO is a measure of subjectivity and opinion that weights the polarity (positive/negative) and the strength (intense/weak) of opinions.

Section 2 summarises the most frequently used techniques for Sentiment Lexicon development and for the Sentiment Classification task; Section 3 describes the Sentiment lexical and syntactic resources we built with NooJ; Section 4 presents the software DOXA, an opinion mining application that applies the NooJ resources to different kinds of opinionated documents and the evaluation of the tool; Section 5 briefly outlines the strengths and the weaknesses of our tool and introduces the future lines of action that our research will take.

State of the art

Many techniques to perform the Sentiment Polarity Classification have been discussed in literature. Lexicon-based approaches always start from this basic assumption that the text sentiment orientation comes from the semantic orientations of words and phrases contained in it. Thus, the SO identification task requires the determination of the polarity of the individual words (Taboada, 2006). The most commonly used SO indicators are adjectives or adjective phrases (Hatzivassiloglo, 1997; Hu, 2004; Taboada, 2006); but recently it has become very common to use adverbs (Benamara, 2007), nouns (Vermeij, 2005; Riloff, 2003) and verbs (Neviarouskaya, 2009) as well. Several methods are used to build and test these dictionaries, such as Latent Semantic Analysis (Landauer 1997), bootstrapping algorithms (Riloff 2003), graph propagation algorithms applied on the web (Velikovich 2010; Kaji 2007), distributional similarity (Wiebe 2000), the use of conjunctions (eg 'and' or 'but'), or morphological relationships between adjectives (Hatzivassiloglou 1997), context coherency (Kanayama 2006), Word Similarity (Mohammad 2009), and lastly, the Pointwise Mutual Information (PMI) based on Seed Words (Turney 2002; Velikovich 2010). Learning and statistical methods usually make use of Support Vector Machine classifiers. Pang et al. (2002) use Support Vector Machine, Naive Bayes and Maximum Entropy classifiers, with diverse sets of features, such as unigrams, bigrams, binary and term frequency feature weights, and others. Finally, as regards the hybrid methods, the works of Andreevskaia (2008) and Dasgupta (2009) must be cited. In order to attain a high level of accuracy in the results, it is not sufficient to dispose of Sentiment Lexicons; indeed, the local context often causes the polarity of the sentences to change. Such is the case of Negation (Choi, 2008, Benamara,

2012), Intensification (Kennedy, 2006; Polanyi, 2006), Irrealis markers and Conditional tenses (Taboada, 2011; Narayanan, 2009). Rule-based approaches that take into account the syntactic dimension of the Sentiment Analysis are those used by Mulder (2004) and Nasukawa (2003).

Method and Resources

In the present work we present a hand-tagged Sentiment Lexicon that has been built with NooJ. Adjectives, verbs and nouns contained in the NooJ Italian dictionaries of simple words have been manually evaluated by excluding the words with a neutral meaning, and by weighting the Prior Polarity (Osgood, 1957) of the words endowed with a positive or negative SO. The polarity of the adverbs has been automatically derived from the adjectives of sentiment, using a NooJ morphological grammar that will be described below. In order to obtain two separate scales for the evaluation of the strength (intense/weak) and of the polarity (positive/negative), every entry of the lexicon of sentiment has been weighted combining four tags: +POS (positive), +NEG (negative), +FORTE (intense) and +DEB (weak). In this way we created an evaluation scale from -3 to +3 and a strength scale from -1 to +1. Contextual Valence Shifters have been taken into consideration thanks to a network of syntactic grammars that computes the words' Prior Polarity, making it consistent with the real textual context of words.

In detail, the NooJ dictionary of Sentiment Adjectives contains over 5,300 entries. Examples of the evaluation and the strength scales are reported in Table 1. Thanks to the morphological grammar shown in Figure 1, it has been possible to derive the dictionary of Sentiment Adverbs from that of the Adjectives. All of the adverbs contained in the Italian dictionary of simple words have been inserted into a NooJ text and the afore-mentioned grammar has been used to quickly populate the new dictionary by extracting the ones ending with the suffix *-mente*, '-ly' and by making such words inherit the adjectives' polarity. The NooJ annotations have been manually checked, producing a set of more than 3,600 adverbs of sentiment.

Entries	Translation	Score
meraviglioso,A+FLX=N88+DRV=ISSIMO:N88+POS+FORTE	'wonderful'	+3
divertente,A+FLX=N79+DRV=ISSIMO:N88+POS	'funny'	+2
accettabile,A+FLX=N79+DRV=ISSIMO:N88+POS+DEB	'acceptable'	+1
insapore,A+FLX=N79+DRV=ISSIMO:N88+NEG+DEB	'flavourless'	-1
cafone,A+FLX=N88+DRV=ISSIMO:N88+NEG	'bumpkin'	-2
disastroso,A+FLX=N88+DRV=ISSIMO:N88+NEG+FORTE	'disastrous'	-3
straripante,A+FLX=N79+DRV=ISSIMO:N88+FORTE	'overflowing'	+1
episodico,A+FLX=N87+DRV=ISSIMO:N88+DEB	'episodic'	-1

Table 1 – Extract of the Sentiment dictionary

Figure 1 – Extract of the morphological grammar used to automatically populate the dictionary of Sentiment Adverbs

The verbs chosen for our sentiment lexicon are the Psychological Semantic Predicates (Gross, 1981; 1995) belonging to the Italian Lexicon-grammar classes 41, 42, 43 and 43B. Between these verbs, a list of over 600 entries has been evaluated and hand-tagged with the same labels used to evaluate the adjectives. The nominalisations of these predicates have been used to manually build the Sentiment dictionary of nouns which includes over 1,000 entries.

In the end, more than 500 Italian frozen sentences containing adjectives (Vietri, 1990; 2011) were evaluated and then formalised with a pairing of dictionary-grammar. Among the idioms considered there are the comparative frozen sentences of the type *N0 Agg come C1*, described by (Vietri 1990)[1].

Although a great part of the works on Sentiment Analysis focuses on the simple lexical valence of negative or positive words, it must be noted that, in many cases, the sentence or the discourse context shifts the valence of individual terms (Polanyi, 2006).

---

[1]Other idioms included in our resources are *N0 essere (Agg + Ppass) Prep C1* (e.g. *Max è matto da legare*, 'Max is so crazy he should be locked up'); *N0 essere Agg e Agg* (e.g. *Max è bello e fritto*, 'Max is cooked'); *C0 essere Agg (come C1 + E)* (*Mary ha la coscienza sporca* ↔ *La coscienza è sporca*, 'Mary has a guilty conscience' ↔ 'The conscience is guilty'), *N0 essere C1 Agg* (*Mary è una gatta morta*, 'Mary is a cock tease'). Given the higher frequency, we only included *C0 essere Agg (come C1 + E)* into the idioms' grammar using its transformation *N0 avere C0 Agg*.

In order find the Semantic Orientation of real sentences written in natural language, a grammar that computes the polarity of the opinion lexicon has been built with NooJ (Fig. 2). In our grammar, adjectives, adverbs, nouns and verbs have been treated separately in four dedicated metanodes. A fifth metanode is dedicated to domain-independent sentiment expressions that are not built around specific sentiment words, but must also be considered opinion indicators. The Sentiment Pattern Extraction and the consequent text annotation are performed using six different nodes (Figure 3) which are enclosed in every metanode of the main graph.

In this work, the metanodes basically work as ‘boxes’ for the Sentiment Expressions, which are given the same label if they are embedded in the same Sentiment box. We will describe below in detail the Contextual Valence Shifters that have been taken into account in the present work: negation, intensification, modality and certain types of comparative constructions.

As regards negation, we included in our grammar negative operators (eg *non*, ‘not’, *mica*, *per niente*, *affatto*, ‘not at all’), negative quantifiers (eg *nessuno,* ‘nobody’ *niente*, *nulla*, ‘nothing’) and lexical negation (eg *senza*, ‘without’, *mancanza di*, *assenza di*, *carenza di*, ‘lack of’) (Benamara, 2012). Negation indicators do not always change a sentence polarity into its positive or negative counterparts (eg *La Citroen non*$_{\textbf{(NegOperator)}}$) *produce auto valide*$_{\textbf{(A+POS)}}$, ‘Citroen does not produce efficient cars’, Negative sentence); they often have the effect of increasing or decreasing the sentence score (e.g. *Grafica non*$_{\textbf{(NegOperator)}}$ *proprio spettacolare*$_{\textbf{(A+POS+FORTE)}}$, ‘The not quite spectacular graphic’, Weakly Negative sentence). That is why we prefer to talk about valence ‘shifting’ rather than ‘switching’.

In order to take Intensification into account, we firstly combined in the grammar the words belonging to the strength scale with the sentiment words listed in the evaluation scale. Moreover, the repetition of more than one negative or positive word, or the use of absolute superlative affixes also have the effect of increasing the words’ Prior Polarity and, for this reason, have been included into the grammar. Intensification and negation can also appear together in the same sentence, eg *Personale alla reception non*$_{\textbf{(Negative\_Operator)}}$ *sempre*$_{\textbf{(AVV+FORTE)}}$ *gentile*$_{\textbf{(A+POS)}}$, ‘Not always kind desk clerks.’, Weakly Negative sentence.

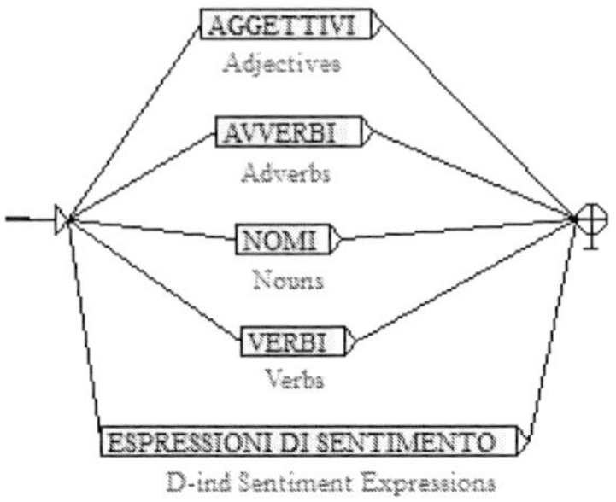

Figure 2 – Main graph of the Contextual Valence Shifters grammar

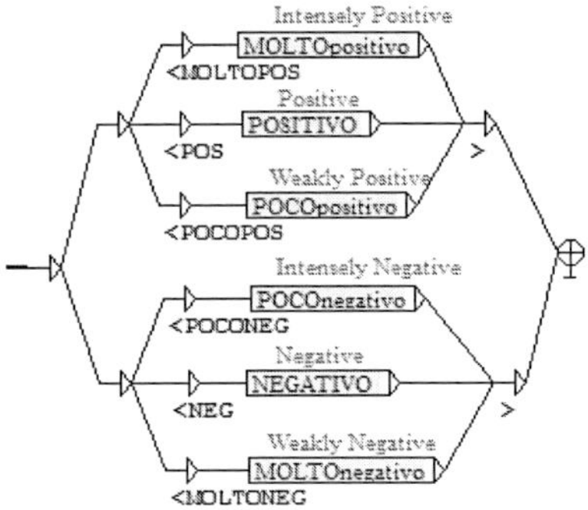

Figure 3 – Using metanodes as boxes for the Sentiment Pattern Extraction

Modality also affects the Semantic Orientation of sentiment expressions. We focused on a particular modality type, among the ones analysed by Benamara (2012), the epistemic category, which refers to the Opinion Holder's personal beliefs and affects the strength and the degree of certainty of opinion expressions. It can be expressed by adverbs of both doubt or necessity and modal verbs such as *dovere* ('have to') and *potere* ('may/can'). In the present work, the above-mentioned adverbs have been respectively considered as downtoners and intensifiers and have been, thus, registered in the strength dictionary.

As far as comparative sentences are concerned, in this work we considered the afore-mentioned comparative frozen sentences of the type *N0 Agg come C1*; some simple comparative sentences that involve the expressions *meglio di*, *migliore di*, 'better than', *peggio di*, *peggiore di*, 'worse than', *superiore a*, 'superior to' *inferiore a*, 'less than'; and the comparative superlative.

Finally, in the Fifth metanode of the Sentiment grammar (Figure 2) we listed and computed many cases in which expressions that do not include the words contained in our dictionaries are also sentiment indicators. For simplicity, in the present work, in this node of the grammar we put the sentences that involve the use of frozen and semi-frozen expressions and words that, for the moment, are not part of the dictionaries.

Experiment and results

The dataset used to evaluate our tools was built using Italian opinionated texts in the form of users' reviews and comments found on e-commerce and opinion websites. It contains 600 texts units (50 positive and 50 negative for each product class) and refers to six different domains, for all of which different websites (such as www.ciao.it; www.amazon.it; www.mymovies.it; www.tripadvisor.it) were exploited. Using the command-line program noojapply.exe, we built a prototype written in JAVA by which users can automatically apply our resources to every kind of text, receiving a feedback of statistics containing the opinions expressed in each case (Figure 4). Using this, we added up the values corresponding to every sentiment expression and, subsequently, we standardised the result for the total number of sentiment expressions contained in the review. Doxa compared this value with the stars that the Opinion holder gave to his review and provided statistics about the opinions expressed in every domain. In Figure 4 we report the analysis conducted on the domain of hotel reviews.

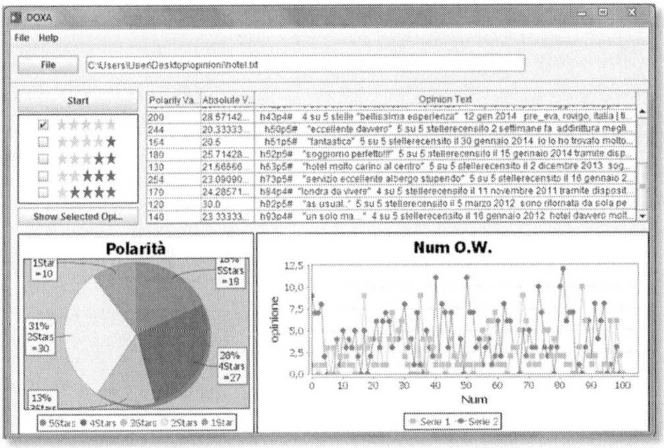

Figure 4 – Sentiment Analysis with Doxa

Because our lexical and grammatical resources are not domain-specific, we observed their interaction with every single part of the corpus, which is composed of many different domains, each one of them characterised by its own peculiarities. Moreover, in order to verify the performances of every part of speech (and of the expressions connected to them) we checked, as shown in Table 2, the Precision and the Recall applying separately every single metanode (A, ADV, N, V, D-ind) of the main graph of the sentiment grammar. The values marked by the asterisks, while reported to be thorough, are not really relevant because of the small number of concordances on which they have been calculated.

As far as the document-level performance is concerned, we calculated the precision twice: in the first case by considering as true positive the reviews correctly classified by Doxa on the basis of a polarity attribution corresponding to the one specified by the Opinion Holder; in the second case by considering as true positive the documents that our tool awarded exactly the same number stars specified by the Opinion Holder.

PRECISION (%)		Cars	Smartphones	Movies	Books	Hotels	Videogames	Average
Sentence level	A	83	84.5	51	77	90.5	82	78
	ADV	78.2	75.8	58.2	84.6	92	50*	73.1
	N	70.4	71.4	43.3	63	79.4	71.4*	66.5
	V	88.2*	57.1*	67.2	73.7	57.1*	100*	73.9
	D-ind	79.3	83.5	64.8	70	87.5	89.4	81.8
	Average	79.9	74.4	56.9	73.7	81.3	78.6	**74.1**
Document level	Polarity	71.0	72.0	63.0	74.0	91.0	72.0	**74.0**
	Intensity	32.0	45.0	25.0	33.0	49.0	34.0	36.3

Table 2 – Sentence-level Precision

RECALL (%)	Cars	Smartphones	Movies	Books	Hotels	Videogames	Average
Sentence-level	72.7	79.6	64.8	65.7	72.1	58.8	69.0
Document-level	100	98.6	100	96.1	98.9	91.2	97.5

Table 3 – Recall on sentence-level and document level performances

As we can see in the last two rows of Table 2, the latter seems to have a very low Precision, but on deeper analysis we discovered that it is quite common for the Opinion Holders to write texts that almost never correspond to the stars they specify. This increases the importance of a software like Doxa, which does not stop at the analysis of the structured data, but enters the semantic dimension of texts written in natural language.

The Recall pertaining to the sentence-level performance of our tool was manually calculated on a sample of 150 opinionated documents (25 from each domain), by considering as false negatives the sentiment indicators which were not annotated by our grammar. The document-level Recall, on the other hand, was automatically checked with DOXA, by considering as true positive all the opinionated documents that contained at least one appropriate sentiment indicator; thus, the documents in which the NooJ grammar did not annotate any pattern were the false negatives that we took into account. Considering the F-measure, the best results were achieved with the smartphone domain (77.0%) in the sentence-level task and with the hotel dataset (94.8%) in the document-level performance.

Conclusion

We conclude this work by anticipating the future line of action that our research will take: we will improve the performances of our system by enlarging the dictionary of verbs and nouns, by building a sentiment dictionary of bad words, by providing the dictionary of multiword expressions with the annotation of sentiment and, lastly, by building a grammar of sentiment expression that is specific for each domain.

Irony (eg *Quel tocco di piccante (...) è gradevole*$_{\mathbf{(A+POS)}}$ *quanto lo sarebbe una spruzzata di pepe su un gelato alla panna*, ‘And the touch of piquancy (…) is as pleasant as a spattering of pepper on a cream-flavoured ice-cream’) and cultural stereotypes (eg *La nuova fiat 500 è consigliabile*$_{\mathbf{(A+POS)}}$ *molto di più ad una ragazza*, ‘The new Fiat 500 is recommended a lot more to a girl’) still remain unresolved problems for the NLP in general and for sentiment analysis. For the moment, we have decided not to deal with with them, but we do not exclude that in the near future we will aim to also tackle these challenges.

References

Andreevskaia, Alina, and Sabine Bergler. 2008. "When Specialists and Generalists Work Together: Overcoming Domain Dependence in Sentiment Tagging." *ACL*.

Benamara, Farah, et al. 2012."How do negation and modality impact on opinions?." *Proceedings of the Workshop on Extra-Propositional Aspects of Meaning in Computational Linguistics*. Association for Computational Linguistics.

Bloom, Kenneth. 2011. *Sentiment analysis based on appraisal theory and functional local grammars*. Diss. Illinois Institute of Technology.

Choi, Yejin, and Claire Cardie. 2008."Learning with compositional semantics as structural inference for subsentential sentiment analysis." *Proceedings of the Conference on Empirical Methods in Natural Language Processing*. Association for Computational Linguistics.

D'Agostino, Emilio. 2005. "Grammatiche lessicalmente esaustive delle passioni Il caso dell'Io collerico. Le forme nominali." *Quaderns d'Italià*.

Dasgupta, Sajib, and Vincent Ng. 2009."Mine the easy, classify the hard: a semi-supervised approach to automatic sentiment classification." *Proceedings of the Joint Conference of the 47th Annual Meeting of the ACL and the 4th International Joint Conference on Natural Language Processing of the AFNLP*: Volume 2-Volume 2. Association for Computational Linguistics.

Gross, Maurice. 1995."Une grammaire locale de l'expression des sentiments." *Langue française* (1995): 70-87.

—. 1981. Les bases empiriques de la notion de prédicat sémantique. *Langages*, 7-52.

Hatzivassiloglou, Vasileios, and Kathleen R. McKeown. 1997. "Predicting the semantic orientation of adjectives." *Proceedings of the 35th annual meeting of the association for computational linguistics and eighth conference of the european chapter of the association for computational linguistics*. Association for Computational Linguistics.

Hu, Minqing, and Bing Liu. 2004. "Mining opinion features in customer reviews." *AAAI*. Vol. 4. No. 4.

Kaji, Nobuhiro, and Masaru Kitsuregawa. 2007. "Building Lexicon for Sentiment Analysis from Massive Collection of HTML Documents." *EMNLP-CoNLL*.

Kanayama, Hiroshi, and Tetsuya Nasukawa. 2006."Fully automatic lexicon expansion for domain-oriented sentiment analysis." *Proceedings of the 2006 Conference on Empirical Methods in Natural Language Processing*. Association for Computational Linguistics.

Kennedy, Alistair, and Diana Inkpen. 2006. "Sentiment classification of movie reviews using contextual valence shifters." *Computational intelligence* 22.2 (2006): 110-125.

Landauer, Thomas K., and Susan T. Dumais. 1997. "A solution to Plato's problem: The latent semantic analysis theory of acquisition, induction, and representation of knowledge." *Psychological review* 104.2: 211.

Liu, Bing. 2010. "Sentiment analysis and subjectivity." *Handbook of natural language processing* 2: 627-666.

Liu, Bing. 2010. "Sentiment analysis: A multi-faceted problem." *IEEE Intelligent Systems* 25.3: 76-80.

Liu, Jingjing, and Stephanie Seneff. 2009."Review sentiment scoring via a parse-and-paraphrase paradigm." *Proceedings of the 2009 Conference on Empirical Methods in Natural Language Processing*: Volume 1-Volume 1. Association for Computational Linguistics.

Mohammad, Saif, Cody Dunne, and Bonnie Dorr. 2009. "Generating high-coverage semantic orientation lexicons from overtly marked words and a thesaurus." *Proceedings of the 2009 Conference on Empirical Methods in Natural Language Processing*: Volume 2-Volume 2. Association for Computational Linguistics.

Mulder, Matthijs, et al. 2004. "A lexical grammatical implementation of affect." *Text, Speech and Dialogue*. Springer Berlin Heidelberg.

Narayanan, Ramanathan, Bing Liu, and Alok Choudhary. 2009. "Sentiment analysis of conditional sentences." *Proceedings of the 2009 Conference on Empirical Methods in Natural Language Processing*: Volume 1-Volume 1. Association for Computational Linguistics.

Neviarouskaya, Alena, Helmut Prendinger, and Mitsuru Ishizuka. 2010. "Recognition of affect, judgment, and appreciation in text." *Proceedings of the 23rd International Conference on Computational Linguistics*. Association for Computational Linguistics.

Pang, Bo, and Lillian Lee. 2008."Opinion mining and sentiment analysis." *Foundations and trends in information retrieval* 2.1-2: 1-135.

Pang, Bo, Lillian Lee, and Shivakumar Vaithyanathan. 2002. "Thumbs up?: sentiment classification using machine learning techniques." *Proceedings of the ACL-02 conference on Empirical methods in natural language processing*-Volume 10. Association for Computational Linguistics.

Polanyi, Livia, and Annie Zaenen. 2006."Contextual valence shifters." *Computing attitude and affect in text: Theory and applications.* Springer Netherlands:1-10.

Riloff, Ellen, Janyce Wiebe, and Theresa Wilson. 2003. "Learning subjective nouns using extraction pattern bootstrapping." *Proceedings of the seventh conference on Natural language learning at HLT-NAACL 2003*-Volume 4. Association for Computational Linguistics.

Taboada, Maite, Caroline Anthony, and Kimberly Voll. 2006. "Methods for creating semantic orientation dictionaries." *Proceedings of the 5th International Conference on Language Resources and Evaluation* (LREC), Genova, Italy.

Taboada, Maite, et al. 2011. "Lexicon-based methods for sentiment analysis." *Computational linguistics* 37.2: 267-307.

Turney, Peter D. 2002. "Thumbs up or thumbs down?: semantic orientation applied to unsupervised classification of reviews." *Proceedings of the 40th annual meeting on association for computational linguistics*. Association for Computational Linguistics.

Velikovich, Leonid, et al. 2010- "The viability of web-derived polarity lexicons." Human Language Technologies: *The 2010 Annual*

Conference of the North American Chapter of the Association for Computational Linguistics. Association for Computational Linguistics.

Vermeij, M. J. M. 2005. "The Orientation of User Opinions Through Adverbs, Verbs and Nouns." *3rd Twente Student Conference on IT*, Enschede June.

Vietri, Simonetta. 1990. "On some comparative frozen sentences in Italian." *Lingvisticæ Investigationes* 14.1: 149-174.

—. 2011. "On a Class of Italian Frozen Sentences." *Lingvisticæ Investigationes* 34.2: 228-267.

Vollero, Agostino. 2010. *E-marketing e Web communication. Verso la gestione della corporate reputation on-line.* Giappichelli.

Yi, Jeonghee, et al. 2003."Sentiment analyzer: Extracting sentiments about a given topic using natural language processing techniques." *Data Mining, 2003. ICDM 2003. Third IEEE International Conference on. IEEE*, 2003.

<MATERIAL> PREDICATIVE ADJECTIVES IN GREEK NOOJ MODULE

ZOE GAVRIILIDOU, LENA PAPADOPOULOU AND ELINA CHADJIPAPA

Abstract

In this paper, the processing of denominal predicative adjectives belonging to the semantic class of <material> is described within the linguistic engine of NooJ. First, our theoretical framework is set: the classes of objects by Gross and the monolingual coordinated dictionaries by Blanco. Second, the description of our data is presented. Third, the utilisation of NooJ dictionaries and grammars for the processing of our data is demonstrated. Finally, the conclusions and the perspectives of our work are drawn.

Introduction

The present work aims to follow up the adjectives quantitative elaboration in the Greek NooJ module (Papadopoulou & Anagnostopoulos 2013). The quantitative data are expected to be complemented qualitatively by the introduction of predicative adjectives belonging to the semantic class of <material>-ie *xrisós* 'gold' basing on the lexicographical data of Papadopoulou and Chatjipapa (2013), which were clustered pursuant to the <classes of objects> by Gaston (1994).

The structure of our paper is as follows. The first part describes briefly the theory of 'classes of objects' by Gross (1994) and the lexicographical model of 'monolingual coordinated dictionaries' by Blanco (2001). In the second part, the existing adjectival data in the Greek NooJ module are reported. In the third part, the processing of the <Material> predicative adjectives within NooJ dictionaries and grammars (Silberztein, 2003) is presented. In the last section of our paper our conclusions regarding the translation equivalence and the dynamic character of NooJ as well as the future perspectives of our work are given.

Theoretical framework

<Classes of objects> (COs) is the main theoretical basis of our work. COs were introduced by Gross (1994) with the aim of providing a homogeneous semantic classification of arguments based on syntactic criteria. His classification concerns a system of retro alimentation between predicates and their arguments according to the semantic content and syntactic behaviour of both.

Considering the following examples:

- *φοράω*/N0:Hum/N1:Conc<ρούχα>
  wear/N0:Hum/N1:Conc<clothes>

- *οδηγώ*/N0:Hum/N1:Conc<μέσα μεταφοράς>
  drive/N0:Hum/N1:Conc<means of transport>

it is observed that two different classes of objects are constructed - <clothes> and <means of transport> - according to the appropriate operators 'wear' and 'drive', which select their arguments by both semantic and syntactic criteria. Although the above examples concern the prototypical case of a relation between predicate-arguments, where by predicate a verb is meant, there is the same application to predicative adjectives:

- e.g. *μεταλλική ντουλάπα* 'metallic closet'

Previous works on adjectives within the framework of CO include, among others, those by Valetopoulos (2003) in Greek and French adjectives and by Catena (2006) in Spanish and French adjectives. The latter applied her adjectival data to the monolingual coordinated dictionaries (MCD).

The concept of classes of objects has been adopted by MCD (Blanco 2001), into whose lexicographical model each lemma is annotated by its CO among other morphological and syntactic-semantic information, in order for each entry to correspond to a lexical unit. In this way, each entry-lexical unit can be linearly associated with its equivalent translation in the target language.

Greek adjectival data in NooJ

To date, the Greek NooJ module contains 9,119 adjectival forms based on the quantitative work by Papadopoulou and Anagnostopoulos (2013). These forms concern adjectives to which the inflectional codification is assigned within the NooJ inflectional grammar and their Spanish and French translation equivalents are merely listed without being further processed semantically.

Contrariwise, the work by Papadopoulou and Chatjipapa (2013), which was carried out within the COs framework, provides a qualitative sample of predicative adjectives belonging exclusively to the semantic class of <material>. Their lexicographical data have been processed within monolingual coordinated dictionaries. Semantic information is provided for each lemma so that each lemma corresponds to a lexical unit. The semantic information concerns the assignation of the four-fold classification proposed by Catena (2006) for the predicative adjectives that are derived from nouns belonging to the class of object <material> (Catena 2006: 32-36):

— <material: X is made of Y material>
— <material: X contains Y material>
— <material: X produces Y material >
— <material: X looks like Y material >

Moreover, the syntactic properties of predicative adjectives have been attributed regarding the syntactic-semantic features of their arguments. It is worth mentioning that the Arg0 of the predicative adjectives presents a series of limitations. The adjectives <material: X is made of Y material> select concrete arguments, the <material: X contains Y material> concrete and locative ones, the <material: X produces Y material> locative and abstract ones belonging to the semantic class of <industrial entity>, and the adjectives <material: X looks like Y material> select concrete arguments.

Furthermore, the translation equivalence in Spanish is provided according to the semantic classes. These data have been used to form the core of our work.

NooJ processing of <material> adjectives

The processing of <material> adjectives within NooJ consists in three main levels: the dictionary, the inflectional grammar and the grammar for paraphrases.

The first level deals with the adaptation of our lexicographical data to meet the formal requirements of NooJ dictionaries, e.g.:

- σιδερένιος,A+FLX=A4+material+DN=σίδερο +ES=de hierro/férreo
- λιπαρός,A+FLX=A1+contenido+DN=λίπος+ES=graso/ grasiento
- σιτοπαραγωγικός,A+FLX=A1+producción+DN=σιτάρι +ES=productor de grano
- κρεμώδης,A+FLX=A10+similitud+DN=κρέμα+ES=cremoso

The macrostructure of the NooJ dictionary of predicative adjectives <material> counts 356 entries in total. The following table presents in detail the number of lemmas that corresponds to each semantic subclass of <material>:

Semantic class	N° entries
<material: material>	168
<material: contains Y>	101
<material: produces Y>	27
<material: looks like Y>	60
TOTAL	356

Table 1 - Macrostructure

The second level refers to the assignment of the inflectional codes to our lemmas within the inflectional grammar of NooJ. For this processing, the inflectional grammar of the Greek NooJ module has been reutilised, without it being necessary to include any additional inflectional paradigm. It should be pointed out that this elaboration functioned as a verification tool for the inflectional codification accuracy of the work by Papadopoulou and Anagnostopoulos (2013), the results of which confirmed the validity of the codes.

The third level concerns the construction of four different grammars, which recognise, parse and paraphrase the adjectival predicates of <material>:

i. σιδερένια πόρτα→ πόρτα από σίδερο
'iron door → door (made) of iron'

ii. λιπαρό φαγητό → φαγητό που περιέχει λίπος
'greasy food → food that contains grease'

iii. σιτοπαραγωγικές χώρες → χώρες που παράγουν σιτάρι
'grain producing states→ states that produce grain'

iv. κρεμώδης αφρός →αφρός που μοιάζει με κρέμα
'creamy foam → foam that looks like cream'

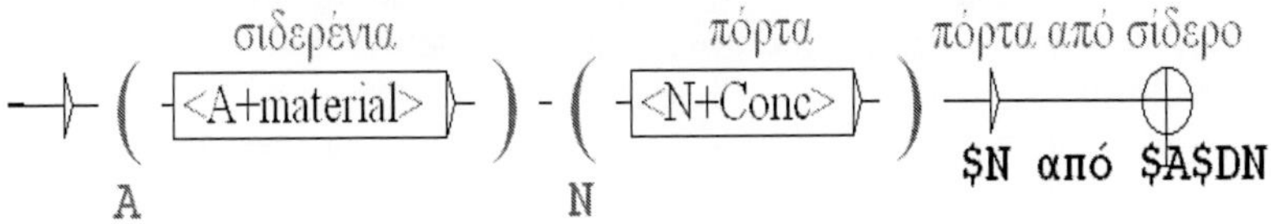

Figure 2- Adjectives <material: X is made of Y material>

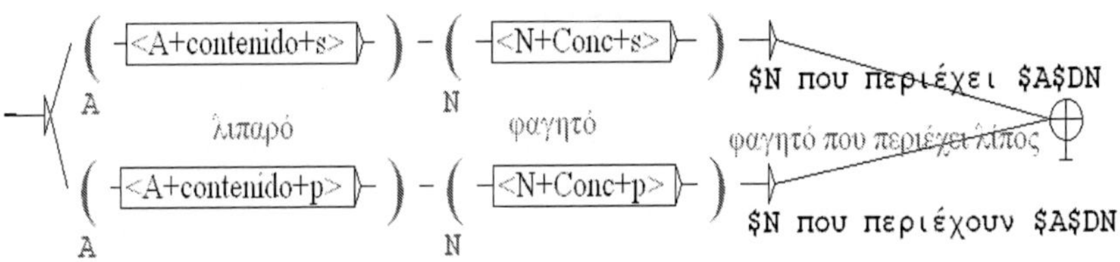

Figure 3 – Adjectives <material: X contains Y material>

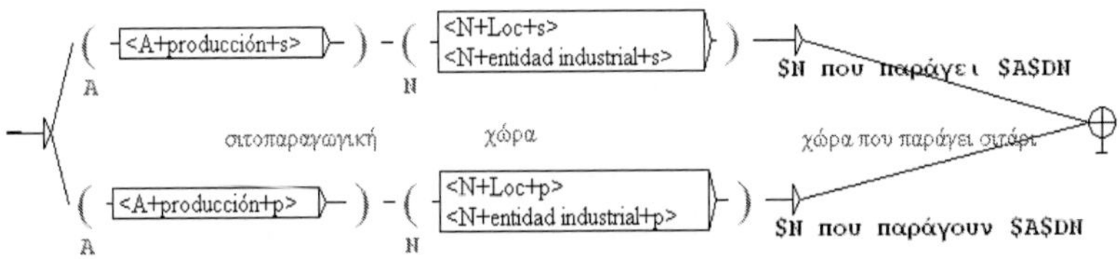

Figure 4 – Adjectives <material: X produces Y material>

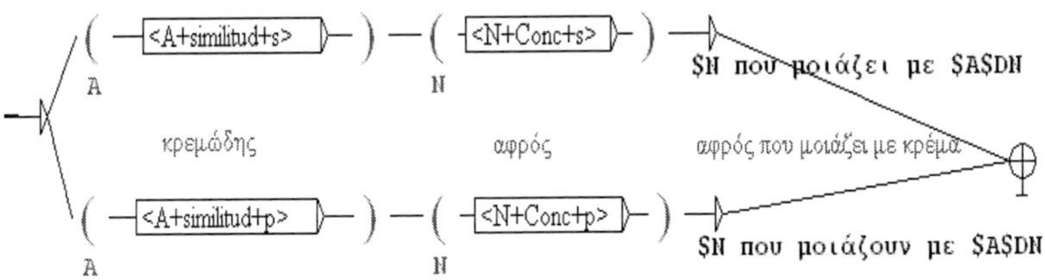

Figure 5 – Adjectives <material: X looks like Y material >

Conclusions and perspectives

The main aim of this work is to suggest a method of improving quantitative lexicographical data in the NooJ module. NooJ functionalities and tools, such as the dictionaries and grammars, as well as the theoretical framework of classes of objects and the lexicographical model of monolingual coordinated dictionaries constitute a reliable framework for a lexicographical treatment of data that provide accurate translation equivalence and paraphrases. Moreover, our method demonstrates that the data in NooJ are not static but rather, can be enriched and improved. Thus, our future work will focus on the enrichment of the Greek NooJ module by processing more semantic classes and making the best use of NooJ linguistic environment.

References

Blanco, Xavier. 2001. Dictionnaires électroniques et traduction automatique espagnol-français. *Langages* 143: 49-70.

Catena, Angels. 2006. *Contribución a la formalización del adjetivo para la traducción automática español-francés*. PhD Dissertation. Bellaterra: Universidad Autónoma de Barcelona.

Gross, Gaston. 1994. Classes d'objets et description des verbes. *Langages*, 115. Larousse, Paris.

Papadopoulou, Lena and Giannis Anagnostopoulos. 2013. Enrichment of the Greek NooJ Module: Morphological Properties. In M. Silberztein, A. Donabédian, & V. Khurshudia, *Formalising Natural Languages with NooJ*. Cambridge Scholars Publishing.

Papadopoulou, Lena and Elina Chatjipapa, 2013. The semantic class <material> of Greek adjectives: Lexicographical treatment and applications on machine translation (GR-ES) and learning Greek. Oral presentation at the 11th International Conference on Greek Linguistics.

Silberztein, Max. 2003. *NooJ Manual*. Available for download at: www.nooj4nlp.net

Valetopoulos, Freidericos 2003. *Les adjectifs prédicatifs en grec et en français: de l'analyse syntaxique à l'élaboration des classes sémantiques*, thèse de 3e cycle. Paris 13.

CROATIAN DERIVATIONAL PATTERNS IN NOOJ

MATEA SREBAČIĆ, KREŠIMIR ŠOJAT AND BOŽO BEKAVAC

Abstract

The paper deals with derivational patterns in Croatian, a Slavic language with rich inflectional and derivational morphology. So far computational processing of Croatian morphology has been predominately aimed at inflectional phenomena. In the introductory part we briefly present CroDeriV, a newly developed resource for the processing of derivational phenomena, which contains 14,300 Croatian verbs. In the main part of the paper, we present the methodology for the rule-based extension of derivational families in CroDeriV with lemmas of other parts of speech (nouns, adjectives, adverbs) developed and applied in NooJ. The ten most frequent verbal roots from CroDeriV are selected as a basis for the drawing-up of rules. The rules describe derivational processes among words of different POS sharing the same lexical morpheme and thus forming a derivational family. The high frequency of the roots used in intra-POS derivation, ie from verb to verb, proved to be a good indicator of richl branching across different POS within a derivational family. At the same time, the selected sample of roots provides a substantial stock of derivational affixes needed for further work, ie for the automatic recognition of derivationally related words in other families with the same rules. Due to extensive allomorphy as well as graphical overlapping of affixes and stems in Croatian, the set of rules was manually constructed for each derivational family discussed in the paper. Finally, the results show that NooJ can be used as a valuable tool for processing Croatian derivational data.

Introduction

This paper deals with derivational patterns in Croatian, a Slavic language with rich inflectional and derivational morphology. Word formation processes in Croatian include compounding and derivation. The language's derivational processes mostly consist of prefixation and suffixation, whereas its inflection is limited to suffixation. The processing of Croatian morphology has been predominantly aimed at inflection. Inflectional classes are extensively covered, for example, by the Croatian Morphological Lexicon (HML) (Tadić, 1994) or morphological grammars in the Croatian NooJ module (Vučković, Tadić, Bekavac, 2010). On the other hand, the processing of derivational morphology, as well as the development of databases such as Catvar (Habash, Dor, 2003) for English or DErivBase (Zeller, Šnajder, Padó, 2014) for German has gained far less attention. In Croatian, derivation is far more productive than compounding, which does not have a very prominent role, unlike in other languages such as German. In this article, we focus on derivational phenomena in Croatian. Specifically, we deal with lexical families – ie sets of words that share the same lexical morpheme and that are derived from the base form through prefixation and/or suffixation. We discuss how derivational processes recorded in CroDeriV, a derivational database for Croatian, are used for the production of morphological rules in NooJ and how these rules can further be used for the development of a morphological parser.

The paper is structured as follows: in Section 2 we briefly present CroDeriV. In Section 3 we describe the most significant derivational processes within selected derivational families. Section 4 deals with derivational rules applied in NooJ. The results of their application are given in Section 5. Future work is outlined in the conclusion.

CroDeriV

CroDeriV is a morphological database that contains data about the morphological structure and derivational relatedness of Croatian words. The morphological structure consists of the segmentation of words into lexical, derivational, and inflectional morphemes. Derivational relatedness is based on mutual lexical morphemes. The database is free for searching at the following site: http://croderiv.ffzg.hr/. The building of CroDeriV can be divided into two phases. The first phase focused on the processing of verbs. At present, CroDeriV contains 14,326 verbs morphologically analysed and grouped into derivational families. All of the verbs were collected in infinitive form from publicly available corpora and dictionaries. The collected verbs were segmented into morphemes using a rule-based approach and checked manually. Those verbs that share the same lexical morpheme were mutually linked. This procedure enabled the recognition of a general morphological structure of all the analysed verbs, as well as the recognition of lexical and derivational morphemes used in derivational processes. The total number of lexical morphemes is 3,386.

The objective in the second phase (database extension), is to incorporate other parts of speech – ie nouns, adjectives, and adverbs – into existing derivational families and to build new ones. In the following section, we describe the procedure we used for this purpose.

Data

In order to incorporate other parts of speech into existing derivational families and build new ones, we used the list of roots from CroDeriV. Our hypothesis was that a high frequency of roots used in intra-POS derivation – ie from verb to verb within a particular derivational family – is an indicator of rich branching across different POS within the derivational family. For example, the root *pis-* (as in *pisati* 'to write') is used in the derivation of 35 verbs and in 174 derivatives of other POS. Apart from the frequency and size of the derivational families, the selection of verbal roots was motivated by two other factors: origin and inflectional class.

We have taken into account only roots of Slavic origin. Our assumption was that their derivational families would reflect typical and productive derivational patterns in Croatian. Finally, we wished to cover various verbal inflectional classes, since different classes usually undergo specific phonological changes at morpheme boundaries. The chosen roots are: *pis-* (*pisac* 'writer', *pisati* 'to write') *glas-* (*glas* 'voice', *glasiti* 'to utter a sound'), *red-* (*red* 'sequence', *redati* 'to line up'), *rez-* (*rez* 'cut', *rezati* 'to cut'), *let-* (*let* 'flight', *letjeti* 'to fly'), *rast-* (*rast* 'growth', *rasti* 'to grow'), *stav-* (*stav* 'stance', 'attitude'; *staviti* 'to put'), *moć* (*moć* 'power', *moći* 'can'), *živ-* (*živ* 'alive', *živjeti* 'to live'), *pad-* (*pad* 'fall', *pasti* 'to fall').

After having established the initial set of verbal roots and infinitives, we started to expand their derivational families with words of other POS. For this purpose, we applied a simple rule-based procedure for the detection of lemmas containing the set of roots given above.[1] The set of lemmas was taken from the HML and various free dictionaries and corpora. We manually checked the results and segmented all the obtained words into morphemes. The final result was that 425 words, belonging to ten derivational families, were analysed for morphemes. This segmentation enabled insight into the morphological structure of nouns,

[1]A more detailed account of these rules is given in Šojat, Srebačić and Pavelić (2014).

adjectives, and adverbs in selected derivational families. The maximum number of prefixes in new members of derivational families was two, whereas we recorded some instances of as many as five suffixes. The new members of the selected derivational families were used in the following step. We grouped all words from this set first according to the same closest derivational suffix, then by the next suffix, and so on. An example is given in Table 1 below. The suffix shared by all words is *-ač*, whereas the other suffixes (e.g., *-iv-* or *-j-*) vary. This kind of representation allowed the detection of possible affixal combinations and can be used for the detection of general derivational patterns in Croatian. The words with the same morphological structure were grouped together, and the generalised derivational patterns of all word groups were used for the development of derivational grammars in NooJ.

Since 79 different suffixes were recorded in the test sample, we decided to focus on those that occur at least five times in the analysed derivational families.

Finally, we extracted all possible combinations in which these suffixes occur and incorporated them in a NooJ grammar.

P	P	R	S	S
	o	glaš	av	ač
	is	pis	iv	ač
	o	pis	iv	ač
	po	pis	iv	ač
	pre	pis	iv	ač
	pro	pis	iv	ač
	u	pis	iv	ač
	za	pis	iv	ač
	o	glaš	iv	ač
	u	ređ	iv	ač
pre	u	ređ	iv	ač
	pri	ređ	iv	ač
ras	po	ređ	iv	ač
	ra	stavl	j	ač
	do	stavl	j	ač
	na	stavl	j	ač
	po	stavl	j	ač
	pred	stavl	j	ač
	sa	stavl	j	ač
za	u	stavl	j	ač

	od	mag		ač
	po	mag		ač
pot	po	mag		ač
		rez		ač
		let		ač
		pis		ač
		glas		ač

Table 1 ⍰ Preparation of the data, P = prefix, R = root S = suffix

Derivational grammars in NooJ

Main structure of the grammar

The main structure of the grammar is divided into three parts: prefixal (Pref), lexical (Root), and suffixal (Suff). The structure of the grammar is presented in Figure 1.

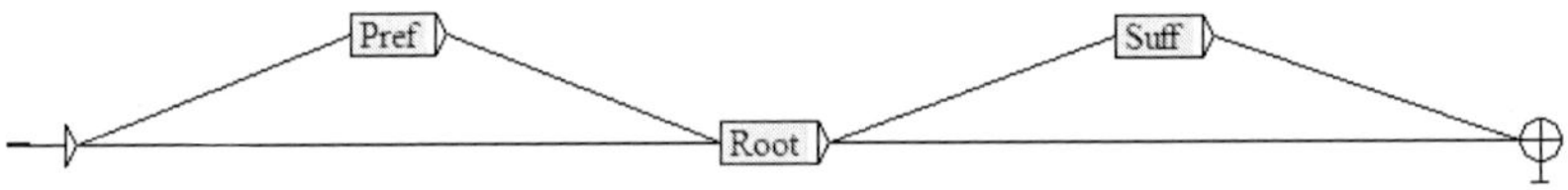

Figure 1 – Main structure of the grammar

Sub-parts of the grammar

The prefixal part consists of two sub-grammars, since the analysed words have up to two prefixes. The overall morphological structure of the prefixal part of the analysed words is as follows:

(P2) + (P1) + R, where P = prefix, R = root, () = optional.

This part of the grammar is based on the list of prefixes and their allomorphs from CroDeriV. Prefixes have a limited set of allomorphs, and by including them in the grammar, we have covered all possible phonological changes at the prefix-root boundary.

The lexical part consists of roots and their allomorphs. As mentioned, we took ten roots of Slavic origin and built their derivational families with all POS included. All allomorphs of roots were extracted from CroDeriV and taken into account in the development of the grammars.

The development of the grammars for the suffixal part required additional effort, due to numerous and diverse phonological changes that occur at the root-suffix boundary. The suffixal part consists of six sub-grammars based on productive suffixal patterns detected in the analysed derivational families (see Figure 2). Each sub-grammar in the suffixal part consists of derivational sub-patterns based on possible suffixal combinations. Unlike prefixes, which are not obligatory, at least one suffix must occur in the morphological structure of inflected words in Croatian.

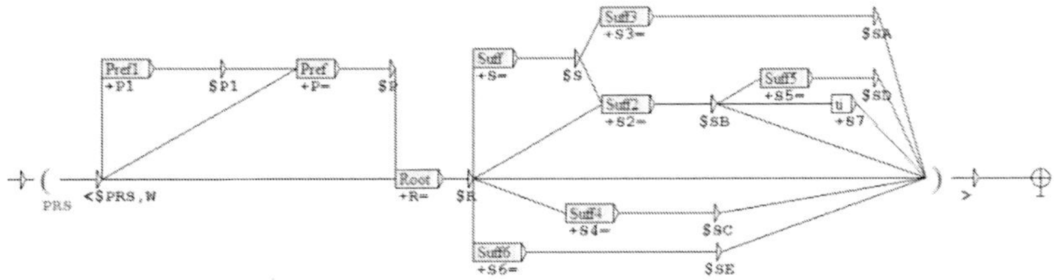

Figure 2 – Elaborated structure of the grammar

Taking all the restrictions into account, approximately 80% of the words from the ten families analysed are covered by the rules described above. These rules can also be applied to other roots, since they are based on generalised patterns of productive suffixes in Croatian.

Results

Generalised derivational patterns produce all the possible combinations of morphemes, which means an over-generation of forms. This can be solved by checking against dictionaries and/or corpora. We used a corpus of 241,248 tokens to check the precision of the method presented here in order to determine whether it is worth applying to the morphological structure of words from unknown derivational families.

In this relatively small corpus, 2,118 word forms were detected and automatically segmented into morphemes. From this number, we have extracted 273 unique forms and 211 lemmas. In other words, based on the initial set of 425 words, we have correctly recognised 49.64% of the instances with a precision of 99%.[2] Although this rate of recall is not quite satisfactory, it would probably rise if the evaluation were to be done on a bigger and more balanced corpus.

[2]Only two lemmas, the personal names *Douglas* and *Rođo*, were not recognised.

Our NooJ grammar also records all the intermediate derivational states, thus enabling the recognition of the complete morphological structure of words (see Figure 3).

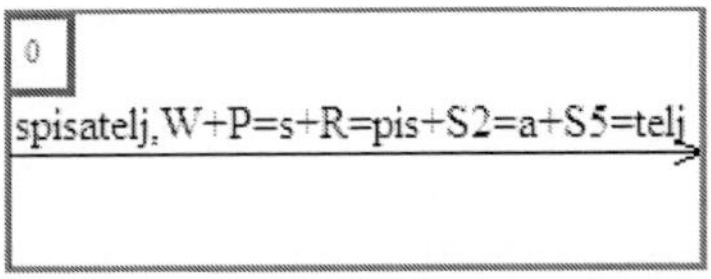

Figure 3 – Morphological structure of the word *spisatelj* 'writer' obtained by the NooJ grammar

Since the grammar is based on productive and generalised derivational patterns, the quick and efficient enlargement of CroDeriV with other POS is possible by adding new roots to the lexical part of the grammar.

Moreover, the methodology itself proved to be effective and valuable in recognising the morphological structure of words, which was more or less carried out manually in the first phases of building CroDeriV.

Conclusion and future work

Preliminary results show that NooJ can be used as a valuable tool for processing Croatian derivational data. Since it records derivational steps used in the formation of particular words, it can be also used as a morphological analyser, which has not yet been developed for Croatian.

The application of the NooJ grammars to the larger set of non-processed data can enable the easier and automatised enlargement of derivational families in CroDeriV with other POS.

The line of processing as described here – ie the recording of all derivational steps – also enables the automatic recognition of words with the same derivational pattern. In future, we plan to process other derivational families via hitherto derivational patterns. We also intend to introduce new derivational patterns via analysing words that remained non-recognised after applying derivational grammars.

Acknowledgements

The research that led to these results was supported by the XLike project (FP7, Grant 288342).

References

Habash, Nizar and Bonnie Dorr. 2003. A Categorial Variation Database for English. In *Proceedings of the North American Association for Computational Linguistics*, Edmonton, Canada, 96-102.

Šojat, Krešimir, Matea Srebačić, and Tin Pavelić. 2014. CroDeriV 2.0: Initial experiments. In *Advances in Natural Language Processing*, edited by Adam Przepiórkowski, and Maciej Ogrodniczuk. Heidelberg, NewYork, Dordrecht, London : Springer, pp. 27-33.

Tadić, Marko. 1994. *Računalna obradba morfologije hrvatskoga književnoga jezika.* PhD Thesis. University of Zagreb, Zagreb.

Vučković, Kristina, Marko Tadić, and Božo Bekavac. 2010. Croatian Language Resources for NooJ'. *CIT. Journal of computing and information technology* 18: 295-301.

Zeller, Britta, Sebastian Padó, and Jan Šnajder. 2014. Towards semantic validation of a derivational lexicon'. In *Proceedings of COLING 2014, the 25th International Conference on Computational Linguistics: Technical Papers*, Dublin City University and Association for Computational Linguistics: Dublin, Ireland, 1728-1739.

THE INFLECTION OF ITALIAN PRONOMINAL VERBS

MARIO MONTELEONE AND MARIA PIA DI BUONO[1]

Abstract

In this paper we describe how to inflect Italian pronominal verbs (IPVs) using NooJ rule-edited inflectional grammars. More specifically, we show how a relatively small set of NooJ instructions correctly inflects 244 pronominal verbs which are actually atomic linguistic units and therefore have to be lemmatised inside electronic dictionaries. We also demonstrate that the set of instructions used to inflect ALU pronominal verbs can be used to tag and parse verbal agglutinations obtained by argument pronominalisation within simple sentences.

Introduction

Unlike all other Italian simple atomic linguistic units (ALUs), the inflection IPVs present substantial peculiarities, and can be considered a topic pertaining not only to morphology, but also to morpho-syntax and, to a certain extent, to formal and semantic idiomaticity. In spite of all this, oddly in Italian literature, IPVs and IPV inflection seem to have never been considered crucial topics to deal with. Even specialised and academy-oriented Italian grammar books do not present any in-depth and/or exhaustive studies on IPVs. We dare to advance the hypothesis that this may be due not to the low attractiveness of the argument itself, but rather to the fact that in the past neither an analytical methodology nor a NLP environment suitable to comprehensively describe and reuse IPVs and IPV inflected forms were used.

---

[1]Mario Monteleone is the author of the paragraphs from I to V. Maria Pia di Buono is the author of paragraphs VI and VII. The authors would like to thank Max Silberztein for his crucial and constant support during all the construction phases of the dictionary.

In the following, we will give full details on the taxonomy we established for these verbs, which is basically based on two main sets, ie morphological IPVs and syntactic IPVs. But as a first instance, it is worth stressing that even in their idiosyncrasy, these verbs present easily predictable and formalisable behaviours of co-reference, co-occurrence and selection restriction. Therefore, embedding an IPV electronic dictionary in NooJ is at the same time a feasible and essential task, as it can considerably help in achieving a fairly detailed description of Italian morpho-syntax, and a more consistent automatic textual analysis.

IPVs: Morphological and Transformational Features

From a morphological point of view, in their canonical form IPVs are the result of an agglutination between an infinitive verb which drops the final *–e*, and a maximum of two pronominal particles such as:

- *-si* in *lavarsi* (to wash oneself, to wash one another), which can be segmented into *lavar-* (from *lavare*) + *-si*;
- *-ce* and *-la* in *avercela* (to be angry with) which can be segmented into *aver-* (from *avere*) + *-ce* and *-la*;
- *-se* and *-la* in *vedersela* (to have a deal with someone), which can be segmented into *veder-* (from *vedere*) + *-se* and *-la*.

In such agglutinations, it is worth noting that the pronominal particles may derive from:

- a process of 'frozen pronominalisation', which cannot be accounted for by means of transformational rules ie which cannot assign an acceptable and/or grammatical deictic function to the pronominal particle *–si*. This happens with forms as *inginocchiarsi* (to kneel down) in which the *–si* does not stand for any noun or predicate argument. Such verbs have one and only one autonomous infinitive form, while forms such as *inginocchiare* can be used only within causative sentences, as for instance *Max fa inginocchiare Luca* (Max makes Luca kneel down);
- a process of pronominalisation/cliticisation which can be accounted for by means of transformational rules inside simple/nuclear sentences. For instance, the sentence *Max si lava* (Max washes himself) is obtained transforming the simple

sentence *Max_0 lava Max_1*, where the *si* refers to the subject *Max*. Therefore, given that:

Max_0=:Max_1

we have:

[T Pron] → *Max lava se stesso (Max=:se stesso)*
[T Clitic]→ *Max si*[2] *lava (se stesso=:si)*

Consequently, the *–si* is agglutinated with the infinitive form of the verb, as previously shown.

IPV Typological Classification

On such basis, and using a strict Lexicon-Grammar (LG) approach, it is possible to establish a first macro-classification for these verbs. We will have a morphological or pure IPV when:

- the agglutinated pronominal particle is not obtained by means of pronominalization ie it does not stand for one or more arguments of a given verb.
- the corresponding non-pronominal infinitive cannot occur as an autonomous ALU inside simple sentences.

At the same time, we will have a syntactic pronominal verb when:

- the agglutinated pronominal particle is obtained by means of pronominalisation ie it stands for one or more arguments of a given verb;
- the corresponding non-pronominal infinitive can occur as an autonomous ALU inside simple sentences.

Therefore, only the inflection of Pure Italian Pronominal Verbs (PIPVs) will be dealt with in this paper, considering that here we will mainly deal with morphology, lemmatisation and inflection. If PIPVs are

---

[2]In such cases, we deal with a very common phenomenon of Italian morpho-syntax which goes by the name of ‘ascent of the clitic’: whenever a simple or compound pronoun is transformed into a clitic, it moves back to the left of the verb, immediately after the N0.

autonomous ALUs, then they need to be lemmatised inside electronic dictionaries, and automatically inflected; on the contrary, Italian syntactic pronominal verbs (ISPVs), in all their occurrences, can be recognised and parsed by means of local grammars.

With simple taxonomic purposes, although ISPVs are not the central theme of this paper, we may note that these verbs can be divided into:

1. **reflexives**, as *pettinarsi* (to comb oneself) in *Max si pettina* (Max combs himself);
2. **possessive reflexives,** for instance:
    a. *lavarsi Nparte_del_corpo* (to wash Nbody_part), as in *Max si lava le mani* (Max washes his hands), which may be paraphrased in *Max lava le sue mani;*
    b. *abbottonarsi Nabito* (to button one's Ndress), as in *Max si abbottona la camicia* (Max buttons his shirt), which may be paraphrased in *Max abbottona la sua camicia*;
3. **pronominal intransitives** as *ammantarsi* (to be mantled with) in *La collina si ammanta di neve* (The hill is mantled with snow), in a binary transformation relationship with *La neve ammanta la collina* (The snow mantles the hill), in which we find a permutation of the two complements but no change in their semantic roles;
4. **pronominal transitives** as *accaparrarsi* (to grab) in *Harry si accaparra l'uovo doro* (Harry grabs the golden egg), which may be paraphrased into *Harry accaparra l'uovo doro per se stesso*;
5. **reciprocals** such as *sposarsi* (to get married) in sentences as *Max e Paola si sposano* (Max and Paola get married).

A further possible ISPV type is the one as in *mangiarsi una mela* (to eat an apple), in which the *–si* is neither deictic nor syntactic. Such constructions have a mere emphatic value, used to stress both the agentivity of the subject or the patientivity of an even non-essential complement, as in:

*…russando**le** tutta la note nelle orecchie…* (… snoring all night long in her ears…)

IPV Morph-Syntactic Features

Contrary to all other Italian inflectional entries, IPVs present specific formal and morpho-syntactic idiosyncrasies that do not allow either the reuse or the adaptation of existing NooJ algorithms and codes; therefore, the inflectional codes, which can be established for IPVs, necessarily have a very low level of productivity.

In this sense, the main constraints come from:

1. the aforementioned 'ascent of the clitic'; in every inflected form, a given clitic not only shifts from the end of the verb to the position immediately before it, but also agrees with the verb in number and person for all analytical forms; gender, number and person for all synthetic forms (ie agglutinated forms);
2. the fact that the numbers of characters to delete from the infinitive and the type of grammatical morphemes to add to the root are almost never specific to each single entry;
3. last but not least, the fact that PIPVs represent a most peculiar morph-syntactic case, in which a simple word such as *inginocchiarsi*, when inflected, produces both simple synthetic forms as *inginocchiati* (kneel down, imperative) and compound analytic forms such as *mi inginocchio* (I kneel down), or *si inginocchiò* (he/she knelt down). This implies that while building NooJ inflection codes for PIPVs, the correct insertion and protection of spaces also have to be predicted.

In addition to what is stated in previous point 1, as for morpho-syntactic features of IPVs, we note the obligatory co-reference of pre-verbal pronoun particles with specific verb persons. Such a feature is a mandatory constraint for all PIPVs, and predicts the following co-occurrences:

- *mi, me* in the first person, singular (as in *mi inginocchio*, I kneel down, and *me la vedrò con lui*, I will have deal with him);
- *ti, te* in the second person, singular (as in *ti inginocchi*, you kneel down, and *te la vedrai con lui*, you will deal with him);
- *si, se* in the third person, singular (as in *si inginocchia*, he/she kneels down, *se la vedrà con lui,* he/she will deal with him);
- *ci, ce* in the first person, plural (as in *ci inginocchiamo*, we kneel down, and *ce la vedremo con lui,* we will deal with him);
- *vi, ve* in the second person, plural (as in *vi inginocchiate*, you kneel down, and *ve la vedrete con lui,* you will deal with him);
- *si, se* in the third person, plural (as in *si inginocchiano*, they kneel down, and *se la vedranno con lui,* they will deal with him).[3]

[3]This kind of constraint is quite different form constraints coming from pronominalisation within simple sentences. For instance, in the sentence *Max si lava la camica* (Max washes his shirt) the verb *lavarsi* is a possessive reflexive which may have the following pronominal synthetic inflected form *lavandosi la camicia* (while washing his shirt). This form can be further agglutinated into *lavandosela*. On the contrary, in the sentence *Max ti lava la camicia* (Max washes your shirt) *lavare* is used as a transitive verb. Therefore, the pronominal

In the following paragraph, we will deal in detail with the structuring of inflection codes of IPVs, also defining with precision which tenses need to inflect either synthetic or analytic forms.

IPV Inflection Codes

As previously stated, IPVs are simple words which, when inflected, produce a considerable number of compound forms; also, the number of characters to delete from the infinitive to obtain inflected forms almost always differs from verb to verb. Finally, for the building of inflection codes, it is crucial that NooJ provides the possibility to insert and protect spaces between words. PIPV inflection codes were built taking duly into account these features, which led us to create 45 inflectional grammars, used to inflect 244 IPVs. The resulting dictionary contains 42,193 entries. An excerpt of the dictionary is given in the following figure:

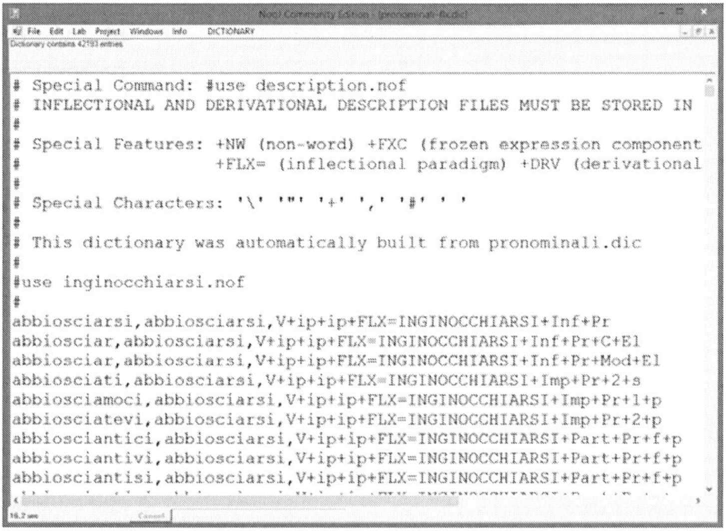

Figure 1 – an excerpt of PIPV inflected dictionary

---

agglutination *lavandotela* (while washing it) will be classified as a (possible) pronominalisation of a transitive verb, and not of an IPV. As for pre-verbal pronominal particles, it is clear that pronominal agglutinations of this last type are esocentric (ie they depend on the specific syntactic behavior of a given verb), while IPV pronominal agglutinations are endocentric (ie they concern and stress the relationships among pre-verbal pronominal particles and verb tenses).

In this dictionary, each IPV produces an average of almost 173 forms, a much higher number than for other non-pronominal Italian verbs, which normally produce a number of inflected forms ranging from 50 to 80, not considering defective verbs.[4] This significant numeric difference is due to the fact that in the inflection codes we also predicted forms such as:

mi fossi inginocchiato (had I kneeled down)

ie all compound forms of the type *auxiliary verb + past participle*. Generally speaking, such inflected forms are not contemplated inside non-pronominal verb inflection codes, since for these verbs it is not possible to infer the correct auxiliary without observing syntactic behaviours within simple sentences. For instance, considering that in Italian we have two main auxiliary verbs, ie *avere* (to have) and *essere* (to be), if we take as an example the verb *correre* (to run), we note that it may take both auxiliaries, as in:

Max è corso a casa (Max ran home, intransitive, auxiliary verb *essere*)

Max ha corso i cento metri ostacoli (Max ran the hundred-meter hurdles, transitive with a restricted class of direct objects, auxiliary *avere*).

On the contrary, we have noted that all IPVs take a sole auxiliary verb, either *essere* or *avere*, and this allowed us to predict within inflection codes also all constructions of the type *auxiliary verb + past participle*, in which the forms of the auxiliary vary according to the verb tense. Moreover, as for past participle forms, it is worth noting the necessity to inflect many IPVs in gender and number, always maintaining agreement with verb tenses. This means that the not only the masculine singular form:

mi fossi inginocchiato

must be predicted, but also the forms:

mi fossi inginocchiata (had I kneeled down, feminine singular)

while for plural tenses we also have to predict:

---

[4]An example of a defective verb is *concernere* (to concern), which only inflects the third persons, both singular and plural, and the present participle.

ci fossimo inginocchiati (had we kneeled down, masculine plural)
ci fossimo inginocchiate (had we kneeled down, feminine plural)

Exceptions to this are verbs like *avercela* (to be angry with), in which *–la* is a feminine singular pronoun used as a clitic yet having no semantic weight and not expressing any kind of relation with a given noun. However, the presence of this clitic imposes restrictions on the inflection of past participle forms, so as to allow only the feminine ones. Therefore, we will have:

se ce l'avessi avuta con Maria (had I been angry with Mary, feminine singular)

and not

**se ce l'avessi avuto con Maria*

in which *avuto* is a masculine singular past participle. The necessity to inflect past participle forms, together with the inflection of constructions of the type *auxiliary verb + past participle*, are the main reasons for the elevated average number of inflected forms for each IPV.

Formal Instructions and Tags Used

To build IPV inflection codes, we chose to use rule-editor grammars instead of Finite-State Automata (FSA), mainly because in this way the instructions to write would be much easier to manage and correct, if necessary.

The morpho-syntactic tags used for IPV inflected forms were:

C	form used in causative sentences
m	masculine form
f	feminine form
s	singular form
p	plural form
Cond	conditional
Cong	subjunctive
El	elided form
FutAnt	future perfect
FutSem	future
Ger	gerund

Imp	imperfect
Imper	imperative
Inf	infinitive
Mod	form used with a modal verb
Part	participle
Pas	past
PasPros	present perfect
PasRem	past perfect
Pr	present
Trap	perfect progressive
TrapPros	present perfect continuous
TrapRem	past perfect continuous
1	first person
2	second person
3	third person
ip[5]	intransitive pronominal
rec[6]	reciprocal
tp[6]	transitive pronominal

Table 1 – morpho-syntactic tags used for IPV inflected forms

The NooJ formal instructions used to inflect IPVs were <B> (backspace), <LW> (go to the left of the word), <RW> (go to the right of the word), <E> (leave the word unchanged)[6]. Generally speaking, to inflect non-pronominal Italian verbs it is sufficient to use the instruction <B>, mainly combining the lexical morpheme of a given verb with all the necessary grammatical morphemes and/or suffixes. For instance, the verb *sognare* (to dream), at the present indicative, is inflected as shown in figure 2:

[5]In the current state of our research, we notice the presence of intransitive pronominal PIPVs such as *ammantarsi*, (to mantle with), reciprocals such as *chiavarsi* (to fuck each other) and transitive pronominals such as *scoparsi* (to fuck someone). It is interesting to note that all the verbs denoting intercourse of the sexual sphere can be used both as reciprocals and as transitive pronominals. However, it is possible that in the development of our research, other morph-syntactic typologies will have to be noted for PIPVs.

[6]For more on the use of these instructions, see Silberztein (1993, 2002).

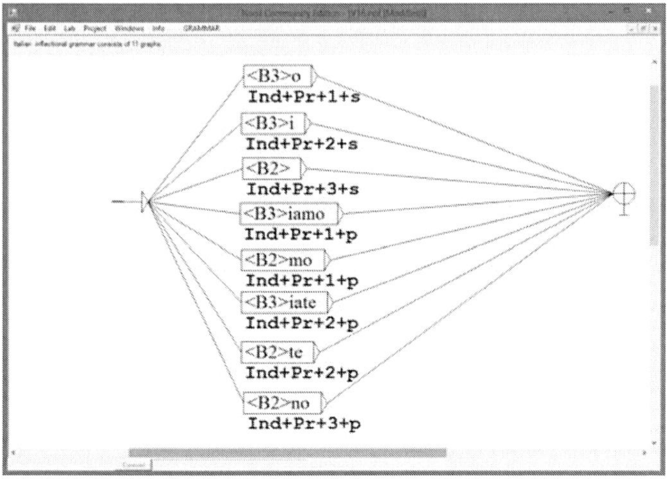

Figure 2 – FSA for the inflection of *sognare*, present indicative.

Inside our Italian electronic dictionary, the verb *sognare* and 53other similar verbs are inflected by means of the code V16. This indicates that all the verbs belonging to V16 have the same inflectional behaviour ie that to obtain, for instance, all their present indicative, second plural persons, it is sufficient to enter the NooJ command "<B2>te". On the contrary, a similar instruction is not always sufficient to inflect IPVs, not only because of the variable number of characters to drop and add for each voice/tense, but also because we have to insert pre-verbal pronominal particles before the inflected verb form itself. Therefore, again for *inginocchiarsi*, the inflection instruction used to obtain the present indicative is structured as follows:

<LW>mi" "<RW><B4>o/Ind+Pr+1+s |
<LW>ti" "<RW><B4>/Ind+Pr+2+s |
<LW>si" "<RW><B3>/Ind+Pr+3+s |
<LW>ci" "<RW><B3>mo/Ind+Pr+1+p |
<LW>vi" "<RW><B3>te/Ind+Pr+2+p |
<LW>si" "<RW><B3>no/Ind+Pr+3+p |

Besides, to obtain the past perfect subjunctive, we use the following instructions:

<LW>ti" "fossi" "<RW><B3>to/Cong+Trap+2+m+s |
<LW>si" "fosse" "<RW><B3>to/Cong+Trap+3+m+s |
<LW>ci" "fossimo" "<RW><B3>ti/Cong+Trap+1+m+p |
<LW>vi" "foste" "<RW><B3>ti/Cong+Trap+2+m+p |
<LW>si" "fossero" "<RW><B3>ti/Cong+Trap+3+m+p |
<LW>mi" "fossi" "<RW><B3>ta/Cong+Trap+1+f+s |
<LW>ti" "fossi" "<RW><B3>ta/Cong+Trap+2+f+s |
<LW>si" "fosse" "<RW><B3>ta/Cong+Trap+3+f+s |
<LW>ci" "fossimo" "<RW><B3>te/Cong+Trap+1+f+p |
<LW>vi" "foste" "<RW><B3>te/Cong+Trap+2+f+p |
<LW>si" "fossero" "<RW><B3>te/Cong+Trap+3+f+p |

In this one as well as in all IPV codes, the insertion of spaces is protected by the instruction " ".

Conclusions and Future Perspectives

So far, not all IPVS have been analysed and included in our dictionary of pronominal verbs; the total number of missing verbs is equal to 65. Some special forms such as *finirla* (to put an end to it), *pagarla* (to pay for it) or *scamparla* (to escape from something) have not yet been examined and inflected. All of these verbs will be the core of our future research.

In addition, we have noted that the inflection schemes of PIPVs may also be used to inflect reflexive and possessive reflexive verbs; we have previously stated that the forms of this type of verbs must be parsed by means of FSA grammars, due to the fact that they are not ALUs but pronominalised forms of transitive verbs. However, if confirmed, the possibility to use PIPV inflection codes for reflexive and possessive reflexive verbs would greatly facilitate and accelerate the building of FSA grammars for verbs such as *lavarsi* (to wash) or *pettinarsi* (to comb), which both inflect as *abbozzolarsi* (to cocoon), as shown in the following example:

mi lavavo,lavarsi,V+rif+FLX=ABBOZZOLARSI+Ind+Imp+1+s
mi lavai,lavarsi,V+rif+FLX=ABBOZZOLARSI+Ind+PasRem+1+s
mi lavassi,lavarsi,V+rif+FLX=ABBOZZOLARSI+Cong+Imp+1+s
ti pettinavi,pettinarsi,V+rif+FLX=ABBOZZOLARSI+Ind+Imp+2+s
ti pettinasti,pettinarsi,V+rif+FLX=ABBOZZOLARSI+Ind+PasRem+2+s
ti pettinassi,pettinarsi,V+rif+FLX=ABBOZZOLARSI+Cong+Imp+2+s

References

De Bueris, Giustino and Annibale Elia, Eds. 2008. *Lessici elettronici e descrizioni lessicali, sintattiche, morfologiche ed ortografiche*, Plectica, Salerno.

Gross, Maurice. 1989. La construction de dictionnaires électroniques. In *Annales des Télécommunications*, vol. 44, n° 1-2: CENT, Issy-les-Moulineaux/Lannion, pp. 4-19.

Monteleone, Mario. 2004. *Lessicografia e dizionari elettronici. Dagli usi linguistici alle basi di dati lessicali*, Fiorentino & New Technology, Napoli.

Silberztein, Max. 1993. *Dictionnaires électroniques et analyse automatique de textes*, Masson, Paris.

—. 2003. *The NooJ Manual* (available at the Web site http://www.nooj4nlp.net/NooJManual.pdf).

—. 2013. *NooJ Computational Devices*. Formalising Natural Languages with NooJ: Selected Papers from the NooJ 2012 International Conference. Edited by Anaïd Donabédian, Victoria Khurshudian and Max Silberztein. Cambridge Scholars Publishing. Newcastle.

Vietri, Simonetta, Annibale Elia, and Emilio D'Agostino. 2004. Lexicon-grammar, Electronic Dictionaries and Local Grammars in Italian. In Laporte Eric, Leclère Christian, Piot Mireille, Silberztein Max Eds. *Syntaxe, Lexique et Lexique-Grammaire. Volume dédié à Maurice Gross*, Lingvisticae Investigationes Supplementa 24, John Benjamins, Amsterdam/Philadelphia, pp. 137-146.

Vietri, Simonetta. 2008. *Dizionari elettronici e grammatiche a stati finiti. Metodi di analisi formale della lingua italiana*, Plectica, Salerno.

Part II:

Syntax and Semantics

Semantic Role Labelling of Communication Predicates

Annibale Elia
and Alberto Maria Langella

Abstract

In this paper we discuss the possibility of tagging the communication predicates. These represent the majority of the Italian lexicon-grammar Class 47. We will show how to achieve this through the use of dictionaries improved with specific syntactical properties and a set of syntactic grammars.

Introduction[1]

In this article we aim to show how to build a dictionary and a syntactical grammar for the annotation of communication predicates in a text

This work will be carried out on Class 47[2] of the Italian lexicon-grammar, the so-called communication predicates class, with verbs like *comunicare* (to communicate), *confessare* (to confess), *confidare* (to confide) etc. These are verbs which share the structural property of having three arguments:

a) an elementary argument such as 'subject'
b) a non-elementary argument such as 'direct object'
c) a third elementary argument linked to the operator by the preposition *a* (to)

We give, in the order presented above, the following semantic roles to the three arguments:

---

[1]A. Elia is author of *Introduction and Class 47: Some Observations* sections; A. M. Langella is author of *The Syntactic Grammar on CP Predicates* and of *An Evaluation of the Tagging* sections.

[2] For a description of Class 47 see Elia, Martinelli e D'Agostino (1981).

a) ‘**AS**’ meaning ‘Agent Speaker’
b) ‘**M**’ meaning ‘Message’
c) ‘**RR**’ meaning ‘Recipient Receiver’

The verbs will be tagged as ‘**CP**’ meaning ‘Communication Predicate’.

Class 47: some observations

The definitional structure[3] of the Italian Class 47 is ***N0um V Ch F a N2***. ***N0*** is in most cases and with very few exceptions a ***Num***, a human noun. ***N1*** is a clause often reduced to a noun to which we can assign the lexicon-syntactic role of ‘message’. The verbs of this class are *annunciare* (to announce), *comunicare* (to inform), *confermare* (to confirm) ecc. In sentences like:

1. *Mario comunica la sua partenza a Giovanni*
   ‘Mario informs Giovanni of his departure’
2. *Mario conferma la sua partenza a Giovanni*
   ‘Mario confirms his departure to Giovanni’

These verbs can be interpreted as ‘communication operators’, with a transfer of information from a ***N0um*** to a ***N2um***. In these sentences the ***N1*** is co-referent to ***N0***. They accept nominalisations like the following:

1a. *Mario dà comunicazione della sua partenza a Giovanni*
‘Mario gives information of his departure to Giovanni’
2a. *Mario dà conferma della sua partenza a Giovanni*
‘Mario gives confirmation of his departure to Giovanni’

The ***N1s*** in sentences number 1, 2 and 3 are in distributional equivalence with clauses like ***il fatto Ch F*** and ***il fatto di Vinf***:

1b. *Mario comunica* ((E+*il fatto*) (*che partirà*))+*di partire*) *a Giovanni*
‘Mario informs Giovanni of the fact that he is leaving’

[3]For an introduction to the concept of definitional structure for Italian see the first two chapters of Elia, Martinelli, D’Agostino (1981).

2b. *Mario conferma* ((E+*il fatto*) (*che partirà*))+*di partire*) *a Giovanni*
'Mario confirms (E+the fact) that he is leaving to Giovanni'

or even with ***di Vinf***:

1c. *Mario comunica di partire a Giovanni*
'Mario informs Giovanni to be leaving'
2c. *Mario conferma di partire a Giovanni*
'Mario confirms to be leaving to Giovanni'

Each verb of this class accepts passivisation with the sole exception of *ansimare*:

1d. *La sua partenza è comunicata da Mario a Giovanni*
'Giovanni was informed of his departure by Mario'
2d. *La sua partenza è confermata da Mario a Giovanni*
'His departure was confirmed to Giovanni by Mario'

Other verbs of this class like *intimare* (to order), *impedire* (to prevent) etc have a co-reference relation between the ***N1*** and the ***N2*** as in the following sentences:

3. *Mario intima la partenza a Giovanni*
'Mario orders Giovanni to leave'
4. *Mario impedisce la partenza a Giovanni*
'Mario prevents Giovanni from leaving'

that is between *partenza* (leave/leaving) and *Giovanni*.

The Syntactic Grammar on CP Predicates

In order to build a syntactic grammar capable of parsing CP sentences like the ones seen above and tagging them (and parts of them) in natural language texts, we have chosen to split the main graph (called CLASS 47 DEF) into four sub-graphs or embedded graphs:

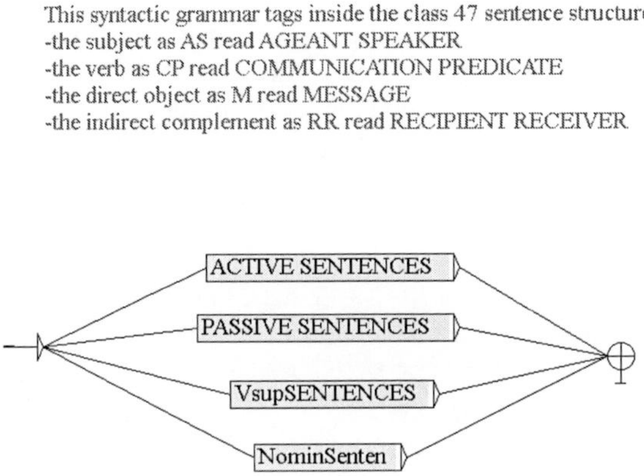

Figure 1 – The Main Graph

The embedded graphs are for (i) the active sentence description, (ii) the passive sentence description, (iii) sentences with verb dropping and finally (iv) sentences with nominalisations. The graph for active sentences is the following:

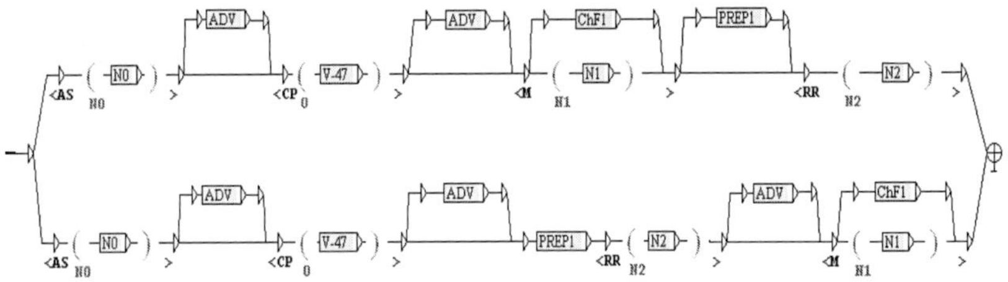

Figure 2 – Graph for Active Sentences

For the main arguments inside the previous graph we have used the special nodes '$(' and '$)' in order to store the embedded node (for example ***N0*** in $(N0$)) and recall its content later in the relevant part of the main graph. The node called 'V-47' contains a description of the possible occurrence of CP operators in simple forms, like *comunicò* (informed), *esternava* (expressed) etc. and compound forms with the auxiliary verb *avere,* like *aveva comunicato* (had informed), *ha esternato* (had expressed) etc. Between the auxiliary verb and the main operator there is even the possibility of an adverb, in order to take into account local and incremental[4] transformation by way of new linguistic material: 1. *Mario aveva comunicato la partenza a Maria* (Mario had informed Maria of his leaving)→ 1a. *Mario aveva rapidamente comunicato la partenza a Maria* (Mario had quickly informed Maria of his leaving).

The graph is used in association with a dictionary called Class 47, of which we give the following sample:

```
annunciare,V+47+FLX=V4+FARE+DRV=Nop1:CPN1
ansimare,V+47+FLX=V3
anticipare,V+47+FLX=V3+FARE+DRV=Nop7:CPN7
articolare,V+47+FLX=V3+DRV=CPN7
asserire,V+47+FLX=V201+FARE+DRV=Nop43:CPN43
assicurare,V+47+FLX=V3+DARE+DRV=Nop7:CPN7
augurare,V+47+FLX=V3+FARE+DARE+DRV=Nop2:CPN2
balbettare,V+47+FLX=V3+FARE+DRV=Nop15:CPN15
```

Figure 3 – A Sample of the Dictionary

where to the usual verbal inflectional codes (FLX=V3, FLX=V40 etc) we have added the information regarding the class ('+47') and the derivational codes to derive nouns from the verbs. The derivational codes for nouns allow them to inherit directly from the dictionary the grammatical properties of the verbs. The syntactic property 'V+47' is useful in order to parse only the verbs belonging to Class 47 and filter out all the rest. According to the Harrisian principles the verbs of Class 47 are *Onon*[5], non-elementary operators, because the direct object can be a clause, like in 2. *Mario comunica il fatto che parte a Maria* (Mario informs Maria about the fact that he's leaving), 2a. *Mario comunica di partire a Maria* (Mario informs Maria that he's leaving). Thus, the paths to the immediate right of the node 'V-47' have to allow such a possibility and we embedded these syntactic patterns in the node labelled as 'ChF1':

[4]For a definition of incremental and non-incremental operators see Harris (1970).
[5]For the typology of the different Harrsian operators in Italian see Langella (2014).

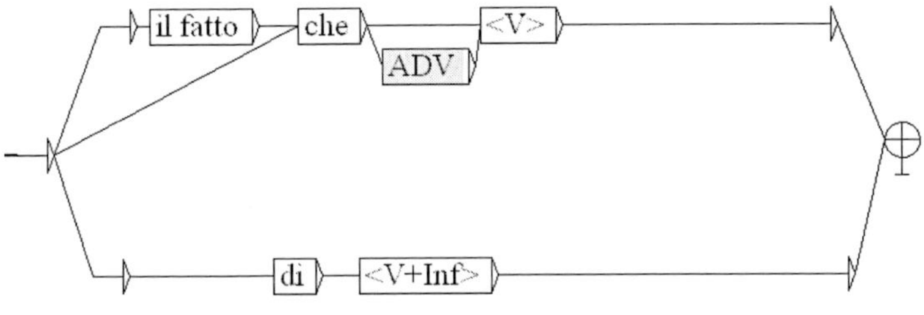

Figure 4 – The Grammar for the Object Clause

Also in this graph, between the node ‘che’ and the node ‘<V>’ we have added the embedded graph ‘ADV’ to take into account sequences like *il fatto che sicuramente partiva* (the fact that he was certainly leaving), *il fatto che rapidamente partiva* (the fact that he was quickly leaving), etc. The path ‘di’/‘<V+inf>’ is meant to parse sequences like *di partire* (to leave), *di mangiar*e (to eat) etc with the preposition *di* plus a verb in the infinitive form. The two paths ‘il fatto’+‘che V’ and ‘di’+‘Vinf’ are, according to the Harrisian principles, in distributional equivalence.

As an alternative path for the direct object, as well as the previous clauses, we have simple nouns. The graph ‘N1’ is the following:

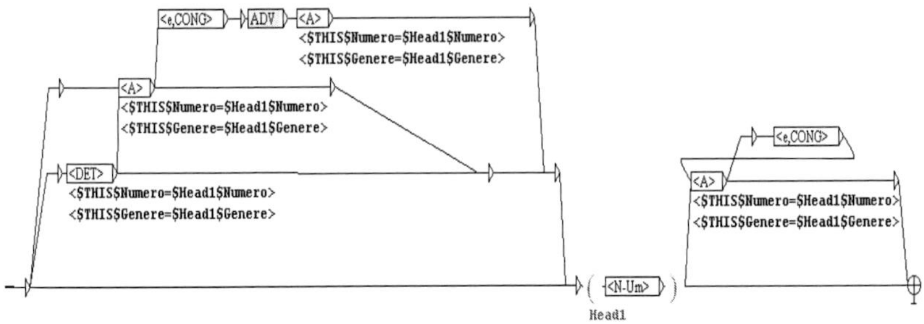

Figure 5 – The Grammar for the Direct Object N1

It can parse direct non-human nouns with the eventual occurrences of adjectives either to the left or to the right in sequences like *la bella notizia* (the good news), *la bella e piacevole notizia* (the good and pleasant news), *la notizia insolita* (the unusual news), *la notizia insolita e entusiasmante* (the unusual and exciting news) etc. The variable ‘$THIS’ and ‘$Head1’have been used to guarantee the agreement between the number and gender of the nouns stored in the variable ‘$Head1’ and the co-occurrent modifiers.

In order to parse the prepositional argument, we have built an embedded graph, called ‘N2’, linked to the main operator via the occurrence of prepositions like *a*, *ad* (to) etc, which are described in the node ‘PREP1’. The structure of the graph ‘N2’ is very similar to the one shown above for the graph ‘N1’:

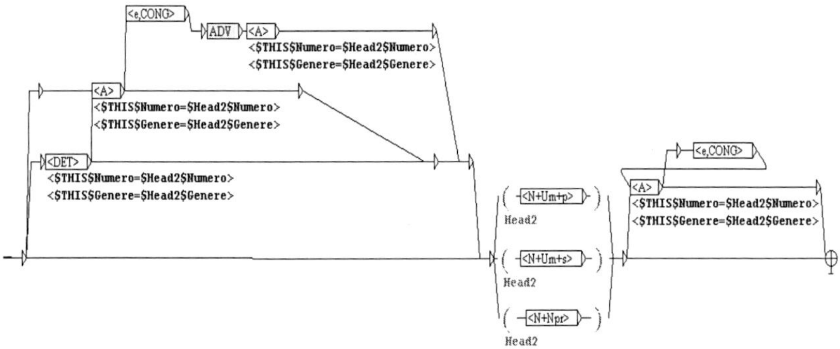

Figure 6 – The Grammar for the Indirect Object N2

The difference is that here we take into account the occurrences of singular and plural human nouns. The special nodes are again used here for the lexical agreement between nouns and modifiers. The type of prepositional arguments described are *a Maria* (to Maria), *alla bella Maria* (to nice Maria), *alla bella e nostalgica Maria* (to nice and nostalgic Maria)etc.

The graph dedicated to the parsing of passive sentences is the following:

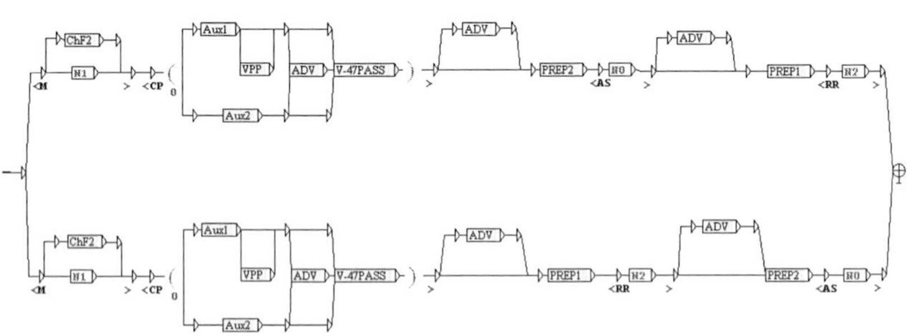

Figure 7 – The Graph for Passive Sentences

It is made up of two main paths. The first one parses sentences like *Il fatto che Mario parta è comunicato da Maria a Giovani* (The fact that Mario is leaving is communicated by Maria to Giovanni), *La partenza di Mario viene comunicata da Maria a Giovanni* (The departure of Mario is communicated by Maria to Giovanni) and so forth. The node 'ChF2' has the following structure:

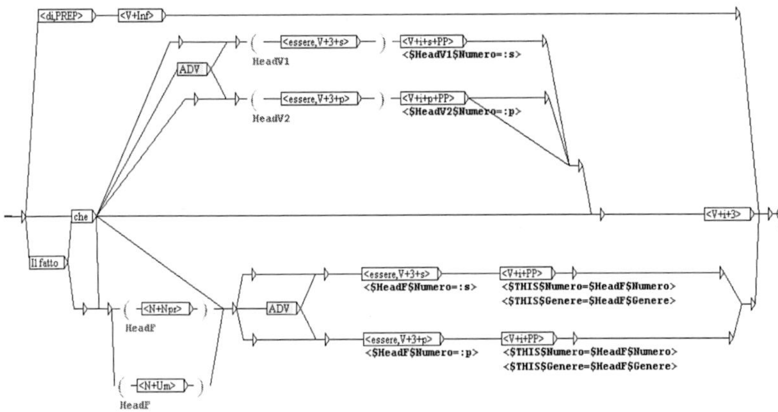

Figure 8 – The Grammar for the Subject Clause of the Passive Sentences

Here again the use of the special nodes '$(' and '$)' accounts for the agreement of the auxiliary *essere* and the verb in the past participle form in sequences like *Il fatto che Maria è partita* (The fact that Maria has left), *Che Maria fosse arrivata* (That Maria has arrived) etc with the possible and eventual parsing of adverbs between *Il fatto che Maria/Che Maria* (The fact that Maria /That Maria) and the auxiliary *essere V+PP.*

The embedded graph 'Aux1' stands for the different forms of the auxiliary verb *essere*, the graph 'Aux2' for the auxiliary *venire*. For sequences like *è stato comprato* (has been bought), *è stato mangiato* (has been eaten) we have built the graph 'VPP' followed by the graph 'V-47PASS'. The first one allows parsing of *stato*, *stata*, *stati* and *state* preceded and followed by eventual adverbs:

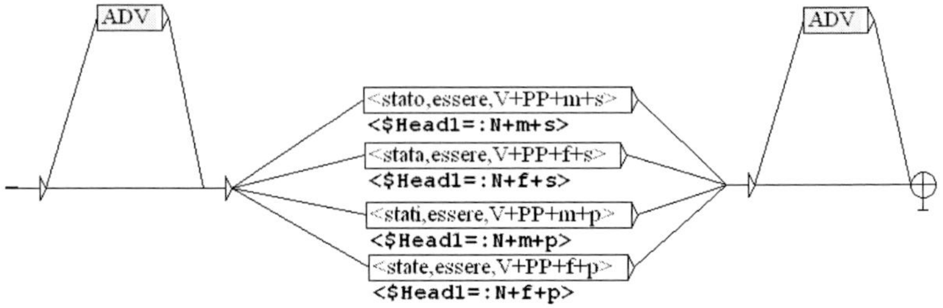

Figure 9 – The Grammar for the Auxiliary Past Participle

whereas the second graph accounts for the past participle forms of the verbs listed in our Class 47:

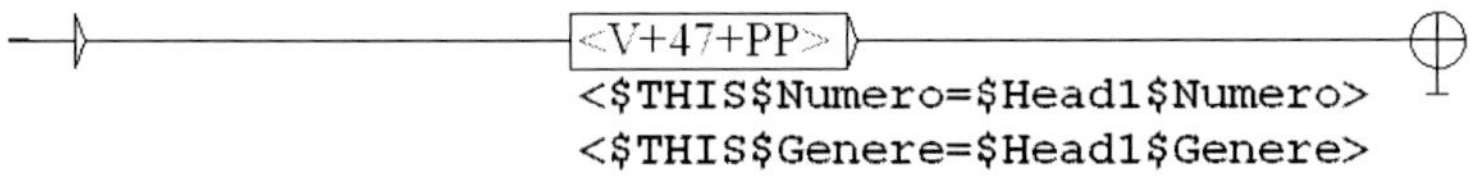

Figure 10 – The Grammar for Past Participle Verbs in Passive Sentences

The verbal forms in the grammar above have a grammatical agreement with the nouns stored in the variable '$Head1'.

From this point on, we have two alternative paths in the graph for passive sentences. One which, via the embedded graph 'Prep2', parses sequences like ***da N a N***, and another that parses a permutation of the above sequence, that is **a N da N**, via the embedded graph 'Prep1'. We shall now demonstrate an example of tagging, reminding you that the following tags are used here:

a) '**AS**' meaning Agent Speaker
b) '**M**' meaning Message
c) '**RR**' meaning Recipient Receiver
d) '**CP**' meaning Communication Predicate

The embedded graph 'VsupSENTENCES' deals with the nominalisation of the active and passive sentences and the embedded graph 'NominaSenten' deals with nominalised sentences with reductions of lexical units as far as zero.

An Evaluation of the Tagging

We have tested the grammar in Figure 1 on a variety of documents belonging to the specialised language of the Italian Public Administration. The text has been tagged and the matched sequences isolated as shown in the following figure:

ome di	chi fa la richiesta/<S<AS><CP>>	con ri
ve alla	descrizione delle attività/<CP><M>	da pr
ività di	comunicazione dei risultati/<CP><M>	degli
illustra	il significato dei termini/<CP><M>	utilizz
ai temi	della comunicazione del movimento/<CP><M>	di rim
ne e di	comunicazione della pubblica amministrazione/<CP><M>	". Tale

Figure 11 – Concordance

The tags have then been added to the text and exported as an XML document. In the excerpt from the XML document which follows, we can see the semantic roles we have devised added to the nouns and to the predicates belonging to Class 47:

Gli Enti/Aziende che desiderano aderire ai servizi, o semplicemente vogliono avere ulteriori informazioni su quanto predisposto da INAIL nell'ambito della cooperazione applicativa, possono contattare l'Istituto al seguente indirizzo:
dcsit-standard-centrocompcoopapp@inail.it
E' importante che nella mail vengano indicate almeno le seguenti informazioni:
1. l'Ente/Azienda interessato,
2. le esigenze,
3. le finalità che motivano la richiesta,
4. Nome e cognome di <AS>chi</AS> fa <CP>la richiesta</CP> con recapito telefonico.
Selezionato il suddetto tab, si apre la pagina 'Utilizza' con l'<CP>elenco</CP> dei <M>servizi divisi</M> per argomento. All'interno quindi della macro area 'Denunce', si potrà selezionare la 'Denuncia/Comunicazione di Infortunio'
Se sono presenti denunce/comunicazioni compilate, ma non ancora inviate, è possibile selezionare quella di interesse anche tramite il "Filtro di ricerca P.A.T." che, selezionata la P.A.T., restituisce l'<CP>elenco</CP> delle <M>relative denunce </M>in lavorazione. La scelta della denuncia da completare deve essere effettuata mediante l'apposita icona della lente di ingrandimento.
Archivio News - Accesso all'<CP>elenco</CP> delle <M>News</M>, ossia le informazioni e gli avvisi agli utenti sugli aggiornamenti

Figure 12 – XML Document

The results are promising and we have between 70% and 80% of correct matches. The incorrect matches must be attributed to the fact that the words belonging to the sentences of Class 47 are far from each other.

Conclusion

We have shown a grammar for the semantic role labelling of Italian Comunication Predicates. The results are good. To improve the tagging precision of the grammar we need to better take into account the co-occurring subclasses of subject nouns and direct object nouns. A further work on possible paraphrases of sentences of this class could allow NooJ to extend the semantic role labelling activity to a greater number of sentences belonging to the class we are dealing with.

References

D'Agostino, Emilio. 1992. *Analisi del discorso. Metodi descrittivi dell'italiano d'uso*. Napoli: Loffredo.

Elia, Annibale. 1984. *Le verbe italien*. Schena-Nizet Press.

Elia, Annibale, Simonetta Vietri, Alberto Postiglione, Mario Monteleone, and Federica Marano. 2010. Data Mining Modular Software System. In *Proceedings of the 2010 International Conference on Semantic Web & Web Services*, pp. 127-133. CSREA Press.

Elia, Annibale, Maurizio Martinelli, and Emilio D'Agostino. 1981. *Lessico e strutture della sintassi*. Liguori Editore.

Gross, Maurice. 1975. *Méthodes en syntaxe*. Paris: Hermann.

—. 1981. Les bases empiriques de la notion de predicat semantique. *Languages* 15 (63): pp. 7-49.

Langella, Alberto Maria. 2014. *Elementi di grammatica dell'italiano su basi matematiche*. Padova: Libreriauniversitaria.it Edizioni.

Silberztein, Max. 2010. Syntactic parsing with NooJ. In *Proceedings of the NooJ 2009 International Conference and Workshop*, pp. 177-190. Centre de Publication Universitaire.

—. 2011. Automatic Transformational Analysis and Generation. In *Proceedings of the 2010 International NooJ Conference*, pp. 221-231. Komotini: Democritius University Editions, 2011.

Vietri, Simonetta. 2013. The annotation of the Predicate-argument structure of transfer nouns. In *Proceedings of the NooJ 2012 International Conference and Workshop*, pp. 89-99. Cambridge Scholars Publishing.

AN ATTEMPT TO RECOGNISE HONORIFIC PASSIVE VERBAL FORM IN JAPANESE WITH NOOJ

VALÉRIE COLLEC-CLERC

Abstract

This paper aims to define a method which makes it possible to identify the distinctive features of the Japanese honorific passive form.

Introduction

The context of our study is the automatic production of polite sentences, which comprises utterances in which the speaker regards the addressee or a third person as superior to him or her, according to psychological or social criteria. One of the possible forms that can be employed is a special use of the passive form, called the honorific passive. Since the Japanese passive form is also utilised to express inconvenience, ambiguity could occur between the two uses. With NooJ graphs, we have tried to correctly distinguish the different meanings of the passive forms. This attempt has led us to recognise true honorific forms in corpora. NooJ graphs are also used as a preliminary step in determining formal rules which could be added to our system of sentence generation. To start with, we discuss the specificities of the Japanese language in natural language processing with NooJ analysis, and briefly introduce referential politeness in Japanese. Then we will present the results we have obtained on testing our NooJ graphs and the conclusions we have drawn.

Japanese writing system

The Japanese writing system is based on three kinds of characters: Chinese-like ideograms, called *kanji*, and two syllabic types, called *hiragana* and katakana. The latter is mostly used for foreign words. This overlapping of characters is shown by the sample sentence underneath:

フランス人の学生が自然言語処理を勉強している。
Furansujinnogakuseigashizengengoshoriwobenkyoushiteiru.
'The French student/s does/do NLP studies.'
フランス (katakana) *furansu* ('France')
人 (kanji) *jin* ('person')
の (hiragana) *no* (genitive marker)
学生 (kanji) *gakusei* ('student')
が (hiragana) *ga* (subject marker)
自然言語処理(kanji) *shizengengoshori* (Natural Language Processing)
を (hiragana) *wo* (object marker)
勉強 (kanji) *benkyou* ('study')
して(hiragana) *shite* ('do')
いる(hiragana) *iru* + (auxiliary, non past neutral form)
。 marker of sentence ending

Segmentation problem

The above-mentioned example shows that standard writing does not separate words by spaces. As *hiragana* can also appear within plain words and in a great number of prefixes and suffixes, the change of writing type is not sufficient for a correct recognition of successions of words. Accurate segmentation is a classic problem in analysing texts automatically. NLP tools often resort to a preliminary segmenting phase with a tokeniser like Chasen, based on a dictionary and statistical data about the succession of the POS (part of speech), but they carry errors and they discard other possibilities by only showing those most frequent occurrences. Improving segmentation requires syntactic knowledge, which can be obtained with NooJ.

NooJ and the Japanese language

In a previous work (Collec-Clerc, 2013), we introduced a Japanese dictionary for NooJ which relies on one of the linguistic resources available from Jim Breen's JDIC, a free multilingual dictionary. The NooJ dictionary also employs names traditionally used for Western POS such as A (adjective), N (noun), V (verb), AV (adverb), etc, if the Japanese syntactic unit has similar functions. In addition, we have used categories specific to the Japanese language: CTR (counter), PART (postpositional particle), PREF (prefix), SUF (suffix). Sub-categories are also employed to describe Japanese specificities inside a given part of speech, for instance i-adjectives (ADJI), no-adjectives (ADJNO). To correctly identify words from stems, inflection and derivation rules were added. Japanese inflections mainly concern 15 verb-groups and i-adjectives. Inflections carry verb tenses, mood, polarity (negative/affirmative) but also politeness level (formal/informal) used by the speaker and special constructions of different uses such as verbal linking of complex forms such as the te-form. For example: 教えてくれる*oshietekureru* consists of the てte-form of 教える *oshieru* (show) and an auxiliary verb indicating the act of giving (くれる*kureru*). Some common nouns and adverbs can be turned into verbs by using the verbal suffix する (*suru*), which has led us to create a derivation rule. We will also explain how this stage of our work, which was dedicated to an accurate distinction of passives, enabled us to enhance the information linked to the lexical resource of our NooJ dictionary.

Complexity of Japanese politeness system

The Japanese inter-personal communication system (待遇表現 *taiguuhyougen*), constrains the choice of uttering forms, distinguishing two axes of relationship: the vertical relationship (上下関係 *jougekankei*) and the horizontal relationship. The vertical relationship deals with the hierarchical role of individuals: superior/inferior (目上 *Meue* /目下 *meshita*). The horizontal relationship deals with the proximity of individuals within, or outside of, the same group. In-group (*uchi*: 内) people can show their true feelings (*honne* 本音) to each other while they must comply with their public position or attitude (*tatemae*: 建前) towards out-group (*soto* : 外) people.

The utterance considers the distance between the speaker and addressee. The speaker may use either the plain form (*futsukei*: 普通形) when the relationship with the addressee is familiar, or the polite form (*teineikei*: 丁寧形) which corresponds to polite language. The choice of language results in an addressee-oriented politeness.

The position of the speaker in the situation of utterance depends on these factors: the speaker or a person who belongs to the speaker's group is the person being referred to in utterances; neither the speaker nor a person who belongs to the speaker's group is referred to. Graduated expressions of politeness can be used in the same utterance and could range from respect to humility. This is called referential politeness and is more often termed the honorific system or *keigo* (敬語). The honorific system is a complex linguistic phenomenon. It presents many linguistic forms: dedicated constructions, nouns, special suffixes or prefixes, auxiliary verbs, suppletive verbs.

In the main verbal constructions of the honorific system, Japanese linguists pointed out the difference between its two components: humility language or *kenjougo* (謙譲語) *and* honorific language *or sonkeigo* (尊敬語).

Kenjougo is used when the speaker or a person belonging to the speaker's group is the referent of the utterance. It conveys a willingness of the speaker to humble himself or herself towards the addressees. *Kenjougo* is also referred to as subject honorific. *Sonkeigo* is used to show respect toward the referents of the utterance when they are different from the speaker or a person who belongs to the speaker's group. It is also referred to as non-subject honorific. *Sonkeigo* is composed of various structures like those shown below as an example:

- Specific constructions with honorific prefixes *o* or *go* （御,お,ご）added to a nominalised verb and the verbal structure *ni naru* (になる). For example, the verb *hairu* (入る: 'enter') converted into a *O-Verb-ni-naru* expression becomes *ohairininaru* (お入りになる),
- suppletive verbs to replace neutral verbs. For example *irassharu* (いらっしゃる: 'come', 'go') instead of *kuru* (来る: 'come') or *iku* (行く: 'go').
- The honorific passive form.

Meanings and use of the passive forms in Japanese

The morphological form of the Japanese passive (*ukemi* : 受身形) is equivalent to Western languages, but its usage differs. The direct passive (*chokusetsuukemi* 直接受身) which corresponds to the Western use, roughly consists in an inverted role between the subject and the object of the active form in order to emphasise the object. Alongside the direct passive, this morphological form can also express potentiality (*kanousei*:可能形), inconvenience (*meiwakuukemi*: 迷惑受身形) and honorification (*sonkeigo* :尊敬語), which explains why it can also be used with intransitive verbs.

The construction of the passive form depends on the group the verbs belong to. *Ichidan*-verbs, namely verbs ending with the sound *iru* or *eru*, add to their stems the passive ending *rareru* (られる), while *godan*-verbs have the final vowel sound of their stem changed before the adjunction of the passive ending *reru* (れる). For example, 聞く (*kiku)* (listen) becomes 聞かれる (*kikareru)* (be listened).

Active form:
Gaikokujin ha Nattou wo taberu/ 'Foreigner/s eat/s *Natto* (fermented soybeans)'
国人は納豆外を食べる。

Direct passive:
Nattou ha gaikokujin ni taberareru/ '*Natto* (fermented soybeans) is eaten by foreigner/s'
納豆は外国人に食べられる。

Ichidan-verbs also possess a potential form which is morphologically identical to their passive. The potential form is used to describe physical or intellectual ability. For instance, the form 食べられる (*taberareru*) is both the potential (is able to eat) and the direct passive form (be eaten) of the verb食べる (*taberu*) (eat).

Potential form:
外国人は納豆が食べられる。
Gaikokujin ha nattou ga taberareru/ 'Foreigner/s can eat *Natto* (fermented soybeans)'.

The adversative passive expresses inconvenience. It indicates an adversative effect, suggesting that someone, generally the subject of this utterance, is negatively affected. Unlike the direct passive, it may be used with intransitive verbs.

Adversative passive:
Ame ni furareta/ '(Unfortunately for the speaker) it was raining'
雨に降られた。
Kodomo ni nakareta/ '(Unfortunately for the speaker) the child cried'
子供に泣かれた。

In these two examples, the subject of the utterance is implicitly the speaker.

Honorific passive:

The honorific passive is a way to speak of a person with respect. Only the verb of the sentence is changed into the passive form while the subject and object remain unchanged. For example, the sentence: *buchou ha shinbun wo yomu*: (部長は新聞を読む: 'the department manager reads the newspaper') can assume an honorific function by switching the verb from the active: *yomu* (読む: 'reads') to the passive: *yomareru* (読まれる: 'be read'). The resulting sentence is: 部長は新聞を読まれる (*buchou ha shimbun wo yomareru*: 'The department manager reads the newspaper') without any syntactic transfer between the subject部長 (*buchou*: 'the chief') and the object新聞 (*shimbun*: 'newspaper').

Recognition of honorific passive

Our work on honorific language prompted us to try to identify honorific forms in a sample of a set of morphologically passive sentences. In real inter-personal situations of communication, the addressee is helped by the context to accurately understand the utterance. In our study we were led to use heuristic rules relying on syntactic characteristics or on basic semantic features of a group of words to have a chance of successful disambiguation.

Let us examine several sentences with different passive meanings:

1- Honorific: 先生が/は魚を食べられる。 *sensei-ga sakana-wo taberaremasu*. 'The teacher eats fish.'

2- Direct/Potential: 日本ではたくさんの魚がたべられる。*nihon-deha takusan-no sakana-ga taberaremasu* 'In Japan people (can) eat a lot of fish (a lot of fish is eaten).'

3- Potential: 先生は 魚が食べられる。*sensei-ha sakana-ga taberaremasu*. 'The teacher can eat fish.'

4- Adversative: (私は) 会長に笑われる。*(watashi-ha) kaichou-ni warawareta*. 'I was laughed at by the company president.'

5- Honorific: 社長が/は冗談に笑われた。*shachou-ga/ha joudan ni warawareta*. 'The company president laughed at the joke.'

In sentences 1 and 5 the honoured people (teacher and company president) can either be designated by the subject-marking particle *ga* (が) or the theme-marking particle *ha* (は).

Sentence 2 can also be construed as a potential form. The topicalisation is realised at the level of location (*Nihon deha*) 日本では: 'in Japan' で (*de* location-marker, *ha* theme-marker).

In sentence 3 the real subject is directly linked to the potential verb (fish and the ability to eat them), which could explain why the possessor of this ability (the teacher) is topicalised ie designated with the theme-marker particle は (*ha*).

In sentence 4 the person who bears the detriment is not necessarily mentioned in the sentence, whereas the agent of the detriment is indicated with the particle *ni* に. This particle is normally used as agent marker in the case of the direct passive.

As we cannot use the context of the utterance, we choose to base our method on internal elements in order to distinguish the honorific passive from the adversative passive. Subsequently, we use both syntactic and semantic approaches. The former mainly consists in analysing the different POS present in the sentence construction, the latter in determining the main semantic features.

Syntactic approach

In a passive form, the particle が (*ga*) determines a subject function, and に (*ni*) an agent function. The Japanese language makes it possible to use zero-pronoun structures, when the referent is the speaker or the listener themselves. The adversative passive implies an agent which is the origin of detriment and a patient who bears the detriment - a sentence in which the adversative agent is designated. Since the honorific passive only implies a morphological transformation of the verb, the same subject remains and there is no named agent. As a result particles are indicative, and can be easily tested in NooJ graphs.

Adversative passive (the subject is not the speaker)

Hanako GA tonari no gakusei NI piano wo asa made hikareta.

'Hanako was annoyed by her neighbouring student who played piano until the morning.'

花子が隣の学生にピアノを朝まで弾かれた。PATIENT+GA, ADVERS.AGENT+NI, VERB+PASS. ENDING

Adversative passive (the subject is the speaker)

tonari no gakusei NI piano wo asa made hikareta.

'I was annoyed by her neighbour who played piano until the morning.'

隣の学生にピアノを朝まで弾かれた。ØPATIENT, ADVERS.AGENT+NI, VERB+PASS. ENDING

Honorific passive (the subject cannot be the speaker)
Ichiryuu no ongakuka GA piano wo asa made hikareta
'The first-rate musician played the piano until the morning.'
一流の音楽家がピアノを朝まで弾かれた。 HONOUREE+GA, ØAGENT, VERB+PASS. ENDING

Semantic approach and enhancement of NooJ Japanese dictionary

An honorific form is generally applied to human beings. This indication enables us to reject some passive forms as non-honorific.

Honorific passive
一流の音楽家がピアノを朝まで弾かれた。
Ichiryuu-no ongakuka-GA piano-wo asa-made hikareta.
Human(Firstrate-GEN musician)-SUBJ morning-until played-PASS-PAST
'The first rate musician played the piano until morning.' (The musician is the honoree+ the time goes quickly)

Adversative passive
一流の音楽家にピアノを朝まで弾かれた。
Ichiryuu-no ongakuka- NI piano-o asa-made hikareta.
[Human(Speaker)-SUBJ] Human(Firstrate-GEN musician)-DAT morning-until played-PASS-PAST
'I was adversely affected by the first rate musician who played the piano until morning.' (The concert was too long).

The importance of the human feature in the honorific passive led us to add 'human' feature in the NooJ dictionary (+HUM) for common nouns.
We decided to treat the proper nouns separately, assuming that they are often used with title-suffix (*san*さん, *sama* 様・さま, *kun* 君, *shi* 氏, *chan* ちゃん) in case of honorification. We decided to create a NooJ graph which lists title-suffixes. We also created a graph containing a list of human common nouns which semantically bear a derogatory value. Indeed, such values automatically exclude honorification.

Application with NooJ

Our objective is to extract the passive honorific from a corpus of sentences. In Japanese, passive constructs are either used before a noun in a noun phrase, or used with the main verb of the sentence. Our graphs include the two possibilities: Honor NP (honorific noun phrase) and Honor sentence (honorific sentence).

A human noun phrase (NP) is a noun with a determiner (adjective or noun and genitive particle) or an honorific suffix.

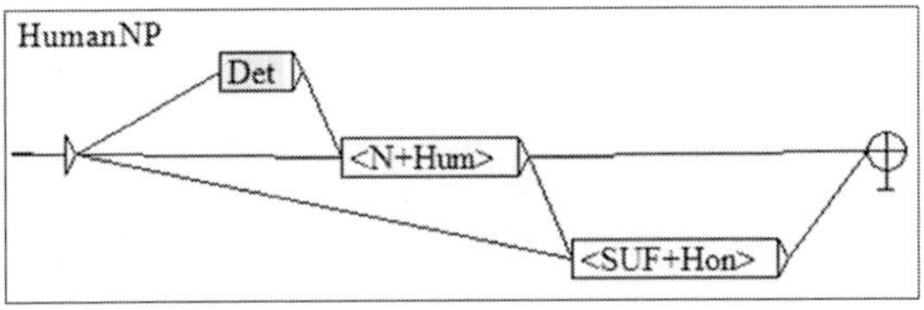

Figure 1 – Human NP graph

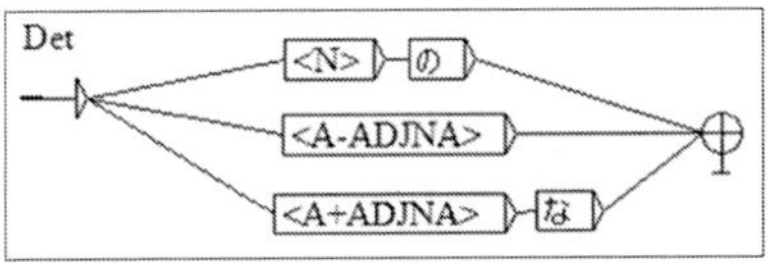

Figure 2 – Determiner graph

An honorific sentence basically consists of a human subject, complements which do not generally bear human features and a verb conjugated in the passive form.

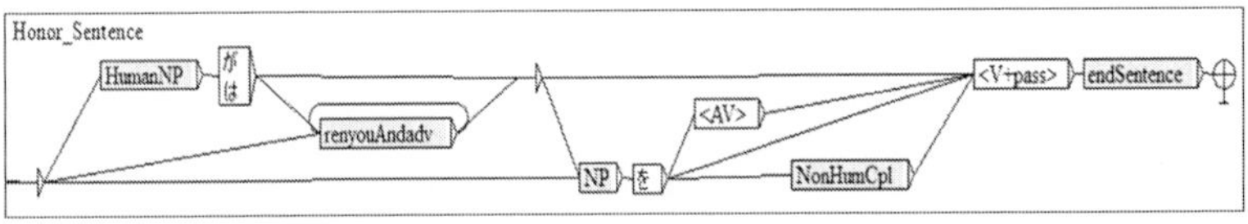

Figure 3 – Honorific sentence graph

Triggering the rejection of a complete sentence with an embedded graph is a difficult task, so we decided to extract all of the passive sentences containing a human subject even if they also have a human agent. Since the presence of an agent excludes the possibility of honorific passive, we labelled the graph with “NoHonorifics” as complementary information.

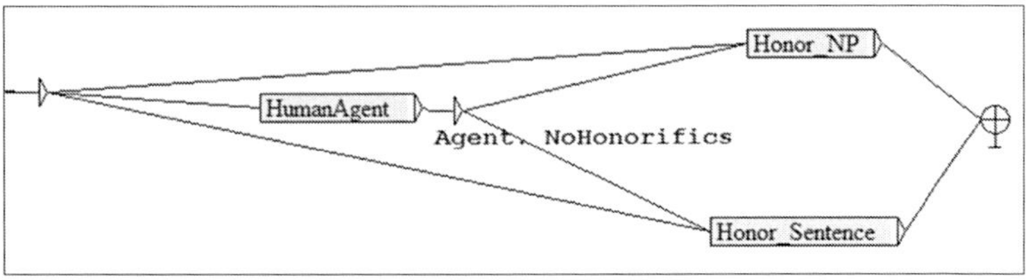

Figure 4 – Main graph

A human agent is the combination of a human noun phrase and the particle に (*ni*) as a postposition.

Testing the graphs

We have applied these graphs to a set of twelve Japanese sentences which present different uses of the passive.

All of the honorific passives were extracted. Four adversative sentences were extracted but with the annotation of “NoHonorifics”.

Before	Seq.	After
:ができませんでした。2. 私は	妹に彼の手紙を破られました。/Agent. NoHonorifics	3. 花子に髪を切られ
)手紙を破られました。3. 花	子に髪を切られた。/Agent. NoHonorifics	4. 金魚に死なれて悲
なれて悲しくてたまらない。5.	先生が書かれたご本	6. 社長さんが出席さ
5. 先生が書かれたご本 6.	社長さんが出席される会議	7. 部長は旅行の間た
長さんが出席される会議 7.	部長は旅行の間たくさん写真を撮られました。	8. 田中さんはいつ帰
写真を撮られました。8. 田中	さんはいつ帰られますか。	9. 先生が問題を配ら
さんはいつ帰られますか。9.	先生が問題を配られました。	そして、テストについて説
が問題を配られました。そして、	テストについて説明されました。	10. ロボットが人間に
が人間に操られている。11.	被験者が与えられた刺激	は次のようである。12.
刺激は次のようである。12.	一流の音楽家がピアノを朝まで弾かれた。	13. 一流の音楽家に
アノを朝まで弾かれた。13.	一流の音楽家にピアノを朝まで弾かれた。/Agent. NoHonorifics	14. 実はこの草は食べ
ど、僕は食べられない。15.	警官に車を止められました。/Agent. NoHonorifics	そして、名前と住所を尋
止められました。そして、名前と	住所を尋ねられました。	16. お父さんは子供に

Figure 5 – Extraction

Out of 12 sentences, two mistakes are reported. Detailed explanations are given underneath.

DIRECT PASSIVE
被験者が与えられた刺激は次のようである。
Hikensha ga atae rareta shigeki wa tsugi no you dearu.
'The patient reacted to the stimulus which was given to him as followed.'
Comment: This sentence contains both a human subject and an agent ('doctor'), which had been omitted.

ADVERSATIVE PASSIVE: 警官に車を止められました。そして、名前と住所を尋ねられました
Keikan ni kuruma wo tome raremashita. Soshite, namae to jūsho wo tazune raremashita.
'I had my car stopped by a policeman. Then I was asked my name and my address.'
Comment: The second part of the sentence was mistakenly extracted. Thus the agent ('by the policeman') who had already been mentioned in the first part was not repeated.

Conclusion

NooJ has proven its ability to process real Japanese sentences without artificial segmentation. Standard patterns of syntactic correctness are easily analysed with embedded grammar graphs. In our present study, the design of these graphs is a way to check assumptions about the difference between the honorific passive and other passive forms. The graphs we built up to illustrate our point of view were tested on a set of sentences. To properly distinguish passive honorific sentences, we have added a human category as semantic information in the NooJ dictionary.

References

Collec-Clerc, Valérie. 2013. Adapting Existing Japanese Linguistic Resources to Build a NooJ dictionary to Recognise Honorific Forms. Formalising Natural Languages with NooJ 2013, In *Selected papers from the NooJ 2013 International Conference* – Edited by Svetla Koeva, Sli Mesfar and Max Silberztein, pp 143-155.

Mami, Iwashita. 2007**.** The meanings and functions of Japanese passive constructions In *Studies in Asian Linguistics University of Sydney* LINCOM 71. 255 p.

Siegel, Melanie. 2000. Japanese Honorification in an HPSG Framework, *Proceedings of the 14th Pacific Asia - Conference on Language, Information and Computation*. pp. 289-300.

Koeva, Svetla, Denis Maurel, and Max Silberztein. 2007. Formaliser les langues avec l'ordinateur: de INTEX à NooJ. *Cahiers de la MSH Ledoux*, Presses Universitaires de Franche-Comté, Besançon.

Sugimura, Ryôichi. 1986. Japanese honorifics and Situation Semantics, In *International Conference on Computational Linguistics*. pp. 507-510.

Tanaka, Satchiko et al, 1983. Keigo wo totonoeru (Treatment of the honorific form), In *Asakura Nihongo Shin-Kôza* vol 5. Ed. Asakura Shoten, Tokyo.

Terruya, Kazuhiro. 2007. Interpersonal grammar of Japanese. In *A Systemic functional grammar of Japanese,* Vol 2, Ch 4, pp135-205.

Tsujimura, Natsuko. 2005. *Japanese Linguistics Vol II syntax and Semantics Vol III Pragmatics, Sociolinguistics and language contact* Ed Routlege London.

Wetzel, Patricia. 2004. Keigo in modern Japan from Meiji to the present, University of Hawai pressStudies In *Japanese Linguistics 1988-90.* Lone Publications, London, 1991. pp. 127-150.

Wlodarczyk, André. 1996. *Politesse et Personne – Le japonais face aux langues occidentales*. Editions L'harmattan.

—. Projet LEXGRAMJP *Lexique et grammaire pour l'analyse du japonais écrit* (JaLexBD–Raoul Blin).

—. Duisburg Universität *Japanisch Grundkursund Intensiv kurs* (Examples of sentences).

A NOOJ MODULE FOR NAMED ENTITY RECOGNITION IN MIDDLE FRENCH

MOURAD AOUINI

Abstract

This paper presents a methodology for the development of a NooJ module for the recognition of named entities in Middle French texts. This module is designed to facilitate the computer-aided analysis of this language by addressing the major obstacles that it presents for morpho-syntactic tagging and the identification of named entities: most notably its non-standard orthography and grammar.

The initial module is based on a training corpus of political texts of French and English origin, in Middle French, dating from the mid-twelfth to the early sixteenth century. This corpus of texts has certain clear characteristics which mean that the nature of the Middle French it contains is notably different from that of literary modern French. Moreover, the grammar of these texts can vary enormously according to the geographical location, social status, education and time period of the author and/or copyist, as well as other factors such as the intended function of the text. There is also significant variation in orthography, which poses problems for analysis.

We have focused on the manual development of rules for the annotation and recognition of named entities such as person, location and organisation. These rules are context-based, and take into account the lemmas and parts of speech of the words surrounding the object of study in order aid disambiguation

Introduction

With the expansion of the internet and the development of digitalisation tools, it is becoming increasingly easy to approach large corpora of texts. The analysis of corpora now plays a major role in domains such as the analysis of user data in social networks, e-reputation management, political discourse and historical sources like medieval texts.

This project began as a result of work on the development of an application designed to facilitate the analysis of medieval texts: PALM (Plateforme d'analyse linguistique médiévales). Part of the European Research Council funded programme called Signs and States. PALM is a network designed to help users compile, analyse and share corpora of medieval texts in digital form. The general aim of the European program 'Signs and States' is to examine how developments in government in the later Middle Ages changed societies not only socially or economically, but also culturally. In this context, we are interested in using NooJ to develop modules that can analyse medieval texts effectively.

Our Middle French corpus contains texts of English and French origin dating from the mid-twelfth to the early sixteenth century. All of the texts are related to political culture. This is a huge remit which one could argue covers the vast majority of texts written in the Middle Ages. For this reason, we have imposed some limits on our choice of texts. The corpus includes texts directly related to the process of government, texts discussing particular political events and texts which consider good and bad rule in a general manner.

This corpus has certain clear characteristics which mean that the nature of the Middle French it contains is notably different from that of literary modern French. The grammar of these texts can vary enormously according to the geographical location, social status, education and time period of the author and/or copyist, as well as other factors such as the intended function of the text.

We distinguish three main features of Middle French texts:

- orthographical variation: the same word can exist in many different forms
- the evolution of grammatical structures: The syntax of the texts is influenced by geographical and chronological factors
- the presence of vocabulary from many languages: in the Middle Ages there were close links between English, French and Latin, and we often find vocabulary drawn from several languages in Middle French texts.

The typology of Named Entities and related work

The Message Understanding Conference MUC (Chinchor, 1998) defined NER as the ability to find and classify names of entities, place names, temporal expressions, and certain types of numerical expressions in texts. This task is intended to be of direct practical value and an essential component of many language processing tasks, such as information extraction (IE), information retrieval (IR), question answering and machine translation (MT).

The hierarchy of named entities includes three types of expressions:

- proper names (ENAMEX) which includes persons, localisation and organisation
- temporal expressions (TIMEX) which includes time and date expressions
- numeric expressions (NUMEX) which includes numbers, percentages, and monetary quantities.

Recently, a number of methods have been used for NER, and we can classify them under three main approaches: statistical, rule-based and hybrid. Statistical methods aim to find the probability distribution $p(y|x)$, where y is the sequence of NE tags assigned to x and x is the sequence of words in the sentence. There are two ways of implementing this approach: either by using a classifier such as Naive Bayes (Pearl, 1988) (Roth et al., 2002) or by using sequence models such as Maximum Entropy Markov Model (MEMM) or Conditional Markov Models (CMM) (McCallum et al., 2000), Conditional Random Fields (CRF) (McCallum et al., 2003). Rule-based methods attempt to use syntactic and semantic patterns written manually or semi-automatically to capture the corresponding named entity (Coates-Stephens, 1993). These rules can be modelled using regular expression or local grammar (Gross, 1997) with NooJ linguistic platform (Silberztein and Tutin, 2005). Hybrid methods combine rule-based methods and statistical methods (Mikheev et al., 1998) to improve the results.

As far as we know, little NER work has been done for medieval vernacular languages, and there has been no study dedicated to Middle French. The present work proposes a rule-based method implemented with the linguistic platform NooJ.

Development of the NooJ Module for NER

In this section, we present our NooJ Module, which is designed to facilitate the computer-aided analysis of Middle French texts by addressing the major obstacles that they present for named entity recognition: most notably their non-standard orthography and grammar.

Construction of a Middle French Dictionary

The first task was to build a dictionary that takes into account specific features of our corpus. As far as we know, there are a few linguistic resources in Middle French which have been built by other teams.

We constructed our own dictionary using some of the existing and heterogeneous resources. We used the entries of *Dictionnaire de Moyen Français* (DMF, 2012), the entries of a list of the most frequent words in the written French language (Fondet & Jejcic, 2011) and the entries of the *Anglo Normand Dictionary* (Totter, 2001). We enriched our dictionary with proper nouns drawn from many glossaries, index editions and encyclopedic information. Finally, we added to our dictionary by extracting words from our corpus.

Due to the absence of standard spelling and the geographically and chronologically influenced variety which characterises late Middle French vocabulary, there are frequently several possible spellings for the same word.

By consulting our corpus, we created graphs representing frequently-occurring morphological rules. For example, nouns could be pluralised by the addition of an 's' but a 'z' or an 'x' might also be used. As an example, the entry for *roi*, meaning 'king', takes the following form.
roi,NC+FLX=ROI+SENS=1

roi here represents the form as it is attested in the text, while NC(*nom commun* or common noun) represents the part of speech. 'FLX=ROI' indicates the paradigm that is to be applied, in this case that linked to the lemma *roi*, which is as follows:

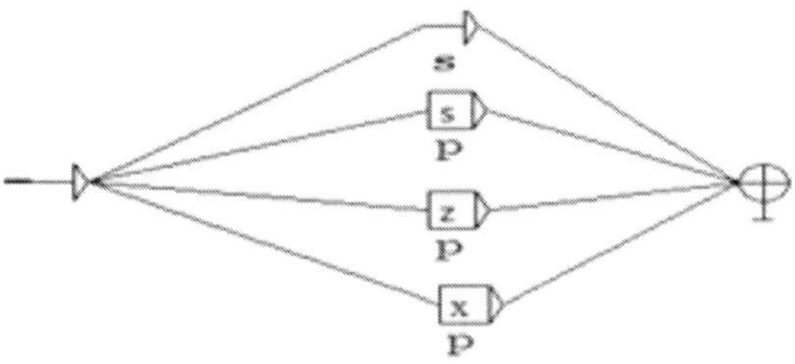

Figure 1 – Graph of ROI paradigm

Working from our corpus, we added all the variants which were not represented by our morphological graph to the dictionary. For speakers of modern French, who are only familiar with the forms *roi* and *rois*, the full entry for *roi* with all its variants will appear strange:

roi,NC+FLX=ROI+SENS=1
rai,roi,NC+FLX= ROI+SENS=1
re,roi,NC+FLX= ROI+SENS=1
ree,roi,NC+FLX= ROI+SENS=1
rei,roi,NC+FLX= ROI+SENS=1
reis,roi,NC+FLX= ROI+SENS=1
etc.

Our dictionary contains many homonyms and ambiguous words. For example, the word *roi* is a common noun which can have two meanings ‘king’ or ‘order, measure’. Another example is the word *duc* with two homonyms which can mean ‘duke’ or ‘bird’ (related to the modern English duck). In order to distinguish between meanings in these kinds of cases, we added an extra level of qualification to the entry: the semantic label SENS which distinguishes them by a number. The detailed definition of each word is easily accessible by consulting the DMF or by processing a text in PALM.

Disambiguation of some frequent words

In this step, we realised that there are some words which are frequent and systematically ambiguous. We developed local grammars to remove these ambiguities automatically. The grammar lists a number of ‘unambiguous’ contexts in which one can disambiguate these words with certainty (Silberztein, 2010).

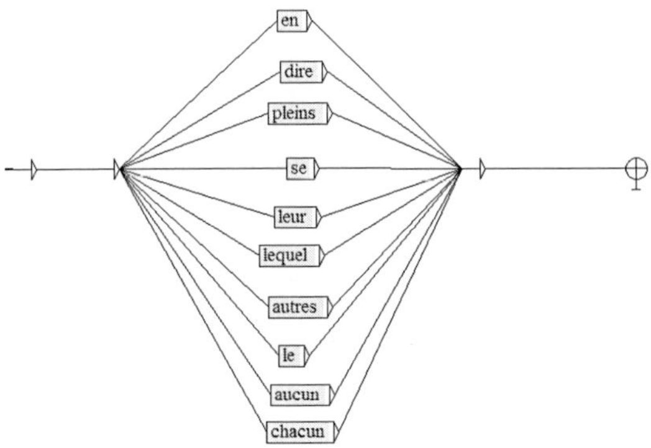

Figure 2 – Graph to disambiguate frequent words

For the example, the form *pleins* can be either an adverb (*pleins*=many) or a verb (*se plaindre*=complain). When preceded by a pronoun like *je,tu, il* etc.' it has to be verb.

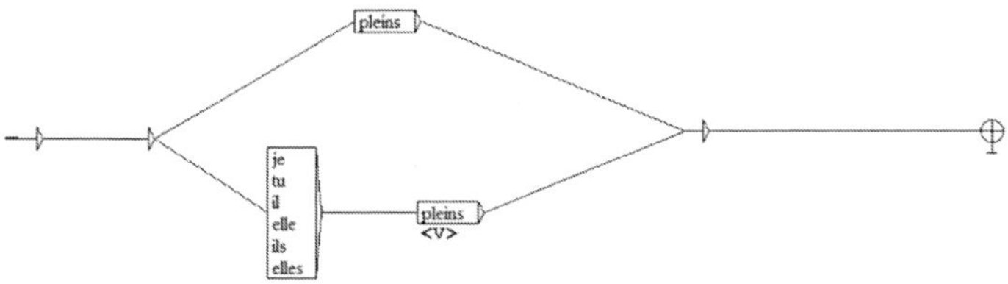

Figure 3 – Graph to disambiguate '*pleins*'

As another example, all the variants of the lemma *se* when followed by a noun have to be annotated <se,PRO>.

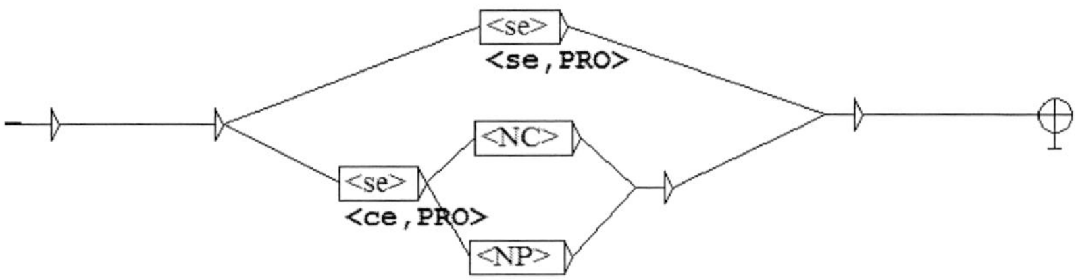

Figure 4 – Graph to disambiguate '*se*'

Building dictionaries of proper names ENAMEX

To recognise ENAMEX in Middle French texts, we began by building dictionaries for names linked to person, location and organisation.

Dictionaries to Recognise Persons

We built four dictionaries used in the graphs to recognise persons: a dictionary of first names, a dictionary of last names, a dictionary of titles and a dictionary of professions.

- *Dictionary of First Names:* This dictionary contains more than 3,000 entries. Each entry contains the following information: part of speech and first name (NP+Prénom). Like the main dictionary, this dictionary has many variants for the same noun. As shown in the following example, we added more than 20 variations of the first name 'Paul' in order to recognise different forms.

paul,NP+ Prénom
paol,paul,NP+ Prénom
paolo,paul,NP+ Prénom
paoul,paul,NP+ Prénom
paullus,paul,NP+ Prénom
paulus,paul,NP+ Prénom
etc.

- ***Dictionary of Last Names:*** This dictionary is composed of more than 2,000 entries. Each entry contains the following information: part of speech and last name (NP+Nom).

- ***Dictionary of Compound Names:*** By consulting and studying our corpus in greater depth, we built this dictionary which contains more than 1,000 entries consisting of sequences of words referring to a person. In the Middle Ages, a person was described according to his features, for instance his country, his town, his profession or other factors. As a consequence, we found many sequences of words referring to people like 'Guillaume de Normandie' and 'Guillaume le Roux' as shown in the following example.

guillaume de castillon,NP+Personne+UNAMB
guillaume de dormans,NP+Personne+UNAMB
guillaume de gennes,NP+Personne+UNAMB
guillaume de graville,NP+Personne+UNAMB
guillaume de meleun,NP+Personne+UNAMB
guillaume de normandie,NP+Personne+UNAMB
guillaume le roux,NP+Personne+UNAMB

- ***Dictionary of titles:*** This dictionary is composed of more than 1,000 entries. Each entry contains the following information: part of speech and title (NC+Titre).

- ***Dictionary of professions:*** This dictionary contains more than 1,000 entries. Each entry contains all paradigms, all variants and the following information: part of speech and profession (NC+Profession) as shown in the following example.

maréchal,NC+Profession
marchal,maréchal,NC+Profession
marescal,maréchal,NC+Profession
marescaus,maréchal,NC+Profession
mareschal,maréchal,NC+Profession

mareschauls,maréchal,NC+Profession
mareschaulx,maréchal,NC+Profession
etc.

Dictionary to Recognise Organisations

We built a dictionary of organisations which is composed of more than 1,000 entries, consisting of religious institutions such as churches and abbeys and other institutions such as castles and parliaments. Each entry contains the following information: part of speech and organisation (NP+Organisation).

Dictionary to Recognise Location

We built a dictionary of location which contains the names of places such as countries and cities. It contains more than 3,000 entries. As shown in the following example, each entry can have many variants, and contains the following information: part of speech and location (NP+Lieu).
italie,NP+Lieu
itaile,italie,NP+Lieu
itaille,italie,NP+Lieu
itallie,italie,NP+Lieu
itayle,italie,NP+Lieu
etc.

Recognition graphs

In this step, we created a series of grammars which enable us to group all elements of the same entity. Each grammar is a sequence of words which consists of triggers and dictionary entries.

Recognition Graph for a Person

By consulting and analysing the corpus, we realised that there are many ways to refer to the name of a person in the Middle Ages. A person can be identified by his first name and last name such as *jehan chambon*, by his title such as *roi Richard (*King Richard), by his profession such as *le juge Bertrand* (Judge Bertrand), by his location such as *John de Paris* (John from Paris), by his organisation such as *Prêtre de cathédrale de Rome* (priest of the cathedral of Rome), by his family ties such as *La cousine de conseiller Edward* (the cousin of councilor Edward) or by some expression such as *Le serviteur d'ame de dieu* (the servant of God). Therefore, we distinguish many patterns as shown in the following graph.

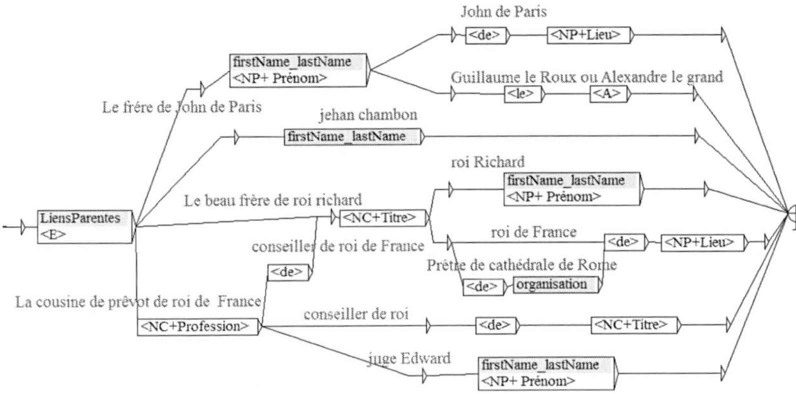

Figure 5 – The main graph to recognise persons

Recognition Graph for location

In our corpus, authors described places using expressions such as *plusieurs belles villes de France* (several beautiful cities of France), *nombreuse villes d'Angleterre* (numerous cities of England), *notre belle ville de Paris* (our beautiful city of Paris) to demonstrate their greatness, beauty and importance. To reflect this, we created the graph 'description' to recognise the description of a place such as *grand nombre de* (large number of), *nombreuses belles* (numerous beautiful). We also created the graph *declencheur* which recognises triggers such as *rue* (street),*ville* (city) or *commune* (municipality). These graphs are used as sub-graphs within a main graph to recognise all patterns, as the following figure illustrates.

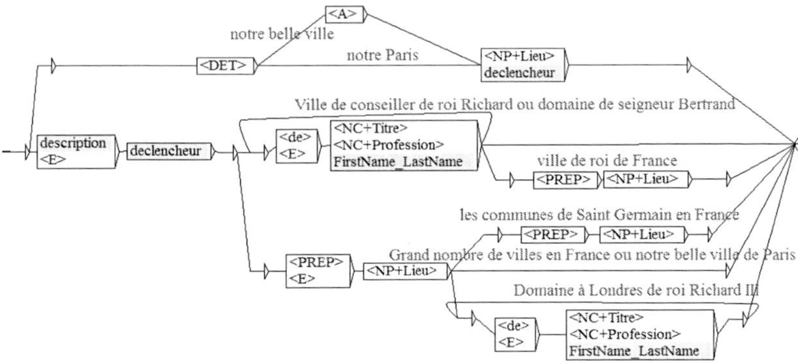

Figure 6 – The main graph to recognise location

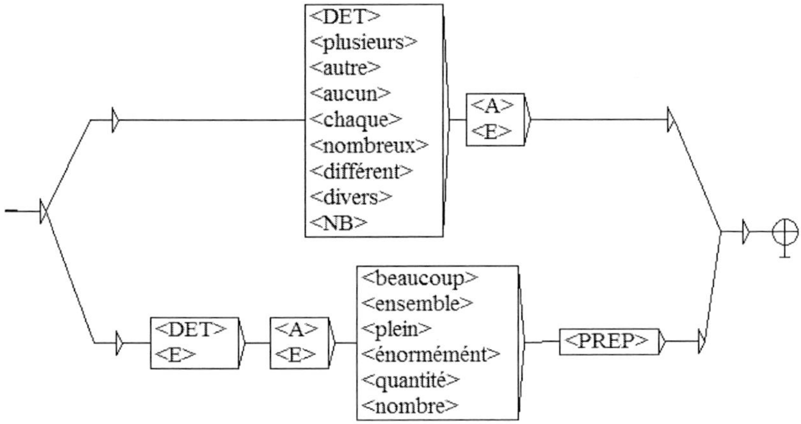

Figure 7 – The graph of description

Recognition Graph for organisations

We distinguish many kinds of organisations such as religious, political, hospital and personal. An organisation was described according to a location such as *hôtel de dieu de Paris* (hospital of Paris) or a person such as *Le cathédrale de Guillaume de Normandie* (William of Normandy's cathedral). Therefore, we distinguish many patterns as shown in the following graph.

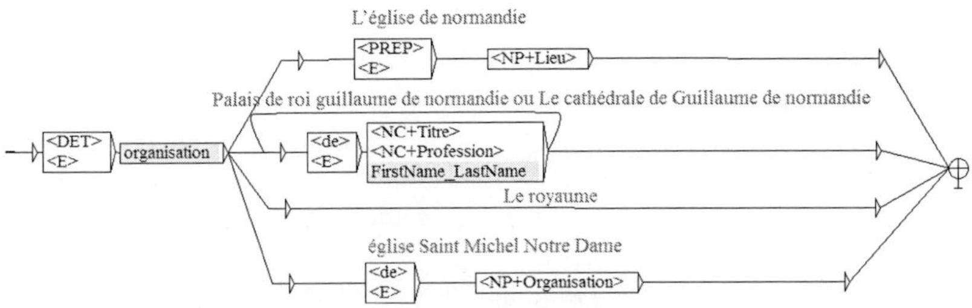

Figure 8 – The main graph to recognise organization

Evaluation of the NooJ Module for NER

To evaluate the performance of our system of ENAMEX recognition, we used recall, precision and F-measure which are based on an understanding and measure of relevance. Precision measures the percentage of selected responses that are relevant, Recall measures the relevant responses that are selected and F-measure is a combined measure that assesses the Precision/Recall tradeoff (F-measure=2PR/P+R).

	Precision	Recall	F-measure
Person	87.00%	79.00%	82.80%
Location	84.00%	75.00%	79.24%
Organisation	82.00%	72.00%	76.67%

The results are good but they are not perfect. This is mainly due to the absence of standard spelling and the geographically and chronologically influenced variation which characterises late medieval vocabulary including names.

Conclusion and Perspectives

Applying advanced methods of computer aided linguistic analysis to medieval texts can have many advantages. Named entity recognition can, of course, assist the work of historians tracing people and places across large corpora of historic texts. However, the development of tools for the treatment of non-standard and highly variable languages also has a broader application.

In this paper, we have presented our rule-based method implemented by a set of dictionaries and transducers with the linguistic platform NooJ to recognise proper names ENAMEX (person, location and organisation).

This work is in progress, our NooJ module works perfectly and the obtained results are promising.
The next step is to add other syntactic rules for disambiguation, enrich our graphs and dictionaries in order to improve results and build graphs and dictionaries to extract numerical entity NUMEX and temporal expression TIMEX.

References

Coates-Stephens, Sam. 1993. The analysis and acquisition of proper names for the understanding of free text. In *Computers and the Humanities, Vol.26*, pp.441-456.

DMF: *Dictionnaire du Moyen Français*, version 2012 (DMF 2012). ATILF - CNRS & Université de Lorraine. Website: http://www.atilf.fr/dmf.

Fondet, Claire and Fabrice Jejcic. 2011. OrthoFonic : un projet de didacticiel pour l'apprentissage de l'orthographe française. In *L'enseignement de l'orthographe en FLE, TRANEL (Travaux Neuchâtelois de Linguistique), n° 54*, Institut des Sciences du langage et de la communication, Université de Neuchâtel, pp. 71-92.

Genet, Jean-Philippe. 2006. Langue et Histoire. In *Actes du Colloque de l'École Doctorale d' Histoire de Paris I, INHA, 20 et 21 octobre 2006,* Edited by Jean-Philippe Genet, Jean-Marie Bertrand, Pierre Boilley, Jean-Philippe Genet et Pauline Schmitt-Pantel, Paris (Publications de la Sorbonne), 2011.

—. 2011. Langue et histoire : des rapports nouveaux. In *Langue et Histoire* edited by Jean-Philippe Genet, Jean-Marie Bertrand, Pierre Boilley, Jean-Philippe Genet et Pauline Schmitt-Pantel, Paris (Publications de la Sorbonne), 2011, p. 13-31.

—. 2012. Political Language in the Late Medieval English Parliament. In *Parlementarische Kulturen*, éd. J. Feuchter et J. Helmrath, Campus Verlag, Francfort-New York.

Gross, Maurice. 1997. The construction of local grammars. In *Finite-State Language Processing*, E. ROCHE and Y. SCHABES (eds.), Cambridge, Mass./London, England: MIT Press, pp. 329-354.

Laferty, John, Andrew McCallum, and Fernando Pererira,. 2001. *Conditional Random Fields:Probabilistic models for segmenting and labeling sequence data.* In ICML-2001.

Li, Xin and Dan Roth. 2002. Learning question classifiers: the role of semantic information. In *Proc. International Conference on Computational Linguistics* (COLING), 556–562

McCallum, Andrew. 2003. Efficiently Inducing Features of Conditional Random Fields. In *Nineteenth Conference on Uncertainty in Artificial Intelligence* (UAI03).

McCallum, Andrew and Feng Fang-Fang. 2003. *Chinese Word Segmentation with Conditional Random Fields and Integrated Domain Knowledge*. Unpublished Manuscript

Mikheev, Andrei. 1998. Feature lattices for maximum entropy modelling. In *Proceedings of the 36th Annual Meeting of the Association for Computational Linguistics and Proceedings of the 17th International Conference on Computational Linguistics*, pp. 848-854, Montreal, Quebec, August 10-14.

Pearl, Judea. 1988. *Probabilistic Reasoning in Intelligent Systems.*

Silberztein, Max and Agnès Tutin. 2005. NooJ: Un outil TAL de corpus pour l'enseignement des langues. In *Application pour l'étude de la morphologie lexicale en FLE*, Article n°alsic_v08_20-rec11, p. 123-134.

Silberztein, Max. 2004. NooJ : an oriented object approach. In *INTEX pour la Linguistique et le Traitement Automatique des Langues*, J. Royauté & M. Silberztein. Presses Universitaires de Franche-Comté.

Silberztein Max, 2008. *Manuel de NooJ.* Université de Franche-Comté.

Morpho-Syntactic Based Recognition of Arabic MWUs Using NooJ

Azeddine Rhazi

Abstract

The aim of the paper is twofold: firstly, to describe Arabic language multi-word-units by classifying and formalising data; secondly, to clarify the relative importance of automatic identification of MWUs from a given corpus to be treated by a module based on morpho-syntactic tagging. It is necessary, on the one hand, to deal with the NLP research on describing natural languages, and on the other, to build a machine translation (MT) annotation module for the idiomaticity of Arabic MWUs, from the lesser to higher degree, using NooJ as a linguistic development environment.

Introduction

As with simple words, associated, fixed phrases, compound nouns, compound verbs, idioms, frozen expressions, collocations, pragmatemes, MWUs (groups of simple words that are often used or associated together (Pecina Pavel, 2009)) are subjects of linguistic and formal descriptions. A correct and exhaustive treatment of this issue has an important impact on Natural Language Processing (NLP). However, it raises some nontrivial questions regarding, for example, morpho-syntactic MWU properties, morphological non-compositionality of MWUs, their syntactic and semantic variation and the role of separators in MWU sequences. In Arabic, as a highly inflected language, the description must be at least partially lexicalised at a morpho-syntactical level.

In this paper we present the initial results on parsing Arabic using NooJ as a linguistic development environment, regarding the linguistic properties of those units, and to the way of NooJ processing which stores and associates simple words and MWUs in the same dictionary. The aim of this study is also to clarify the relative importance of the automatic identification of MWUs from a given corpus to be treated by NooJ module based on morpho-syntactic tagging of Arabic MWUs according to their degree of idiomaticity.

My own reaction, in this work, is the implementation of an incremental finite-state transducer (using a local grammar of Arabic MWUs). In fact, the work is a development of the project of Arabic MWUs based on approximately 65,000 MWUs as entries. The objective of the first step is to identify given structures; the classification begins with the clustering technique, from similar to hierarchically ascending classification based on a subset of term units (Ibekwe and SanJwan, 2002).

The new developments in this article regard the processing of MWUs using NooJ platform; we propose an implementation and formalisation of this category of sequence into the Arabic corpus, taking into consideration inflexion of each lexical entry (gender, number, the status of concordances, free annexation, and tokenisation), in the context of developing recognition tools and linguistic resources. This helps NooJ users disambiguate and filter out the semantic annotation, by building a specific annotational module for Arabic MWUs, and makes it as easy to use as possible for Arabic system users.

The treatment of MWUs as sequences follows a very specific field and pathway, focusing on those particularly ambiguous MWU forms in relation to the semantic annotation, as in the following types:

a. **Fixed Expressions**: These expressions are lexically, syntactically and morphologically rigid. An expression of this type is considered as a word with spaces (a single word that happens to contain spaces), such as:

(2) الاتحاد الأوروبي; *al-alittihad alouroubbi* (the European union)
(3) حيص بيص; *haysa baysa* (problem).

b. **Semi-Fixed Expressions**: These expressions can undergo variations, but the components of the expression remain adjacent. The variations are of two types, morphological variations where lexical items can express person, number, tense, gender etc, such as the examples in (4) and (4.1), and lexical variations, where one word can be replaced by another as in:

(4) شوط إضافي ; *Chawtun idaafiyun* (overtime).
(4.1) شوطان إضافيان ; *Chawtan idaafiaane* (double overtime).

c. **Morpho-Syntactically**: Flexible Expressions. These are the expressions that can either undergo reordering, such as passivisation, or allow external elements to intervene between the components such as (5), where the adjacency of the MWUs is disrupted or interrupted in (6).

(5) حمية غذائية ; *Himyatun rhadaaiyatun* (alimentary regime)
(6) حمية غذائية صحية / ضعيفة;*Himyatun rhadaiyatun sihiyatun* (good alimentary regime / bad alimentary regime)

This means we can be faced with an ambiguity regarding its semantics and the general text comprehension: almost any semantically-related MWU form can refer at the same time to other semantic fields, having a completely different morpho-syntactic behaviour. Work is currently in progress with a large coverage of MWU inflection types, precisely for a cross-language standard morpho-syntactical description of Arabic MWUs.

Motivation

A significant problem faced by NLP research on describing the Arabic language has become the main challenge of text lexical analysis. The greatest also, in translating MWUs might be the degree of idiomaticity, as many MWUs have, to some extent, an idiomatic sense. For example, it is hard for a system to predict an expression like 'to kick the bucket' which has a meaning that is totally unrelated to the meaning of (to kick), (the) and (bucket) while appearing to conform to the grammar of English.

In fact, an idiom cannot be translated literally because in many cases, it does not exist in an equivalent form in the target language; attention has already been paid to syntactic and/or semantic (non-) equivalence (Conenna, Merilla & al, 1990). Also, not every MWU in the source language has the same equivalent in the target language as well. For example, the German MWU (*ins Auge fassen*) can only be translated by the English one-word term 'envisage'. Hence, in the context of developing tools and linguistic resources, many applications undertake to build a Machine Translation (MT) module based on MWU generation.

What are MWUs and what do they represent for MT?

An MWU is a lexeme made up of a sequence of two or more lexemes, separated by spaces, as mentioned above. Moreover, fixedness and opacity are the main features of these expressions, as well as the idiosyncratic meaning and discontinuity of their elements (Pecina, Pavel, 2009). They have properties that are not predictable from the properties of the individual lexemes or their normal mode of combination. MWUs can also be described as 'idiosyncratic interpretations that cross word boundaries (or spaces)'. (Sag et al., 2002: 2). Unfortunately, MWUs remain an obstacle for automatic recognition and identification.

In fact, NLP and MT environments process simple and multi-words at the same one time. Challenges posed to MT by MWUs include syntactic structure and patterns of idiomaticity and fixedness at a semantic, pragmatic and statistical level, flexibility, and reductivity.

Approach

The most promising approach to the challenge of treating and translating MWUs is example-based MT, since in this case each MWU can be listed as an example with its translation equivalent in the target language. For rule- based MT it would be too difficult to define rules to translate MWUs, due to the magnitude of different kinds. Nevertheless, an example based MT system has to apply different rules for the translation of continuous and discontinuous MWU sequences, as it is harder to identify a discontinuous MWU in a sentence where words are inserted between the different components of one structure.

MWUs are, alongside disambiguation, one of the two key problems for NLP and especially for MT (Sag et al. 2002). In terms of lexical productivity, the number of MWUs in a speaker's lexicon is estimated to be of the same order of magnitude as the number of single words. Hence, the proportion of MWUs will rise as a system adds vocabulary for new domains, because each domain adds more MWUs than simple words.

A combined approach is, in this case, generally adopted for carrying out a large-coverage of Arabic linguistic resources for, at the same time; simple and complex words although different practices co-exist. Our suggestion for treating MWUs is an appropriate system for the storage (building a corpus) and band management of MWUs data, as well as the implementation of task-related procedures to the creation of automata for these type of dictionaries.

Examples of lexical entries

It is of utmost importance to specify that one MWU can be a compound, a fragment of a sentence, or a sentence. The group of lexemes (with spaces) which make up an MWU can be continuous or discontinuous, but it is not always possible to mark an MWU with a part of speech, as an MWU may be more or less frozen (or half-frozen). For example:

To kick the bucket, < قضى نحبه >
Which means 'to die' rather than:
to hit a bucket with one's foot.

In this example, which is an endocentric compound, the part of speech may be determined as being a verb. The MWUs is half-frozen, in the sense that not all variation is possible, a certain degree of variation is possible but not everything, as in the following MWUs morpho-syntactical variation:

Example of Arabic MWUs corpora	
MWUs	English translation
تجاوز الخطوط الحمراء	*Exceeds the red lines*
formal classification of Arabic MWUs	
V+N0+N1+N2	Tajaawaza/ Ø/alkhutut /alhamraa
Arabic MWUs Morpho-syntactical transformations	
Morphological transformations of the head of MWUs (verb)	Formal structures (subclass) V + S +N1+N2
تجاوز **العدو** الخطوط الحمراء	تجاوز / Ø / **ال** / **عدو** / ال / خطوط / ال/ حمراء

Figure 1 – Morpho-syntactical variations of Arabic MWUs

Processing Arabic MWUs

Attempting to classify the lexical entries, we describe the morpho-syntactical properties of the elaborated data by demonstrating an Arabic MWU dictionary as well as the graphs created for their processing and automatic recognition in the corpus. The development of morphological grammars embracing certain classes and subclasses of MWUs not currently present in any dictionary provided the lexical source for the dictionary. To annotate the structure head of the MWU you must take context into account in order to disambiguate and filter out the semantic annotation.

A first application is simple MT consultation and information extraction from corpora having no specific tags. MT contains a morphological analyser that can perform research and treatment in texts using regular expressions, including forms, lemmas, syntactic categories or lexical information for example, to search in a corpus all nouns with the same derived head end.

Experiment on a corpus

Arabic MWUs: < qada Amrune nahbahu> قضى عمرو نحبه ‘to die’ is more frozen than the other examples. Let us add that a tense variation is allowed for the verb but we cannot determine the part of speech for the whole expression since it is a sentence, as in the following examples:

Exceeds the red lines تجاوز الخطوط الحمراء
Just around the corner قاب قوسين أو أدنى
Extended redundancy sun (arising) امتَدّت أطنابُ الشمسِ
Scored prized أحرز قصب السبق
Hit the ground (long travel) ضرب في الأرض
Kick the bucket قضى نحبه

Lexical entries of Arabic MWUs

For these reasons it is evident how problematic lexical automatic analysis of Arabic texts is; the following examples illustrate how the opaque meaning is crucial: as in: Qada Amrun nahbahu **قضى عمرو نحبه** (kick the bucket) = (humorous to die), when we apply the morpho-syntaxical properties and local grammar for this type of Arabic sequences in (13.1; **13**.2; 13.3; 13.4):

Qada Amrun nahbahu قضى عمرو نحبه (kick the bucket) = (die)

قضوا نحبهم / قضت نحبها / *يقضي نحبه
safha bayda بيضاء صفحة (freedom from commitments)
صفحة بيضاء = (clean slate)
ا ل / صفحة / ال / بيضاء
صفحا / ت / بيضاء
*صفحة حمراء
(*a red clean slate)
Attaawun almuthmir التعاون المثمر
(Fruitful cooperation)التعاون المثمر
Attaawun (X) almuthmir X* التعاون المثمر
Etc...

Preprocessing graphs

Recognition graphs will be developed alongside tasks involving the automatic treatment of morpho-syntactic and morpho-lexical phenomena according to lexicon-grammar tables.

Arabic MWUs can be subdivided into six categories:

1. V+N
2. V+ N0 +N1
3. V+N0 +P
4. V+N0+(N+P+N)
5. V+N0+(P+N+P+P)
6. V+N0+(N1+N2)

as represented in the following graph of Arabic MWU categories (fig 2 and the example represented in fig 3 respectively):

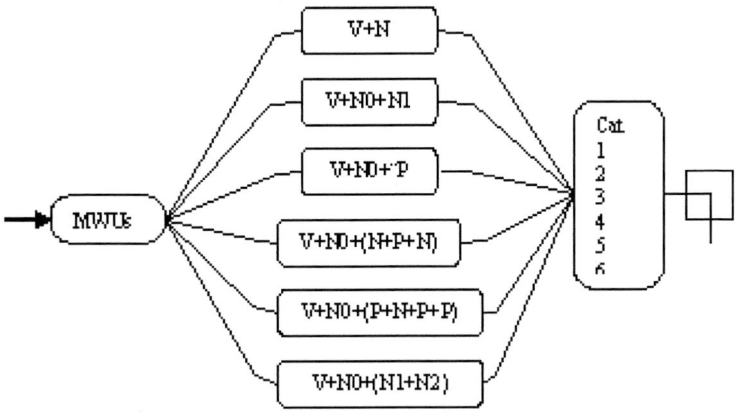

Figure 2 – Category 1 Graph

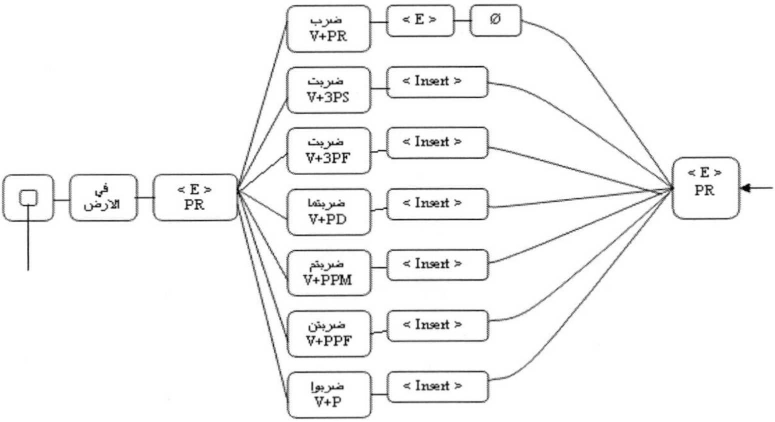

Figure 3 – " Daraba X fii Al ardi" Graph

Conclusion and future perspectives

Work is in progress with a large coverage of Arabic MWUs, taking into account the annotation from the more complex to the atomic sequences, The NooJ processing of Arabic MWUs is,therefore, a tool for expanding the dictionaries with new entries in a systematic way (covering large and diverse areas of the lexicon's inventory of MWUs) and establishing the resources to be used on available specialized on-line dictionaries based on Arabic lexical-semantic data.

As an agglutinative language, an Arabic module for developing automata for the inflection types in the established format is necessary for:

- exploring large databases and spotting different head word inflection types using the existing automata
- extracting thematic MWU dictionaries, using semantic relations encoded in the database, and employing inheritance to the task
- using MT as an environment for MWU extraction, processing the obtained material with the already designed dictionaries and encoding the appropriate candidates among the unrecognised tokens.

References

Attia, Mohammed, Total Antonio,Tounsi Lamia, Pecina Pavel, Genabith Josef van. 2010. *Automatic Extraction of Arabic Multiword Expressions, proceeding of the Workshop on Multiword Expressions: from theory to Applications* (MWE 2010) Beijing. August 2010, pp.18-56,

—. 2008. *Handling Arabic Morphological and Syntactic Ambiguity within the LFG Framework with a View to Machine Translation.* Ph.D. Thesis. The University of Manchester, Manchester, UK.

—. 2005. Developing Robust Arabic Morphological Transducer Using Finite State Technology, In *The 8th.Annual CLUK Research Colloquium 2005*, University of Manchester.

Baldwin, Timothy. 2004. Multiword Expressions, an Advanced Course, *The Australasian Language Technology Summer School* (ALTSS 2004). Sydney, Australia.

Connena, Mirella. 1995. Les expressions figées en français et en Italien : problèmes lexico-syntaxiques de traductions, In *Contrastes N°10. 95.*

Laporte, Eric. 1988. La reconnaissance des expressions figées lors de l'analyse automatique, In *Langage n°90.*

McCarthy, Michael. 2009. Collocations In *Ise*, *How words work together for fluent and natural English Self-study and classroom use* Cambridge.

Mesfar, Slim. 2008. *Analyse morpho-syntaxique automatique et reconnaissance des entités nommés en arabe standard,* Thèse en vue de l'obtention du titre de docteur en Informatique, Université franche comté, France.

Pecina, Pavel. 2009. *Lexical association measure: Collocation Extraction*, Institute of Formal and Applied Linguistics, Editor in chief: Jan Hajič.

SanJuan, Eric, Fidelia Ibekwe-SanJuan. 2002. Terminologie et classification automatique des texts, *JADT 2002, 6eme journées internationales d'analyse statistique des données textuelles.*

Silberztein, Max. 1993 *Dictionnaires électroniques et analyse automatique du textes,* Masson.

—. 2006. NooJ's Linguistic Annotation Engine. In *INTEX/NooJ pour le Traitement Automatique des Langues*, S. Koeva, D. Maurel, M. Silberztein Eds, Cahiers de la MSH Ledoux. Presses Universitaires de Franche-Comté, pp. 9-26.

—. 2011. Variable Unification with NooJ v3. In *Automatic Processing of Various Levels of Linguistic Phenomena*. Kristina Vuckovic, Bozo Bekavac, Max Silberztein Eds. Cambridge Scholars Publishing: Cambridge.

LOCAL GRAMMARS FOR PRAGMATEMES IN NOOJ

LENA PAPADOPOULOU

Abstract

The main objective of this work is the processing of local grammars that certain pragmatemes comprise in their structure. To do so, first the concept of pragmatemes is outlined. Second, the lexicographical model (PragμatLex) that we adopted is described. Third, local grammars that we constructed for this purpose are presented. Finally, the perspectives of our work are drawn.

Introduction

Since the birth of the Greek NooJ module (Chatjipapa, Gavriilidou & Papadopoulou 2008) the Greek community has focused on the construction of dictionaries comprising exclusively lexical units. The present work serves to introduce data that do not correspond to lexical units but to phrastic units and concretely to pragmatemes.

Pragmatemes are non-free phrases that are restricted by a given communicative situation. For example, typical *formulae*, felicitations and greetings, such as *metá timís* 'Yours faithfully' (closing a formal letter), *xróña polá* 'Happy birthday' (to felicitate somebody on his birthday) and *kaliméra* 'Good morning' (to greet someone when meeting him before noon) are considered to be pragmatemes.

There are pragmatemes that enclose in their structure a local grammar. This type of pragmateme is at the core of our present work. However, before proceeding to their processing, the concept of pragmatemes will be defined and the lexicographical model for their treatment by Blanco (2010) –PragμatLex - will be presented.

‘Pragmatemes’ and ‘PragμatLex’

A prototypical pragmateme AB is a compositional phraseme whose signified ‘A⊕B′ is restrictedly constructed by the conceptual representation of the given extralinguistic situation (SIT) (Mel’čuk 1998; Blanco, to appear).

The above definition has been provided within the frame of Meaning⇔Text Theory and concretely by the two-fold categorisation of non-free phrases which corresponds to semantic phrasemes and pragmatic phrasemes (Mel’cuk 1988). The main difference between semantic and pragmatic phrasemes is that the signified of the first is restrictedly constructed by the semantic representation:

- *cítrinos típos* ‘gutter press, lit. yellow press’

while the signified of the latter is restricted by the conceptual representation:

- *kaló savatocíryako* ‘Have a nice weekend’

and quite often by the semantic representation as well (Papadopoulou to appear):

- *ónira γliká* ‘sweet dreams ’

It has to be pointed out that by the term ‘conceptual representation’ the speaker´s perception of the world on the basis of a certain communicative situation (SIT) is meant (Mel’čuk 2012). Henceforth, the definition of the communicative situation in the lexicographical treatment of pragmatemes is crucial.

SIT plays the lead in PragμatLex, which is a lexicographical model exclusively for pragmatemes (Blanco 2010, 2013, to appear) written in XML in order to be compatible with NLP systems (eg Figure 1, 2 and 3).

<ARTICLE language="el">
<Lemma>**Με γεια {Art$_{def+acc}$ N$_{clothes+acc}$}**</Lemma>
<Morphosyntax>**PREP N**</Morphosyntax>
< TRANSLATION language="es">**-**</ TRANSLATION language="es">
<Keyword>**ρούχο**</Keyword>
<SIT>**expresión oral a una persona que lleva nueva**

ropa</SIT>
<SPEECH ACT>**felicitar**</SPEECH ACT>
<SS>~ **X a Y por Z**</SS>
<LF>-</LF>
<CODA>-</CODA>
<SYNONYM>-</SYNONYM>
<ANTONYM>-</ANTONYM>
</ARTICLE language="el">

Figure 6 – Pragmateme *meyá* ‘0 equivalence’ in PragμatLex

<ARTICLE language="el">
<Lemma>**ανάλωση κατά προτίμηση πριν από**</Lemma>
<Morphosyntax>**N PREP N ADV PREP**</Morphosyntax>
< TRANSLATION language="es">**consumir preferentemente antes del**</ TRANSLATION language="es">
<Keyword>**συσκευασία**</Keyword>
<SIT>**escrito en un envase de alimentos**</SIT>
<SPEECH ACT>**avisar**</SPEECH ACT>
<SS>~ **X a Y por Z**</SS>
<LF>-</LF>
<CODA>-</CODA>
<SYNONYM>-</SYNONYM>
<ANTONYM>-</ANTONYM>
<PARADIGM>-</PARADIGM>
</ARTICLE language="el">

Figure 7 – Pragmateme *análosi katá protímisi prin apó* ‘best before’ in PragμatLex

<ARTICLE language="el">
<Lemma>**Συλλυπητήρια**</Lemma>
<Morphosyntax>**N**</Morphosyntax>
< TRANSLATION language="es">**condolencias**</ TRANSLATION language="es">
<Keyword>**πένθος, κηδεία**</Keyword>
<SIT>**expresión escrita u oral de compasión hacia alguien en duelo**</SIT>
<SPEECH ACT>**compadecerse**</SPEECH ACT>

```
<SS>~ X[=of X, Aposs, Adj (p.ej. προεδρικά συλλυπητήρια)]
a Y por Z</SS>
<LF>
        <Magn>βαθιά, θερμά<ολόθερμα</Magn>
        <Ver>ειλικρινή<εγκάρδια<ολόψυχα</Ver>
        <Oper>εκφράζω, απευθύνω, δίνω, στέλνω,
        λέω</Oper>
        <V0>συλλυπούμαι</V0>
        <A0>συλλυπητήριος</A0>
</LF>
<CODA>
        <01>Γεροί να είστε να τον θυμάστε</01>
        <02>Να ζήσετε να τον θυμάστε</02>
        <03>Ζωή σ΄ εσάς</03>
        <04>Ζωή σε λόγου σας</04>
</CODA>
<SYNONYM>-</SYNONYM>
<ANTONYM>συγχαρητήρια</ANTONYM>
<PARADIGM>-</PARADIGM>
</ARTICLE language="el">
```

Figure 8 – Pragmateme *silipitíria* 'condolences' in PragμatLex

PragμatLex is structured in multiple levels in order to render an exhaustive description of each pragmateme. The canonical form of the pragmateme is considered to be the lemma. The microstructure of the dictionary consists in the definition of the SIT, the lexical unit that defines the SIT (keyword of the SIT), the pragmateme´s morphosyntax, the translation equivalence into the target language -where available, the speech act performed, the coda, the semantic structure, the lexical functions, the synonyms and the antonyms of the pragmateme. Moreover, there is a field, into which the paradigms of the pragmatemes are assigned. Such paradigms concern the decomposition of the local grammar that a lemma may comprise, as we can see in the following example (Papadopoulou 2013: 487):

- EL: ipoxreotiká foráte {cierto equipo} [en la entrada de una obra]
  ipoxreotiká foráte *krános*
  ipoxreotiká foráte *jalyá* prostasías
  ipoxreotiká foráte *otoaspíδes*
- EN: {certain equipment} required[in the entry of a construction site]

Hard hats required
Safety glasses required
Ear protection required

NooJ processing

The first step in the processing of pragmatemes was the adaptation of our data in order to meet the formal requirements of NooJ dictionaries. Thus, for example, the pragmatemes in the figures 1, 2 and 3 are represented in the following way in the NooJ dictionary, respectively:

- Με γεια,PR+PRAGMATEMA+ES=0+KW=nuevo+SIT= expresión oral a una persona que lleva nueva ropa +SA=felicitar+SS=X a Y por Z+CODA=-+SYNONYM=- +ANTONYM=-
- ανάλωση κατά προτίμηση πριν από,NP+PRAGMATEMA+ES= consumir preferentemente antes del +KW=συσκευασία+SIT= escrito en un envase de alimentos+SA=avisar +SS=X a Y por Z +CODA=-+SYNONYM=-+ANTONYM=-
- συλλυπητήρια,N+PRAGMATEMA+ES=condolencias+KW=πένθ ος/κηδεία+SIT=expresion escrita u oral de compasion hacia alguien en duelo+SA=compadecerse+SS=X a Y por Z+Magn=βαθιά/θερμά<ολόθερμα+Ver=ειλικρινή<εγκάρδια<ολόψ υχα+Oper=εκφράζω/απευθύνω/δίνω/στέλνω/λέω+V0=συλλυπούμ αι+A0=συλλυπητήριος+CODA=Γεροί να είστε να τον θυμάστε/Να ζήσετε να τον θυμάστε/Ζωή σ΄ εσάς/Ζωή σε λόγου σας+SYNONYM=-+ANTONYM=συγχαρητήρια

The second step consisted in the construction of local grammars within the syntactic grammars of NooJ. Although the grammars are not characterised by their complexity, they present a great utility at the time of their application to texts, as they can parse a large number of pragmateme forms, which otherwise would be space and time consuming, For example, the local grammars for the internal structure of the pragmatemes in Figures 1, 2 and 3 are the following, respectively:

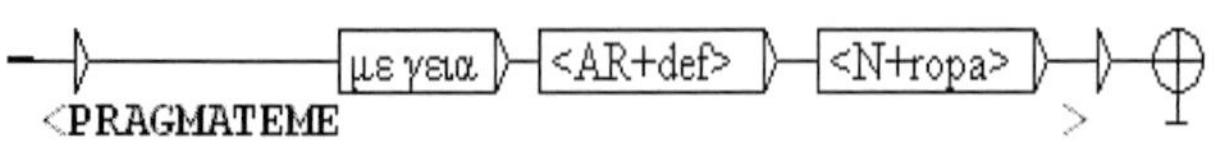

Figure 9 – Pragmateme *meyá* '0 equivalence' in NooJ

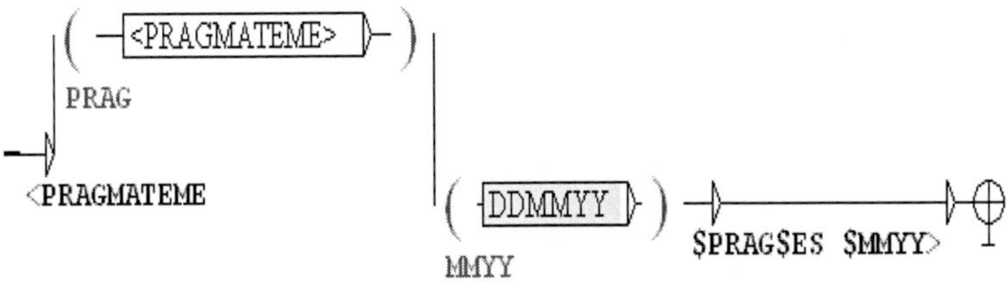

Figure 10 – Pragmateme *análosi katá protímisi prin apó* 'best before' in NooJ

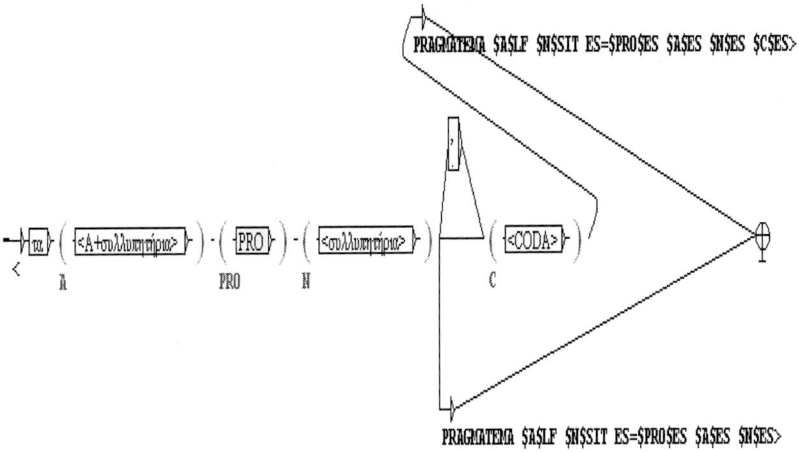

Figure 11 – Pragmateme *silipitíria* 'condolences' in NooJ

Perspectives

The present work is the first step taken towards the processing of pragmatemes within NooJ. Our future work will focus, on the one hand, on the improvement of the Greek NooJ module by the enrichment of the pragmateme dictionary and the parallel elaboration of pragmateme local grammars and, on the other hand, on the introduction of our lexicographical data into the Spanish NooJ module, given that our main work is on the Greek-Spanish language pair.

References

Blanco, Xavier. 2010. Los frasemas composicionales pragmáticos. In S. Mejri, & P. Mogorrón, *Opacité, Idiomaticité, Traduction*. Universitat d'Alacant.

—. 2013. Équivalents de traduction pour les pragmatèmes dans la lexicographie bilingue Français-Espagnol. *Lexicographica*. Volume 29, Issue 1, pp. 5–28.

—. to appear. Microstructure Évolutive pour un Dictionnaire de Pragmatemes. In *Actes des Journées Lexicologie, Lexicographie et Traduction*. Paris: AGence Universitaire de la Francophonie.

Chatzipapa, Elina, Zoe Gavriilidou, and Eleni Papadopoulou. 2008. The New Greek NooJ Module: morpho-semantic issues, In *Blanco, X.; Silberztein, M. (eds) 2008*: *Proceedings of the 2007 NooJ International Conference*, Cambridge: Cambridge Scholars Publishing, pp. 96-103.

Mel'cuk, Igor. 1988. Semantic description or lexical units in an explanatory combinatorial dictionary: Basic principles and heuristic criteria. International Journal of Lexicography 1 (3), pp. 165-188.

—. 1998. Collocations and Lexical Functions. Στο A. P. Cowie, Phraseology: Theory, Analysis, and Applications (σσ. 23-53). Oxford: Clarendon Press.

—. 2012. *Semantics. From Meaning to Text.* Amsterdam/Philadelphia: Benjamins Publishing Company.

Papadopoulou, Eleni. 2013. Pragmatemes: theory and their 'première' in Greek. Στο Z. Gavriilidou, A. Efthymioy, E. Thomadaki, & P. Kambakis-Vougiouklis, *Selected Papers of the 10th I.C.G.L.* (σσ.480-491)

Papadopoulou, Lena. to appear. My deepest condolences: Lexical functions of Greek pragmatemes [in a funeral]. Selected *Papers of the 10th I.C.G.L.*.

RESOURCES FOR IDENTIFICATION OF CUES WITH AUTHOR'S TEXT INSERTIONS IN BELARUSIAN AND RUSSIAN ELECTRONIC TEXTS

YURY HETSEVICH, TATSIANA OKRUT, BORIS LOBANOV AND YAUHENIYA YAKUBOVICH

Abstract

The aim of this paper is to give a general outline of the ongoing work in the processing of cues with text insertions by the author. We describe the main stages of the characters' gender identification in Belarusian and Russian electronic texts. The identification is based on punctuation marks and the detection of gender indicators.

Introduction

A literary text may include not only the author's words but also the words of other characters. As such, creators of audiobooks often use different speakers or synthesised voices so that a text reflects more closely the unique speech characteristics of the characters. It stands to reason, then, that the manual marking of a text for reading by different speakers or speech synthesisers takes a lot of time.

Text-to-speech systems (TTS systems) may serve as an alternative way of creating audiobooks. In only a short amount of time, such systems are able to create an electronic audio file from an electronic text.

Nowadays some ideas for this kind of text analysis already exist. For example, the online system Text Analysis Demo[1] makes it possible to

[1]http://www.alchemyapi.com/api/demo.html

identify characters and their statements[2] in a text, which is an important factor in the identification of the speakers' gender in TTS systems. A group of European scientists has also developed algorithms for character identification and automatic determination of the roles with the help of NooJ syntactic grammars [3]. As for the Slavic languages, the work of Croatian scientists on direct speech identification should be noted [4], although they do not consider the problem of gender identification. Programs for the creation of audiobooks such as MP3book2005[3] and AUDIOBOOK[4] are also quite developed in this area. These have special inbuilt units for logical analysis of dialogues, which can provide markings for distinguishing between the words of the author and various characters in a dialogical text. In AUDIOBOOK, steps were taken to read dialogues in character, but the program does not cover all of the cases. It does not take into account cue structures with more than one insertion of the author's words. In addition, it is unable to identify the gender of a character for indicators such as 'verb + masculine noun' combination in the author's words:

– Трэба напісаць 'яць', – адказвае вучань.

(– We should write 'яць', – the pupil (he) answers.)

It should also be noted that AUDIOBOOK works better with Russian and English speech engines, and that the units for logical analysis of dialogues do not include work with any other languages but Russian.

Thus, our main goal is to develop algorithms for direct speech processing and to provide identification of the characters' gender using the insertions of the author's words in direct speech. The algorithms can subsequently be used in a TTS system.

Data collection and processing procedures for identifying the gender of a character

The authors have developed 3 types of syntactic grammars for direct speech processing – one for all direct speech identification and two for gender-dependent direct speech identification (masculine and feminine gender detection).

We have selected some texts in Belarusian and Russian to identify the specific features of dialogical text (the so-called training set). As NooJ processes a text at the paragraph level, for the development of algorithms

---

[2]http://www.alchemyapi.com/api/entity/quotations.html

[3]http://mp3book2005.ru/1. htm

[4]http://kom-pas.narod.ru/audiobook_net.htm

each text paragraph was separately analysed by experts in the following order (see examples in Table 1):

— marking the paragraphs with direct speech (figure 1 was used as a label)

— marking the cues of male and female characters

— marking the words of a character and the author's words (italics – the characters' words, regular font – the author's words)

Marks of direct speech	Gender of speaker	A paragraph of the Belarusian training text
1	F	- *Бацька вады,* - шэптам сказала Майка.
1	M	- *Бацька вод,* - паправіў Алесь. - *Вось так і Дняпро пачынаецца недзе.*
1	F	- *Жывая вада,* - сказала Яня.
0	-	І яна апусцілася на калені і зламала пальчыкамі крыштальную паверхню.
1	F	- *Піце. Будзеце жыць сто год...*

Table 1 – An excerpt from the Belarusian training corpora with manual marking for direct speech

On the basis of manual text analysis, the following syntactic structures were revealed in direct speech:

Direct speech apart from the author's text:
– C (! | !! | !!! | ? | ?! | … | .).
Direct speech followed by the author's text:
– C (, | ! | !! | !!! | ? | ?! | … | .) – A (… | .).
Direct speech with one or more insertions of the author's text:
– C (, | ! | !! | !!! | ? | ?! | … | .) – A (, | … | . | : | .) – C (, | ! | !! | !!! | ? | ?! | … | .) (– A (, | … | . | : | .) – C (, | ! | !! | !!! | ? | ?! | … | .)).

The structures contain the following annotations: C – the words of a character (speaker), A - the author's text, brackets (,) – the beginning and the end of a choice set with punctuation marks, | - symbol *or* (separation of punctuation marks in a choice set).

Grammar for direct speech identification

The data obtained was used to develop a NooJ syntactic grammar for the automated identification of all paragraphs containing direct speech (DS_All) (Figure 1). The grammar has the same view for both the Belarusian and Russian languages. Its main parts – graphs Speaker and Author – serve to identify the character's words and the author's words, respectively.

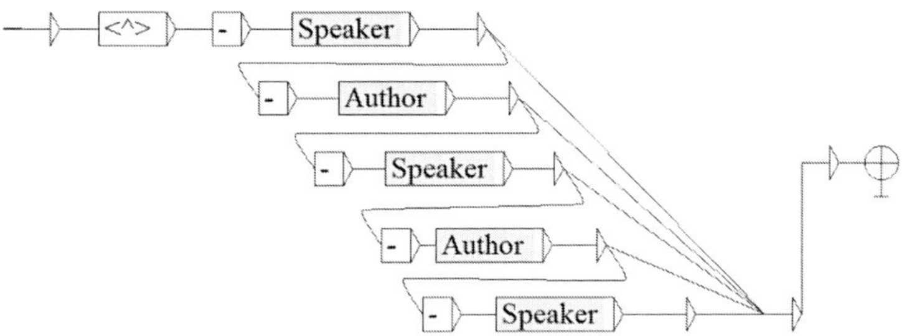

Figure 1 – A general view of the DS_All grammar (identical for Belarusian and Russian)

According to the grammar DS_All, any direct speech sentence starts with a dash followed by the characters' words; Speaker (numbers, different word forms and punctuation marks may be included), which in turn may end with a full stop, comma, exclamation mark, question mark, or a combination of these punctuation marks (combinations with quotation marks are also possible). If there is no author's text after the character's words, the grammar stops. This is how the structure of the first type is identified. If there is any combination of punctuation marks with a dash after the character's words, the grammar continues working and enables the graph Author (various word forms and such punctuation marks as a comma, a full stop or brackets may be included). This is how the structure of the second type is identified.

The grammar can identify from one to two text insertions by the author in direct speech through processing the algorithm in consecutive order: Speaker–Author–Speaker. This provides the identification of direct speech with the structure of the third type.

DS_All can be applied sequentially to any Belarusian or Russian electronic text through NooJ. The results of the application of the grammars are presented in the form of a concordance in Figure 2.

Before	Seq.	After
ıе дзяўчына.	- Вось бачыце, шкада толькі, што вы ад нас далёка, а то б...	- А хіба тут ням
а Алеськаю?	- А хіба тут няма каму гэтай справай заняцца? Вось мой к...	Саханюк і бацн
засмяяліся.	- Не, я ўжо зусім страціў там ласку, дзякаваць Богу.	Айцец Кірыл за
- сказаў ён.	- Апрача таго, я чуў, што ў яе жаніх ёсць ужо.	- Ці мала на св
ііх ёсць ужо.	- Ці мала на свеце дурняў, - зноў дадаў а. Кірыл.	Матушка вяла
а вяла сваё:	- Ну, то што? Хіба жаніхам свіней не падкладаюць?	- Гэта было б н
ідкладаюць?	- Гэта было б не па-хрысціянску.	- Затое ж па-ка

(a)

Before	Seq.	After
и продолжал:	- А как один повесился - это чистая хохма. Мужи...	- Ужас, - сказал
‹усил и начал:	- А как у нас все было - это чистый театр. Я на су...	- говорю, - у нег
- Нормально.	- А конкретнее?	- Трудолюбивый
ик в кармане.	- А корова? - удивилась Белла.	- Что - корова?
. Чего уж там!	- А кто будет фотографировать? - спросила Эви.	- Мишка все сде
ıли сомнения.	- А кто меня, спрашивается, разбудил?	- Я разбудил. Но
о мы за люди.	- А кто тормознуться хотел?	- Я хотел, на вр

(b)

Figure 2 – The results of applying the DS_All grammar to Belarusian (a) and Russian (b) texts

Grammars for the characters' gender identification from the author's text

In the Belarusian and Russian languages, singular past tense verbs may have gender attributes, for example, *направіў* 'he corrected' and *сказала* 'she said' for Belarusian, *высказался* 'he spoke' , *высказалась* 'she spoke' for Russian. As such verbs may often occur in the author's commentaries to direct speech, and some nouns have themselves gender attributes, they may serve as gender indicators and be considered suitable for the gender identification of the characters.

On the basis of the grammar DS_All, two separate grammars were developed – one for masculine gender identification (DS_M), and one for feminine gender identification (DS_F). For this purpose, we have modified the graph Author and added resources for gender identification (Fig. 3). In Figure 3, one can see the subgraph VERBSmasculine. It includes a list of masculine verbs, which were selected at the stage of manual marking of texts in the Belarusian and Russian languages. A similar list of verbs was created within the subgraph VERBSfeminine for feminine gender identification.

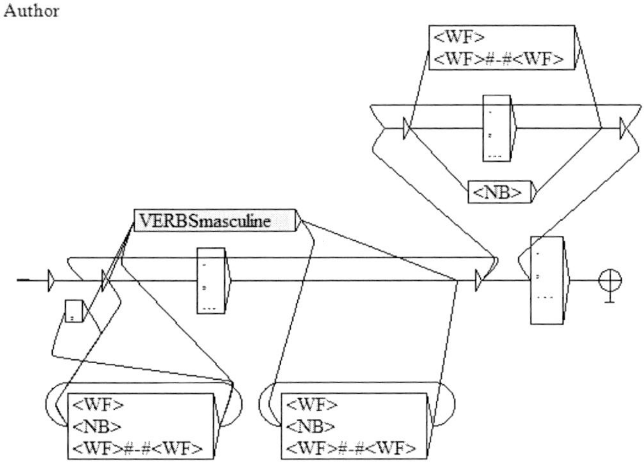

Figure 3 – The subgraph Author, DS_M

Subsequently, we created dictionaries for the Belarusian and Russian languages (Figure 4), where verbs were presented in pairs in the masculine and feminine forms.

It should be noted that in the Belarusian dictionary for verbs that have 'у' at the start of a word (like in *уздыхнула*), a special paradigm ЎVERB1 was added. It takes into account the transition of 'у' into 'ў' after vowels.

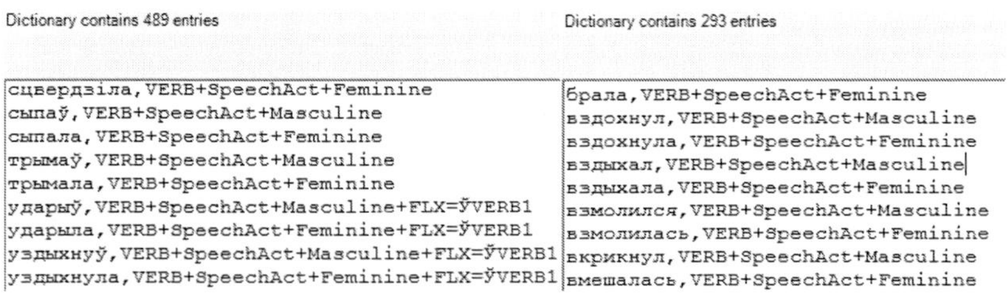

(a) (b)

Figure 4 – Excerpts from the Belarusian (a) and Russian (b) dictionaries of verbs in masculine and feminine forms

Thus, instead of the subgraphs VERBSmasculine and VERBSfeminine, special tags (categories) were used: VERB, SpeechAct (a semantic mark, verbs as comments to direct speech) and Masculine/Feminine (Figure 5).

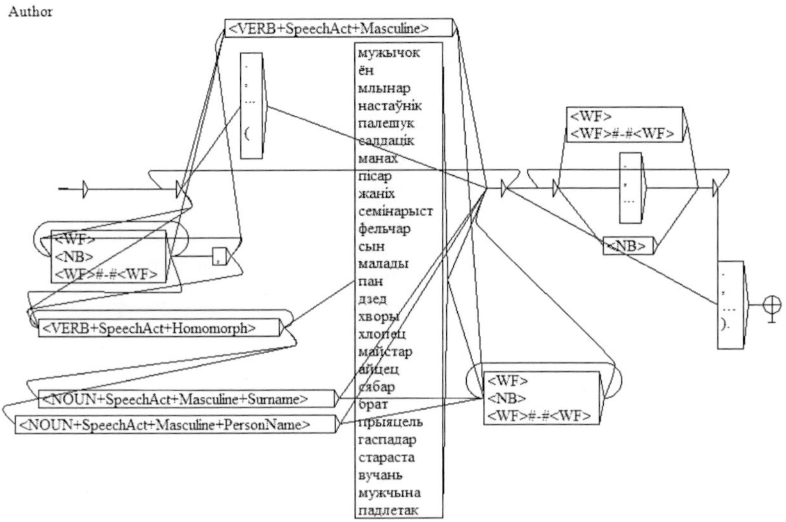

Figure 5 – The subgraph Author, DS_M for Belarusian

In the development process we also investigated the problem of grammatical homoforms. For instance, the verb form *кажа* 'say' (the present tense form of the Belarusian verb *казаць* 'to say') can refer both to the masculine and to the feminine genders, which makes it impossible to use such verbs separately in the identification of the characters' gender. To solve this problem, an additional 'verb-noun' combination of graphs was created, where the first graph with <VERB+SpeechAct+Masculine> annotation includes the grammatical homoforms of verbs which refer to the act of speaking, and the other graph represents a list of nouns having gender attributes (eg *дзед* 'grandfather') (the graphs are represented in Figure 5). Separate dictionaries were created for first names and surnames. These are linked to the grammars DS_M and DS_F through the following sequence of tags: <NOUN + SpeechAct + Masculine + PersonName>, <NOUN + SpeechAct + Feminine + PersonName>, <NOUN + SpeechAct + Masculine + Surname>, and <NOUN + SpeechAct + Feminine + Surname>.

In all, concerning dictionary resources for the Belarusian module, we have created a dictionary of past tense verbs presented by pairs for masculine and feminine genders (489 entries); a dictionary of verbs in the present and future tenses that serve as comments to direct speech but do not allow us to identify the character's gender (14 entries); dictionaries including masculine first names (676 entries) and surnames (324 entries). The dictionaries containing feminine names and surnames are still under development. The resources for the Russian language also include a dictionary of past tense verbs presented by pairs for masculine and feminine genders (297 entries) and a dictionary of verbs without gender attributes (14 entries). The other dictionary resources for the characters' gender identification in electronic texts in Russian are under development.

In order to use the outputs of the grammars in the SAPI 5.1 TTS system, it is necessary to adapt a text to a SAPI TTS XML format[5]. Therefore, to select an appropriate speech synthesiser, a syntactic grammar should provide annotations of the following kind:

<VOICE Required='name=[a synthesiser's name in a TTS system]'>
...A text for synthesis...
</VOICE>.

Thus, in Figure 6 one can see that the speech synthesisers BorisBel and AlesiaBel will be respectively applied to the characters' words (Speaker) and to the author's words (Author).

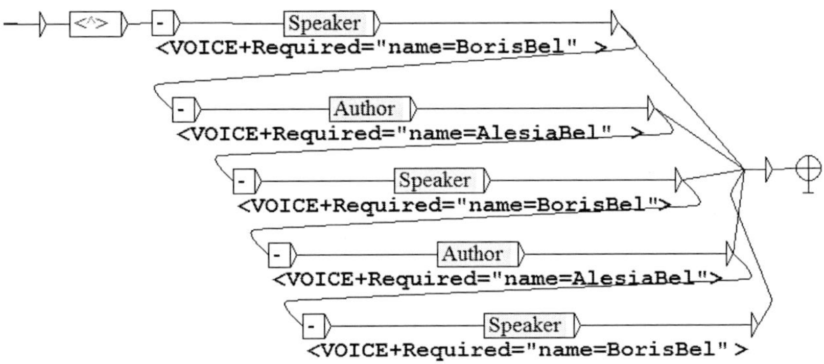

Figure 6 – The DS_All grammar following adaptation for SAPI 5.1

After being processed by the grammars DS_M and DS_F adapted for SAPI 5.1, the sentences in Table 1 will be annotated as in Figure 7. A female voice, AlesiaBel, is applied to the author's words, and voices ElenaBel and BorisBel are used for the female and male characters' words.

[5]XML TTS Tutorial (SAPI 5.3), http://msdn.microsoft.com/en-us/library/ms717 077%28v= vs.85%29.aspx

Such annotation allows us to input texts into the TTS system SAPI 5.1, where the indicated voices switch over automatically (Figure 8).

```
<VOICE Required="name=BorisBel">- Добры дзень,</VOICE>
<VOICE Required="name=ElenaBel">- сказаў настаўнік вучаніцы.</VOICE>
<VOICE Required="name=AlesiaBel">- Добры дзень, Мікалай Пятровіч,</VOICE>
 <VOICE Required="name=ElenaBel">- адказала Таня.</VOICE>
<VOICE Required="name=BorisBel">- Ці рашылі Вы задачку па трыганаметрыі
нумар 123,</VOICE>
 <VOICE Required="name=ElenaBel">- працягнуў настаўнік.</VOICE>
```

Figure 7 – The sentences from Table 1 after being annotated with VoiceXML tags

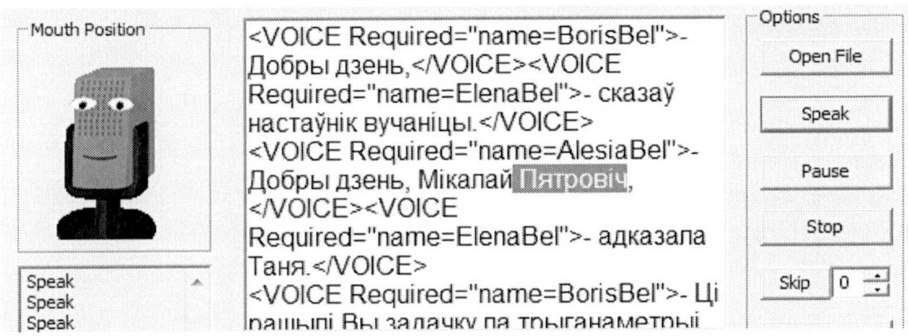

Figure 8 – Speech synthesis of the annotated sentences

Multi-coloured marking of a text

A further application for the above-mentioned annotation is the multi-coloured marking of a text for visual presentation of the author's words and of the female and male characters' words. Such marking may be used by an editor in order to quickly analyse direct speech in a text and to select an optimal number of speech synthesisers or speakers.

To provide multi-coloured marking, the authors have developed the VoiceXmlToColorReplacer software. The program processes VoiceXML-files and allows the conversion of VoiceXML-tags of speech synthesisers into HTML-tags with different styles of direct speech visual presentation.

After a text passes through the VoiceXmlToColorReplacer software, the characters' cues and the author's insertions are marked in different colours: namely, the author's words (AliesiaBel) are in black, the male characters' cues (BorisBel) – in blue, and the female characters' cues (ElenaBel) – in red (Figure 9).

- Бацька вады, - шэптам сказала Майка.
- Бацька вод, - паправіў Алесь. - Вось так і Днявпро пачынаецца недзе.
- Жывая вада, - сказала Яня.
I яна апусцілася на калені і зламала пальчыкамі крыштальную паверхню.
- Піце. Будзеце жыць сто год...

Figure 9 – An excerpt of a Belarusian text with multi-coloured marking of direct speech

Evaluation

Evaluation is conducted using precision, recall and F-measure. The results of the evaluation are given in Tables 2 and 3 for the Belarusian and Russian languages, respectively. In evaluation, we use the following categories: N – cues identified as appropriate by linguistic experts; M – cues correctly processed by the grammar; L – all cues found by the grammar.

The Belarusian test set includes 23,867 word forms; 955 paragraphs; 481 paragraphs with direct speech; 233 paragraphs with the author's text insertions, where 165 are cues of male characters and 68 are cues of female characters. The Russian test set contains 34,056 word forms; 2,669 paragraphs; 1,658 paragraphs with direct speech; 551 paragraphs with author's text insertions, where 456 are cues of male characters and 95 are cues of female characters.

Grammar Name	Precision (P)	Recall (R)	F-measure, %
	(M/L)	(M/N)	2*P*R*100 / (P+R)
DS_All	461/462 = 0,995	461/481 = 0,958	97,6
DS_M	143/145 = 0,986	143/165 = 0,866	92,2
DS_F	57/58 = 0,982	57/68 = 0,838	90,4

Table 2 – Evaluation of the Belarusian Syntactic Grammars' Performance for Direct Speech and Identification of Characters' Gender

Grammar Name	Precision (P)	Recall (R)	F-measure, %
DS_All	1628/1658 = 0,982	1628/1658 = 0,982	98,2
DS_M	339/339 = 1	339/456 = 0,743	85,3
DS_F	90/90 = 1	90/92 = 0,978	98,9

Table 3 – Evaluation of the Russian Syntactic Grammars' Performance for Direct Speech and Identification of Characters' Gender

Conclusion

In this paper we have presented our ongoing work on direct speech processing. We can conclude that rather good operating results have been obtained and that the algorithms developed have shown themselves suitable for use in combination with a TTS system. However, the resources developed still require some improvement: further work needs to be done on the extension of dictionary resources of verb-indicators identifying gender, the extension of the punctuation base (dash and quotation types etc), and the expansion of the test corpora.

Acknowledgements

We would like to thank the linguist Adam Morrison for his help in revising the language of this paper.

References

Jurić, Tereza, Marija Stupar, Damir Boras. 2012. Direct Speech Recognition in Text. In *Selected Papers from the NooJ 2011 Intern. Conf. Automatic Processing of Various Levels of Linguistic Phenomena,* Vučković K., Bekavac B., Silberztein M. Eds. Cambridge Scholars Publishing, Newcastle, 2011, pp.122–127.

Lendvai, Piroska, Tamás Váradi, Sándor Darány, and Thierry Declerck. 2010. Assignment of character and action types in folk tales. In *Selected Papers from the NooJ 2010 Intern. Conf. Formalising Natural Languages with NooJ*, Gavriilidou Z., Chatzipapa E., Papadopoulou L., Silberzstein M. Eds. Democritus University of Thrace, Greece. pp.102–111.

Paraphrases V↔N↔A in One Class of Psychological Predicates

Alberto Maria Langella
and Simona Messina

Abstract

According to the principles of the Lexicon-Grammar methodology developed by Maurice Gross (1975), we will discuss the possibility of producing paraphrases of the Class 41 Lexicon-Grammar predicates. This goal will be achieved via the new NooJ[1] transformational engine. Class 42 and 43, with very few psychological predicates, will be dealt with in a paper to be published soon.

Introduction[2]

The study focuses, in the Lexicon-Grammar of the Italian language[3], on nouns and adjectives that are morphologically and phonologically related to Class 41 of verbs with complement clauses[4].

Most of the verbs in this class are 'psychological' verbs or verbs that have both their own meaning and a 'psychological' metaphorical meaning that is widely accepted by dictionaries; they express sensations or feelings experienced by *Nhum* in N_1 and inspired by the subject N_0 (Gross, 1995).

---

[1]The Italian Module for NooJ is developed by Simonetta Vietri at the University of Salerno.

[2]S. Messina is author of *Introduction* and *The Corpus* sections; A.M. Langella is author of *The Transformations Provided, Dictionary and Graph for Paraphrases, The Production of Paraphrases* sections.

[3]See Elia, Martinelli, D'Agostino (EMDA 1981); Elia (1984); D'Agostino (1992); Vietri (1985, 2004).

[4]For a lexicon-grammar description of the class 41 see Elia (1984).

The definitional structure of this class[5] for the Italian is ***Ch F V Num***. The first position is a clause often reduced to a noun. We have sentences like the following:

1) *Il modo in cui Mark sta parlando imbarazza Maria*
   'The way Mark is speaking embarrasses Mary'
2) *Il fatto che lei stia partendo angoscia John*
   'The fact that she is leaving anguishes John'

.

The possible transformed sentences with nouns and adjectives as operators[6] have the following form:

1a) *Il modo in cui Mark sta parlando è un imbarazzo per Maria*
    'The way Mark is speaking is an embarrassment to Mary'
2a) *Il fatto che lei stia partendo è un'angoscia per John*
    'The fact that she is leaving is an anguish to John'
1b) *Il modo in cui Mark sta parlando è imbarazzante per Mary*
    'The way Mark is speaking is embarrassing to Mary'
2b) *Il fatto che lei stia partendo rende John angosciato*
    'The fact that she is leaving causes John to be anguished'

The previous sentences 1a and 2a are nominalisations of the above shown sentence number 1. The sentences 1b and 2b are adjectivalisations of sentence number 2.

In this class not all entries accept transformed sentences with nouns and adjectives as operators.

In order to produce correct paraphrases we have to discriminate between each entry. Now we will discuss which kind of transformations we have produced and how to do that with the combined use of a paraphrase grammar and a dictionary.

The Corpus

The lexicon consisted of DELA system electronic dictionaries used in the Department of Political, Social and Communication Sciences at the University of Salerno and De Mauro-Paravia and Gradit dictionaries.

[5]Ibid.
[6]For the typology of the different Harrisian operators in Italian see Langella (2014).

On the basis of some previous studies on the adjectives related to Class 41 and other classes with complement clause[7], in this work we concentrate on paraphrase V↔N↔A.

We have selected 996 nouns and 1,278 adjectives which are morpho-phonologically related to the 576 verbs with complement clauses of Class 41.

Class 41 contains 599 verbs and we have included only psychological predicates in the verbal list. For nouns and adjectives, it should be noted that some of the suffixes are extremely productive and the speaker can use a potentially much larger repertoire than that contained in dictionaries; for this reason each list is open and it is possible to increase the lexicon with other entries.

This initial list was then checked to restrict the sample to lexical entries with which there is a full paraphrase between the verbal sentence and the nominal and/or adjectival sentence. This resulted in a set of sentences in paraphrastic relationship, consisting of 570 verbal sentences, 297 nominal sentences and 384 adjectival sentences. Some verbs have been excluded, because it is difficult to obtain a sentence possible in common use.

The Transformations Provided

We have focused on the nominalisations and the adjectivalisations of the psychological predicates of Class 41. Other transformations taken into account are some which can very often occur with these previous two. The types of transformations are named as follows:

1) **+ProN0** = Pronominalisation
2) **+RIDF0** = Reduction of Sentence F0
3) **+1VsupN** = Nominalisation of type 1
4) **+2VsupN** = Nominalisation of type 2
5) **+1VsupA** = Adjectivalisation of type 1
6) **+2VsupA** = Adjectivalisation of type 2
7) **+PASSIVO** = Passive Paraphrase

For each type of transformation we give a pair of sentences as example:

[7]See Messina 2012, 2013 and 2014.

1) **[ProN0]** *Il fatto che John stia parlando preoccupa Mary*
'The fact that John is speaking worries Mary'
→*Il fatto che lui stia parlando preoccupa Mary*
→'The fact that he is speaking worries Mary'

2) **[RIDF0]** *Il fatto che John stia parlando preoccupa Mary*
'The fact that John is speaking worries Mary'
→*John preoccupa Mary*
'John worries Mary'

3) **[1VsupN]** *Il fatto che John stia parlando preoccupa Mary*
'The fact that John is speaking worries Mary'
→*Il fatto che John stia parlando è una preoccupazione per Mary*
→'The fact that John is speaking is a worry for Mary'

4) **[2VsupN]** *Il fatto che John stia parlando preoccupa Mary*
'The fact that John is speaking worries Mary'
→*Il fatto che John stia parlando dà preoccupazione a Mary*
→'The fact that John is speaking gives worrying to Mary'

5) **[1VsupA]** *Il fatto che John stia parlando preoccupa Mary*
'The fact that John is speaking worries Mary'
→*Il fatto che John stia parlando è preoccupante per Mary*
→'The fact that John is speaking is worrying for Mary'

6) **[2VsupA]** *Il fatto che John stia parlando preoccupa Mary*
'The fact that John is speaking worries Mary'
→*Il fatto che John stia parlando rende Mary preoccupata*
→'The fact that John is speaking causes Mary to be worried

7) **[PASSIVO]** *Il fatto che John stia parlando preoccupa Mary*
'The fact that John is speaking worries Mary'
→*Mary è preoccupata dal fatto che John stia parlando*
→'Mary is worried by the fact that John is speaking'

In addition to the previous 7 basic transformations we have provided the possibility of combining them in sentences like the following:

1) Il fatto che John stia parlando preoccupa Maria
→'Lui preoccupa Mary' **[ProN0] + [RIDF0]**
→'He worries Mary'

2) Il fatto che John stia parlando preoccupa Maria
→'Lui è una preoccupazione per Mary' **[ProN0] + [RIDF0] + [1VsupN]**
→'He is a worry for Mary'

Dictionary and Graph for Paraphrases

To generate paraphrases with support verb[8] plus nouns and adjectives morphologically-related to the psychological predicates, we have created ad-hoc derivational grammars. They have to be added to the lexical information stored in the dictionary of Class 41 verbs. This allows these nouns and adjectives to inherit the grammatical properties of the related verbs.

The dictionary has been devised as follows:

Entry	S-Lemma	Category	Aux	DRV	FLX	MorfSynt	SynSem
abbacchiare	abbacchiare	V	a	Nop1:PPN1+Aop1:PPA1+Aop2:PPA2	V11	t	41+VsupN+1VsupA+2VsupA+PASSIVO
abbacchiare	abbacchiare	V	a	Nop2:PPN2+Aop1:PPA1+Aop2:PPA2	V11	t	41+VsupN+1VsupA+2VsupA+PASSIVO
abbagliare	abbagliare	V	a	Nop2:PPN2+Aop1:PPA1+Aop2:PPA2	V11	t	41+VsupN+1VsupA+2VsupA+PASSIVO
abbattere	abbattere	V	a	Nop3:PPN3+Aop3:PPA3	V68	t	41+VsupN+2VsupA+PASSIVO
abbellire	abbellire	V	a	Nop3:PPN3+Aop4:PPA4	V201	t	41+VsupN+2VsupA+PASSIVO
abbindolare	abbindolare	V	a	Nop1:PPN1	V3	t	41+VsupN+PASSIVO
abbrutire	abbrutire	V	a	Nop3:PPN3+Aop4:PPA4	V201	t	41+VsupN+2VsupA+PASSIVO
abbuiare	abbuiare	V	a		V11	t	41+PASSIVO
accalorare	accalorare	V	a	Nop2:PPN2	V3	t	41+VsupN+PASSIVO
accasciare	accasciare	V	a	Nop2:PPN2	V4	t	41+VsupN+PASSIVO
accattivare	accattivare	V	a	PPA1:Aop2+PPA2:Aop2	V3	t	41+1VsupA+2VsupA+PASSIVO

Figure 1 – Sample of Dictionary for Class 41

We have two different derivations for adjectives and one for nouns. For example the property DRV=Aop1:PPA1 allows NooJ to derive the adjective *abbacchiante* from the verb *abbacchiare* (to depress). This adjective is then inflected according to the code PPA1. The property

[8]For a definition of support verb and their variants see D'Agostino (2012).

DRV= PPA2 derives the adjective *abbacchiato* from *abbacchiare*. DRV=Nop1 derives the nouns *abbacchiamento* and *abbacchiatura* and their lexical variants form *abbacchiare*. If the derivations are missing, it means that that particular entry allows no adjectival and nominal paraphrases. The transformational properties like +1VsupA, +2VsupA etc have been added in order to allow the transformational grammar to select only the lexical units required for the specific transformation performed. Let us show the transformational grammar devised:

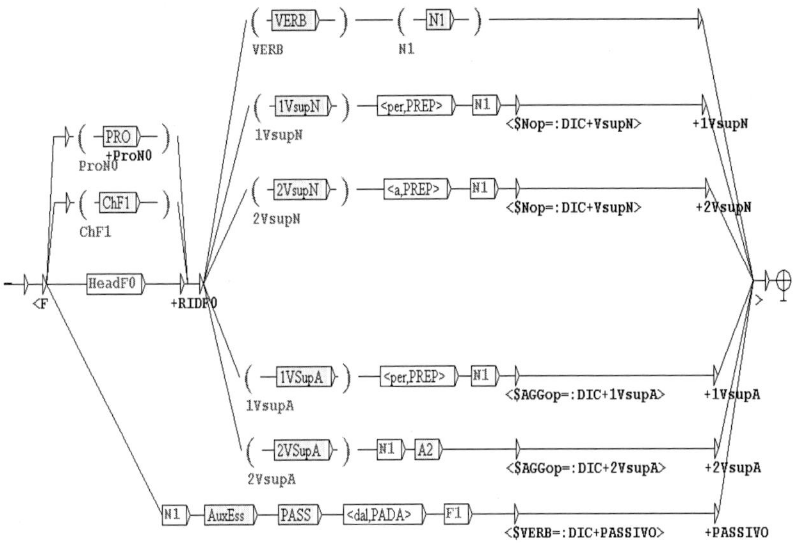

Figure 2 – Paraphrase Grammar for Class 41

In Figure 3 the path producing the +1VsupN transformation has the lexical constraint <$Nop=:DIC+VsupN>, which allows only the lexical entry of Class 41 with the syntactical property +VsupN to pass through that path. The lexical entry *abbacchiare*, as shown in figure 2, has four relevant transformational properties, which are +1VsupA, +2VsupA, +VsupN and +PASSIVO. The first three are nominal and adjectival paraphrases while the last one is the traditional passivisation. The transformational properties +RIDF0 and +ProN0 are definitional because of their applicability to the entire Class 41. *Abbattere* (to depress) has, unlike *abbacchiare,* only three properties, lacking +1VsupA. This is a sentence like

1) *Il calcio abbatte Maria*
'Soccer depresses Mary'

which in Italian, unlike English, has no paraphrase similar to

2) *Il calcio è abbattente per Maria**
'Soccer is depressing for Mary'

The subjects can be nouns or even clauses. The grammar devised for them is as follows:

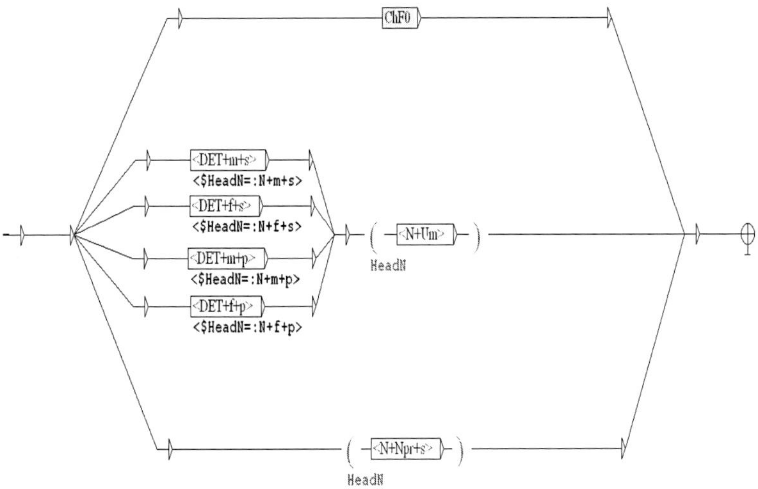

Figure 3 – The Grammar for the Subject (Nouns and Clauses)

The grammar built for the direct object is very similar to the previous one except for the absence of a possible clause:

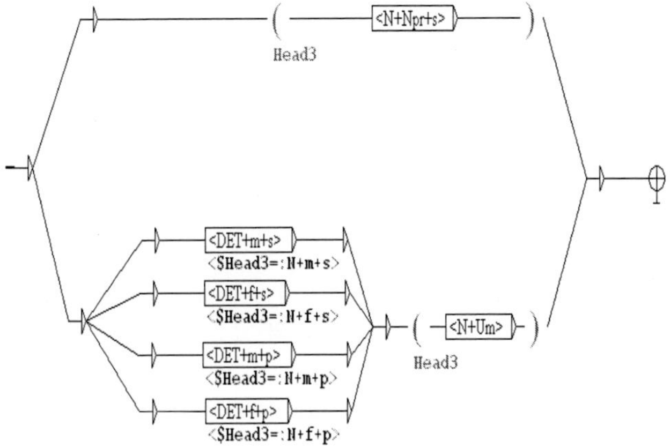

Figure 4 – The Grammar for the Direct Object

Regarding the kind of support verbs generated by our transformational grammar, we have devised embedded graphs such as the following one:

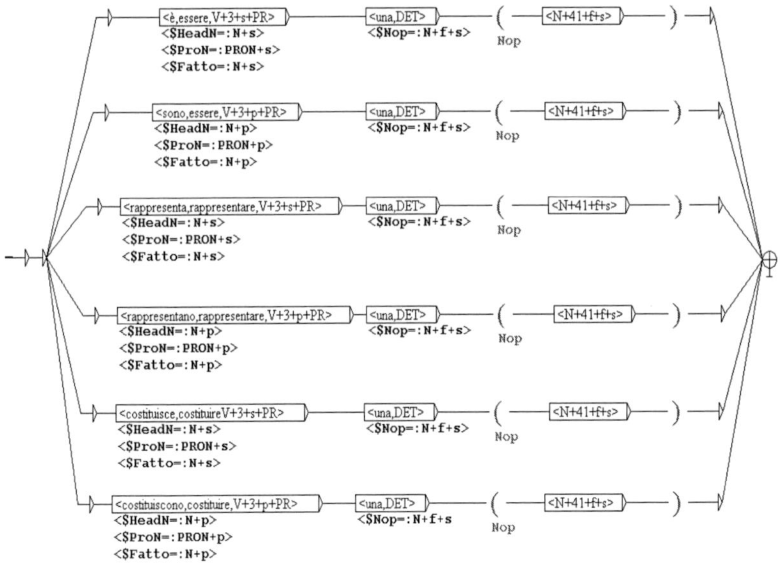

Figure 5 – The grammar for Support Verb in "+VsupN" Transformation Path

The previous grammar can generate a sequence constituted by support verb plus determinant plus feminine and singular nouns of Class 41. We have again used the lexical constraints in order to guarantee the grammatical agreements between the support verb with the subject and between the determinant and the noun.

The Production of Paraphrases

If we enter the sentence *Il fatto che Mario sia venuto preoccupa Maria* (The fact that Mario has come worries Maria) the NooJ transformational engine will produce this:

```
# Dictionary generated automatically
#
il fatto che Mario sia venuto dà preoccupazione a Maria,F+2VsupN
il fatto che Mario sia venuto è preoccupante per Maria,F+1VsupA
il fatto che Mario sia venuto è una preoccupazione per Maria,F+1VsupN
il fatto che Mario sia venuto fa diventare Maria preoccupata,F+2VsupA
il fatto che Mario sia venuto fa essere Maria preoccupata,F+2VsupA
il fatto che Mario sia venuto preoccupa Maria,F
il fatto che Mario sia venuto rappresenta una preoccupazione per Maria,F+1VsupN
il fatto che Mario sia venuto rende Maria preoccupata,F+2VsupA
il fatto che Mario sia venuto trasmette preoccupazione a Maria,F+2VsupN
lui dà preoccupazione a Maria,F+ProN0+RIDF0+2VsupN
lui è preoccupante per Maria,F+ProN0+RIDF0+1VsupA
lui è una preoccupazione per Maria,F+ProN0+RIDF0+1VsupN
lui fa diventare Maria preoccupata,F+ProN0+RIDF0+2VsupA
lui fa essere Maria preoccupata,F+ProN0+RIDF0+2VsupA
lui preoccupa Maria,F+ProN0+RIDF0
lui rappresenta una preoccupazione per Maria,F+ProN0+RIDF0+1VsupN
lui rende Maria preoccupata,F+ProN0+RIDF0+2VsupA
lui trasmette preoccupazione a Maria,F+ProN0+RIDF0+2VsupN
Maria è preoccupata dal fatto che Mario sia venuto,F+PASSIVO
Mario dà preoccupazione a Maria,F+RIDF0+2VsupN
Mario è preoccupante per Maria,F+RIDF0+1VsupA
Mario è una preoccupazione per Maria,F+RIDF0+1VsupN
Mario fa diventare Maria preoccupata,F+RIDF0+2VsupA
Mario fa essere Maria preoccupata,F+RIDF0+2VsupA
Mario preoccupa Maria,F+RIDF0
Mario rappresenta una preoccupazione per Maria,F+RIDF0+1VsupN
Mario rende Maria preoccupata,F+RIDF0+2VsupA
Mario trasmette preoccupazione a Maria,F+RIDF0+2VsupN
```

Figure 6 – Automatic Transformations for Class 41

We can see the basic 7 transformations we have devised for our grammar. They have sometimes been applied alone and in some other cases they act as combinations of more transformations.

Conclusions

This article should be regarded as just the beginning of an extensive work still to do on the different paraphrases constellations of the Italian Lexicon-Grammar classes. We feel it is very important to stress the importance of studying each lexical entry by itself and evaluating its different types of nominalisations and adjectivalisations.

Only after careful study of its lexical-syntactic properties can we devise derivational codes in order to derive the nouns and the adjectives related to the verbs. Different syntactic information, for example the properties +Vsup1, +Vsup2 etc have to be added to each entry in order to allow the paraphrase grammar to generate correct transformations and to discriminate between the ones allowed by each lexical entry.

References

D'Agostino, Emilio. 2012. Varianti di verbi supporto in italiano. In *Lessico e lessicologia*, Silvana Ferreri (eds.) In *Proceedings of the XLIV SLI International Conference "Linguistica educativa, lessico e lessicologia*", University of Tuscia, Viterbo, 27/29 September 2010), pp. 142-156, Roma, Bulzoni.

—. 1992. *Analisi del discorso. Metodi descrittivi dell'italiano d'uso*. Napoli: Loffredo.

De Mauro, Tullio. 2000. *Dizionario della lingua italiana*, Torino: Paravia.

—. 2007. *GRADIT,. (Grande dizionario italiano dell'uso)*. Tullio De Mauro Ed. Torino: UTET.

Elia, Annibale. 1984. *Le verbe italien*. Schena-Nizet Press.

Elia, Annibale, Maurizio Martinelli, and Emilio D'Agostino. 1981. *Lessico e strutture della sintassi*. Liguori Editore.

Gross, Maurice. 1975. *Méthodes en syntaxe*. Paris:Hermann.

—. 1995. Une grammaire locale de l'expression des sentiments. In *Langue Française*, 105, pp. 70- 87, 1995.

Langella, Alberto Maria. 2014. *Elementi di grammatica dell'italiano su basi matematiche*. Padova: Libreriauniversitaria.it edizioni.

Messina, Simona. 2012. Analisi di una classe di aggettivi nel lessico-grammatica dell'italiano. In *Lessico e lessicologia*, Silvana Ferreri (eds.) (*Proceedings of the XLIV SLI International Conference "Linguistica educativa, lessico e lessicologia"*, University of Tuscia, Viterbo, 27/29 September 2010), pp. 81-95.

—. 2013. Six classes of adjectives with complement clauses in the lexicon-grammar of the Italian language. In *Pre-Proocedings of 32nd*

International Conference on Lexis and Grammar, University of Algarve, Faculdade de Ciências Humanas e Sociais, Campus de Gambelas, Faro (Portugal), 10-14 September 2013. Jorge Baptista, Mario Monteleone (eds.), 205-210, Universidade do Algarve, 2013.

—. 2014. La parafrasi aggettivale dei verbi a completiva. *International conference "Discorso e cultura nella lingua e nella letteratura italiana"*, University of Craiova, 20 - 21 September 2013, Elena Pirvu (eds.). Firenze: Franco Cesati, pp. 179-194.

Silberztein, Max. 2010. Syntactic parsing with NooJ. In *Proceedings of the NooJ 2009 International Conference and Workshop*, pp. 177-190. Centre de Publication Universitaire.

—. 2011. Automatic Transformational Analysis and Generation. In *Proceedings of the 2010 International NooJ Conference*, pp. 221-231. Komotini: Democritius University Editions.

Vietri, Simonetta. 2008. *Dizionari elettronici e grammatiche a stati finite. Metodi di analisi formale della lingua italiana*. Salerno: Plectica.

—. 2012. Transformations and Frozen Sentences. In *Proceedings of 2011 NooJ International Conference and Workshop*, pp. 166-180. Cambridge Scholars Publishing.

—. 2013. The annotation of the Predicate-argument structure of transfer nouns. In *Proceedings of the NooJ 2012 International Conference and Workshop*, pp. 89-99. Cambridge Scholars Publishing.

—. 1985. *Lessico e sintassi delle espressioni idiomatiche.* Napoli: Liguori.

PART III:

APPLICATIONS

NEAR LANGUAGE IDENTIFICATION USING NOOJ

BOŽO BEKAVAC, KRISTINA KOCIJAN AND MARKO TADIĆ

Abstract

In this work we take a linguistic knowledge-aware approach tailored for a specific pair of languages. We use NooJ as a core part of a system designed for automatic identification of near languages, Croatian and Serbian in particular. We use several levels of NooJ processing capabilities. First, we apply specially- designed lexical transducers for the detection of the typical morphological issues in language. Then we apply the syntactic grammars for the detection of syntagmas characteristic of the Serbian and Croatian languages. Finally, we measure discrepancies between properties of texts provided by text processing. The output is generated according to a predefined voting principle using AutoHotkey program. Our results show high precision of 99.82 % for language identification of Croatian and Serbian texts.

Introduction

Many machine learning approaches to language identification tasks have been developed in the last two decades. Most of them use language-independent algorithms that distinguish well between clearly different languages.

The motivation for this paper was to develop a system that would enable automatic detection of texts written in two similar languages, Croatian and Serbian. In this paper we understand language identification as the task of automatically detecting the language(s) present in a document based on the content of the document. This task is nontrivial principally for two main reasons:

1. it is difficult to decide between many languages from the huge closed set of known languages,

2. some languages are very similar and it is hard to distinguish between them.

We focus on the latter case where strong similarities between certain languages make them very hard to correctly classify using standard methods that have been proposed in the literature (eg Tiedemann & Ljubešić 2012). Many authors use machine learning methods in this task, but we opted for a rule-based ie grammar driven approach, using NooJ as a core part of a system designed for the automatic identification of near languages. Tiedemann & Ljubešić (2012) use document classification techniques for discriminating between Bosnian, Croatian and Serbian while Ljubešić et al. (2007) use the list of most frequent Croatian words with second-order Markov model classification and a rule of forbidden words for distinguishing Croatian texts from those written in the Serbian or Slovenian language.

In the following sections we will define some of the differences between Croatian and Serbian, explain our algorithm for language identification and show the morphological and syntactic grammars used in the process. Finally, we will evaluate the system and propose some future works.

Differences between Croatian and Serbian

Although in literature one can still sometimes find the double-barrelled name Serbo-Croatian (sometimes also named BCS or BCMS (complex), covering Bosnian, Croatian, Montenegrin and Serbian), it should be noted that this combined name is anchored in an outdated 19th century Slavistic tradition stemming from Šafarík's classification of South Slavic languages. These languages, undoubtedly evolving from a common ancestor, were used for centuries by completely different cultures (Croatian in Catholic, Bosnian in Muslim, and Serbian and Montenegrin in Orthodox societies), which were exposed to different influences, both political (the Ottoman empire ruled Serbia, Montenegro and Bosnia for approximately 400 years, while Croatia was never conquered and acted as *Antemurale Christianitatis*) and linguistic (Serbian, Bosnian, Montenegrin belong to the Balkan language union, thus sharing some common linguistic features while Croatian was never a member of this union and was influenced more by German and Italian).

Today, after more than 20 years of absence of this unification and due to historically entirely different standardisation processes, these languages diverge more and more. After all, the formulations in the Constitutions of the Republic of Croatia and the Republic of Serbia clearly differentiate between these languages and refer to them as Croatian and Serbian only.

One of the largest differences between Croatian and Serbian is the present form of the proto-Slavic vowel *jat* (see Table 1). In contemporary standard Serbian it reflexes as a vowel 'e' and in contemporary standard Croatian it reflexes as trigraph '*ije*' or digraph '*je*', eg 'milk' reflexes as *mlijeko* (hr) and *mleko* (sr). Another very frequent difference is the formation of verbs with borrowed roots: eg 'to employ' – *angažirati* (hr) vs. *angažovati* (sr). These are only some obvious differences between the two languages, but for the sake of clarification it should be noticed that there are many more differences displayed in Table 1 together with frequencies of patterns found in corpora. This list should not be considered as completely exhaustive and conclusive.

The form of the future tense is yet another frequent structural difference at the morphological level that we have identified and used in our model. To be more specific, where Croatian uses the analytic form (verb in the infinitive form preceded or followed by the auxiliary verb) as in *sastat će se/ će se sastati* (will meet), *izabrat će/ će izabrati* (will elect), Serbian uses the synthetic form, merging the two words and omitting the final consonant t, as in *sastaće se, izabraće,* etc (see paths that start with number 4 in Table 1).

On the syntactic level, Croatian uses more infinitives (*pokušava izabrati*) and noun constructions (*ratifikacije*, *uporaba*), while for the equivalent in Serbian, content verb constructions are used, especially *da* + verb (*da ratifikuje, da izabere, da koriste, da nema potrebe*).

In this chapter we give a short overview of only those differences used in our language identification system.

NooJ Language Resources

Four lexical grammars were built for the recognition of words that are similar in Croatian and Serbian. They are all marked with low priority (1 to 4) which means that they are introduced in a cascaded manner to the lexical analysis after all other Croatian lexical grammars. Thus, only words that are left as 'UNKNOWN' in the text, after the Croatian lexical grammars have been applied, are being tested and, if recognised, annotated as Serbian words <SR> with one of these four grammars.

In general, all four grammars use the same paradigm: find an unknown word, check if the Croatian lexicon has its alternation (ie for *angažovati* (sr) it checks the lexicon for *angažirati* (hr) – including all the possible endings) and if found, the recognised word is annotated as a Serbian word.

Otherwise, it is left unmarked. A more detailed description of grammars is found in the following subsections.

Morphological grammars

Where Croatian uses the ending '*-irati*' for verbs, Serbian uses '*-ovati*' instead. The first morphological grammar is designed to recognise this type of phenomena. If the word satisfies given criteria (1 marked as UNKNOWN after applying the main Croatian resources; 2 after character replacement, the 'new' word is recognised as a word from the Croatian dictionary) it is marked as a Serbian word (SR), the additional notation of the number-letter combination that defines the path that recognised the word (1a-1g, 4h-4i) and with the Croatian translation:

<word, SR+1a+CRO=Croatian translation>.

The number from the number-letter combination that marks the path of a recognition is the number of the morphological grammar used (where the number corresponds to the order in which the grammar was used), and the letter defines the order in which the path was added to the grammar (no special reason lies behind the naming of the paths other than to help us find the errors if spotted and help us count which paths are more common in the text). By following this naming logic, it is quite obvious that paths 1a to 1g belong to graph number 1 and paths 3a to 3s belong to graph number 3. However, paths 4h and 4i were added afterwards, when writing the fourth grammar which recognises the analytical future. Since there are verbs that need both transformations (from the first and fourth grammars) in order to be recognised as Croatian, we added them to the first grammar using the fourth grammar notation. The same was also applied in grammars 2 and 3 and only for the infinitive forms of recognised verbs. We did this since it was necessary to recognise infinitives (marked as HRINF) for our syntactic grammar (see Figure 5). Thus, the verb to employ: *angažirati* (hr) -> *angažovati* (sr) will pass through path 1a (the second path from the top in Figure 1) in all its forms except when used in future tense form. Then it will be recognised via path 4h (the first path from the top in Figure 1).

Our first morphological grammar recognises all the Serbian words that use *-ov, -ova, -u, -uje, -eo, -kov* in place of *–irat, -ir, -ira, -io, -cir, -zir* provided that some other restrictions are met (eg that a recognised word is marked as a verb in short infinitive form <V+INFk> for the path 4h, or that a word is a noun for the path 1g in the manner shown in Figure 1.

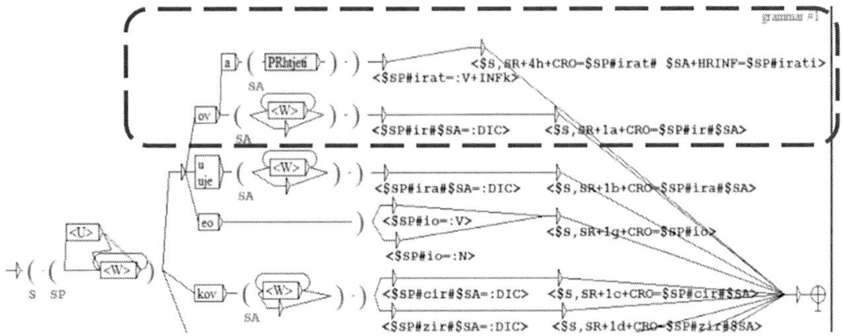

Figure 1 – 1st morphological grammar

Another morphological issue we were able to identify is the reflex of the common proto-Slavic vowel *jat* (see Figure 2), ie usage of a letter ‘e’ in a number of Serbian words where Croatian uses ‘*ije/je*’ as in ‘children’: *djeca* (hr) -> *deca* (sr) or ‘splitting’: *cijepanje* (hr) ->*cepanje* (sr).

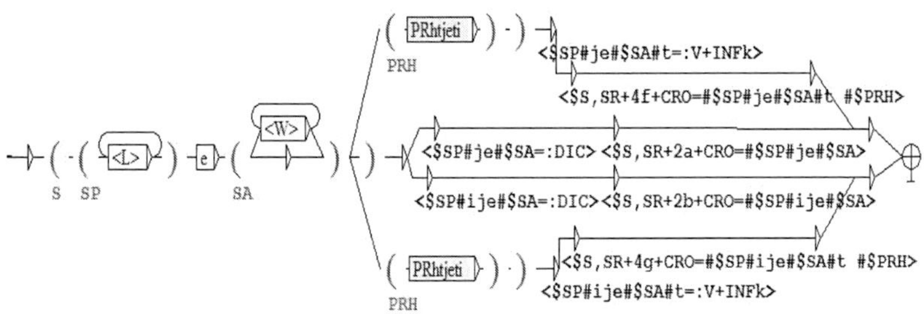

Figure 2 – 2nd morphological grammar for recognising vowel *jat*

The grammar in Figure 3 uses the same logic as the previous two grammars but with different sets of letters ie ‘*demokr**aci**ja*’ (hr) -> ‘*demokr**ati**ja*’ (sr); ‘*u**bojs**tvo*’ (hr) -> ‘*u**bis**tvo*’ (sr); ‘*kriti**zira**ju*’ (hr) -> ‘*kriti**ku**ju*’ (sr). The complete list of changes is given in Table 1.

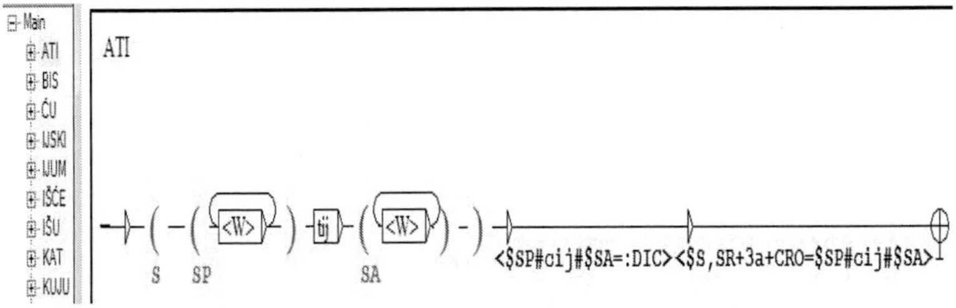

Figure 3 – 3rd morphological grammar for additional lexical differences

The fourth lexical grammar checks for the analytical future when two verbs are used for the construction of the future tense (main verb + auxiliary verb *htjeti* in its clitic form) are found in inversion. Croatian uses these two verbs side-by-side *voljet ću* (I will love). At first glance, it appeared as though we would need to build a syntactic grammar to solve this problem. However, Serbian merges these two verbs into one *voleću* (I will love). For this reason, we were able to construct another morphological grammar (see Figure 4), using, once again, the same paradigm as in the previous morphological grammars.

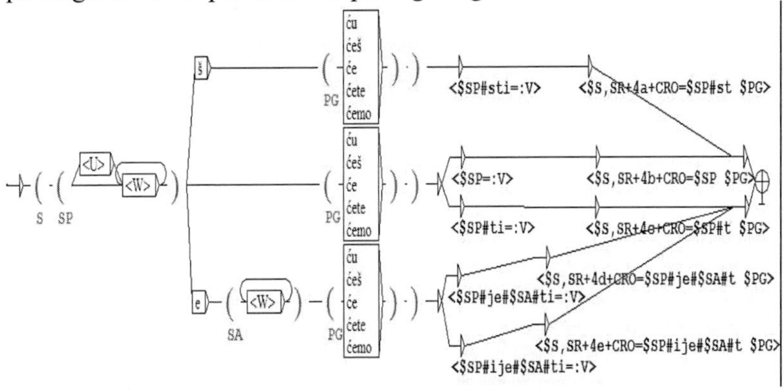

Figure 4 – 4th morphological grammar – future tense

Syntactic Grammar

The syntactic grammar was built to recognise constructions **verb *da* verb**, characteristic of the Serbian language. In this expression, the first verb (one of 9 modal verbs) can be in any tense in both languages, while the second term always remains in the present tense in Serbian and it keeps the infinitive form in Croatian. Thus the sentence 'I wish to learn' uses the following Serbian construction: '*Ja želim da naučim*' while the Croatian sentence uses the infinitive as in '*Ja želim naučiti*'.

Figure 5 shows the main VdaV grammar that has 5 different paths (A1-A5). The A1 path recognises constructions where the second verb is the same in both languages, including coordinations such as, for example, 'I wish to sing and dance', or 'I wish to sing and not to dance'. The A2 and A3 paths recognise constructions where the second verb is different in both languages. Where they differ, is that in path A2, the second verb has been recognised by one of the previous morphological grammars and in path A3 it was not. Paths A4 and A5 recognise those occurrences found in the corpus where there may have also been non-modal verbs in the position of the first verb. In addition, path A4 has a Dative noun after the first verb and Accusative noun, adjective or pronoun. Path A5 has a reflexive second verb. The same paths are described for the modal verb 'to need' (hr/sr *trebati*) but in a separate subgraph (Figures 6, 7 and 8) due to its gender-related particularities.

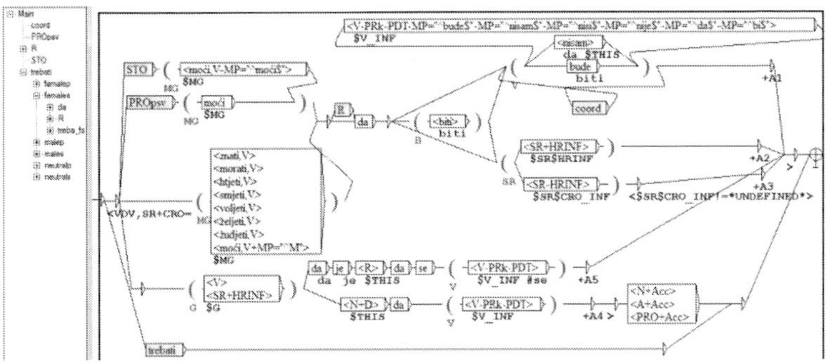

Figure 5 – Syntactic grammar VdaV

As Figure 6 shows, the modal verb *trebati* has more context described since it behaves differently depending on the words (type, case, gender) that precede it.

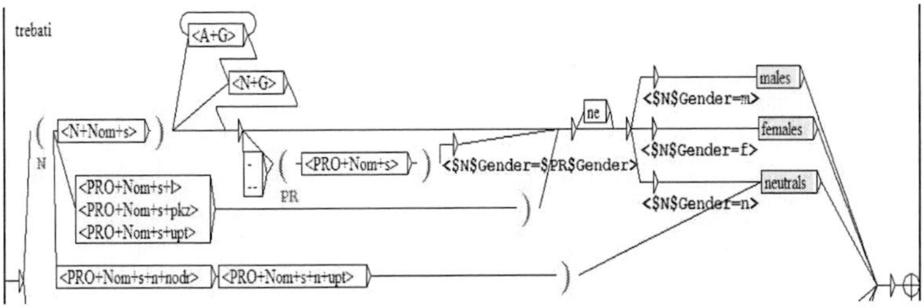

Figure 6 – Subgraph of VdaV grammar

Its subgraphs for female gender subjects and sub-subgraph are shown in Figures 7 and 8 respectively.

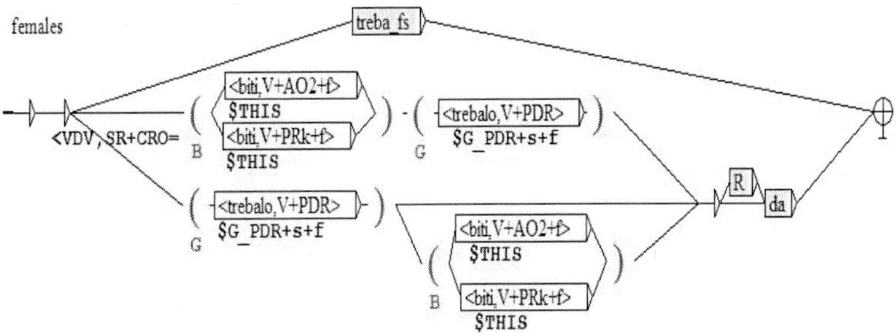

Figure 7 – Subgraph of VdaV grammar for female main verbs

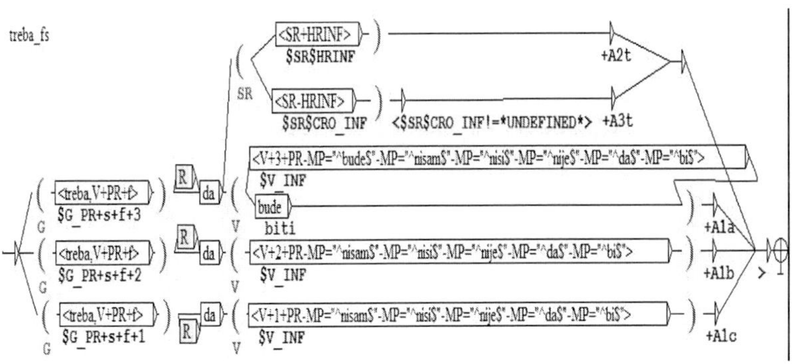

Figure 8 – Sub-subgraph for female singular forms of verb *trebati*

The following examples are recognised with VdaV grammar:

A1a: *Evropa treba da ide* -> *Evropa treba ići* (Europe needs to go)
A1b: *vi treba da uradite* -> *vi trebate uraditi* (You need to do)
A1c: *to treba da koristim* -> *to trebam koristiti* (I need to use that)
A2: *teško moći da ignorišu* -> *teško moći ignorirati* (hardly may ignore)
A2t: *tek treba da formulišu* -> *tek trebaju formulirati* (only just need to formulate)
A3: *Vlada ne bi trebalo da finansira* -> *Vlada ne bi trebala financirati* (Government shouldn't need to finance)
A3t: *Evropa treba brzo da preduzme* -> *Evropa treba brzo poduzeti* (Europe needs quickly to take)
A4: *imaju hrabrosti da podignu javnu svest* -> *imaju hrabrosti podići javnu svijest* (have the courage to raise the global awareness)
A5: *(jedno od rešenja) moglo bi da bude da se uvede (krajnji rok)* -> *(jedno od rješenja) moglo bi biti uvođenje (krajnjega roka)* ((one solution) could be the introduction (of the deadline))

Results

Results for each path described in morphological grammars 1-4 and syntactic grammar (paths A1-A5) are shown in Table 1. Paths are ordered alphabetically, although paths 4f and 4g are described in grammar 2, paths 4h and 4i in grammar 1, and paths 4j, 4k, 4l, 4m and 4n in grammar 3.

# of path	Description	# of occur-rences
1a	ov->ir	93
1b	u|uje -> ira	861
1c	kov->cir	82
1d	kov->zir	64
1e	s->r	4
1f	s->zir	238
1g	eo->io	451
2a	e->je	13 018
2b	e->ije	6 365
3a	tij->cij	162
3b	bis->bojs	144
3c	ću->šu	4
3d	ion->ijsk	273
3e	ijum->ij	110
3f	šć->št	131
3g	iš->iraj	58
3h	kat->kt	176
3i	kuj->ziraj	8
3j	pred->pre	169
3k	pšt->pć	849
3l	sa->su	646
3m	si->ci	384
3n	su->zu	27
3o	ta->ća	84
3p	tič|tic->tječ	65
3r	tič|tic->tjec	151
3s	tkov->tc	0
4a	š->st	6
4b	0->0	376
4c	0->ti	408
4d	e->je	0
4e	e->ije	21
4f	e -> je	21
4g	e -> ije	33
4h	ova -> irat	2
4i	sa->rat	4
4j	sa->su	3
4k	si->zi	1
4l	si->ci	2
4m	ta-> ća	1
4n	tič|tic -> tjec	1

# of path	Description	# of occur-rences
A1	With Cro verb	10 282
A1a		435
A1b		4
A1c		44
A2	With known infinitive form of SR verb	22
A2t		1
A3	With unknown infinitive form of SR verb	997
A3t		102
A4	<V><N+D> da <V><N+Acc>	340
A5	<V> da <biti> <R> da se <V>	2

Table 1 – Detailed description of recognised paths.

The Algorithm

Based on three key distinctions between observed languages described above, we measured the frequency of:

1. unknown tokens
2. syntactic constructions Verb+da+Verb
3. syntactic constructions Verb+Verb-infinitive

Based on obtained frequencies from particular texts we set scoring points for each category for each language (hrPOINTS and srPOINTS). At the end, points scored from each category are added up. Based on the sum obtained, a decision is made about the language of the text. Each time, before processing, hrPOINTS and srPOINTS are set to zero.

After applying Croatian language resources we count the frequency of unknown tokens in a particular text. Based on the percentage of unknown tokens, specific points are awarded to the Croatian or Serbian language in the following manner:

```
if (percentageUNK > 1.2 and percentageUNK <= 5)
    srPOINTS = srPOINTS+5
else if percentageUNK > 5
    srPOINTS = srPOINTS+9
else if percentageUNK < 0.2
    hrPOINTS = hrPOINTS+9
else
    hrPOINTS = hrPOINTS+5
```

The next step is to count the frequencies of *Verb+da+Verb* syntactic constructions from the observed text. Based on the percentage of such constructions we award the points in the following way:

```
if percentageVdaV > 0.4
    srPOINTS = srPOINTS+4
else
    hrPOINTS = hrPOINTS+4
```

This threshold is set relatively high because some (older) authors of Croatian texts tend to use such constructions that are today observed as more characteristic of the Serbian language. The grounds for this may be found in historical reasons of strong language influences (or interferences), since speakers of both languages lived for seven decades in the same country.

The final step is to count the occurences of *Verb+VerbInf* syntactic constructions from the observed text. The points are awarded, based on the percentage of such constructions, in the following way:

```
if percentageVVinf > 0.00001
   srPOINTS = srPOINTS+3
or else
   hrPOINTS = hrPOINTS+3
```

This threshold is set very low because these constructions are very typical for the Croatian language and very rarely found in Serbian texts. Scoring points correspond to the importance of observed differences for particular languages.

Implementation and Evaluation

All stated modules of the near-language identification system are finally processed through the AutoHotkey[1] program in order to automatically collect results and interpret them using NooJ. The findings of processing are presented to the user in the following form:

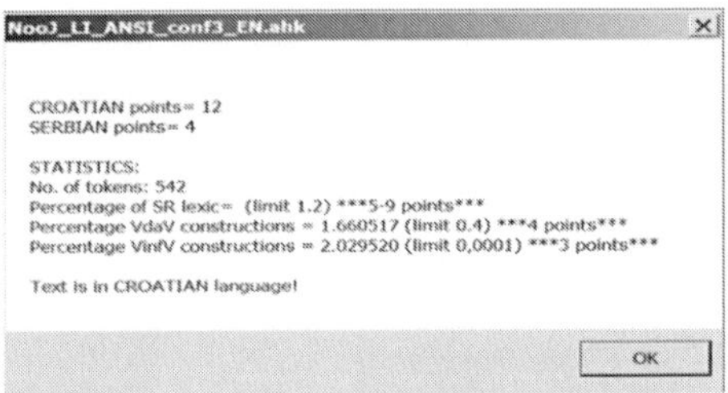

Figure 9 – Presentation of the results of processing

The evaluation is carried out on 1,500 documents from the SETimes corpus (Agić, Ljubešić 2014). The corpus consists of 'news and views from Southeast Europe' from news portal SETimes[2], which is published in ten languages: Bulgarian, Bosnian, Greek, English, Croatian, Macedonian, Romanian, Albanian and Serbian.[3] It is important to emphasise that many news items are very short articles consisting of around 100, 150 or 200

---

[1]http://www.autohotkey.com/
[2]http://setimes.com
[3]http://nlp.ffzg.hr/people/nikola-ljubesic/

tokens. Evaluation is made on texts not known to the system and larger than 150 tokens which are written in Croatian or Serbian. Our results show that our system is achieving very high precision of 99.82 % in language identification of Croatian and Serbian texts.

Conclusion

This work proved that usage of NooJ in combination with the voting approach could achieve hitherto unseen results in the task of detection of near languages. Misclassification happens only with very short articles consisting of 100 to 150 tokens. This should not be considered a drawback of the system since many state-of-the-art machine learning systems have the same problem with very short articles. This is explained by the fact that very often such short texts do not provide sufficient evidence about the language properties on criteria considered. Moreover, we believe that the precision of the system could be further improved using the list of forbidden words which we will try to show with our future work on the project.

References

Agić, Željko and Nikola Ljubešić. 2014. The SETimes.HR Linguistically Annotated Corpus of Croatian. In *Proceedings of the Ninth International Conference on Language Resources and Evaluation (LREC'14)*, 1724–1727. Reykjavik. Iceland.

Bekavac, Božo, Sanja Seljan, and Ivana Simeon. 2008. Corpus-Based Comparison of Contemporary Croatian, Serbian and Bosnian. In *Proceedings of the 6th International Conference on Formal Approaches to South Slavic and Balkan Languages.* 33–39. Dubrovnik, Croatia.

Ljubešić, Nikola, Nives Mikelic, and Damir Boras. 2007. Language Indentification: How to Distinguish Similar Languages? In *Proceedings of the 29th International Conference on Information Technology Interfaces. ITI 2007.* Budin L. et al. (eds.). Zagreb: SRCE. 541-546. Dubrovnik, Croatia.

Silberztein, Max. 2003. *NooJ Manual*. (223 pages) http://www.nooj4nlp.net/NooJManual.pdf.

Tiedemann, Jörg and Nikola Ljubešić. 2012. Efficient Discrimination between Closely Related Languages. In *Proceedings of the 24th International Conference on Computational Linguistics (COLING'12)*, 2619–2634. Mumbai, India.

Vučković, Kristina, Marko Tadić, and Božo Bekavac. 2010. Croatian Language Resources for NooJ. *CIT. Journal of Computing and Information Technology*, 295–301.

TRANSLATING ARABIC RELATIVE CLAUSES INTO ENGLISH USING NOOJ PLATFORM

HAYET BEN ALI, HÉLA FEHRI AND ABDELMAJID BEN HAMADOU

Abstract

In this paper, we aim to present an approach to solving the problems resulting from the translation of Arabic sentences containing relative clauses into English. However, rather than dealing with all relative pronouns we concentrate our efforts on the relative pronouns 'who' and 'that'. We propose a method based on NooJ dictionaries and translation rules (Silberztein and Tutin, 2005). To the dictionaries, we added semantic information (object, animal etc), alongside other grammatical aspects, in order to choose the right relative pronoun ('who' or 'that'). Furthermore, we built a morphological grammar to solve the agglutination problem and syntactic grammars to translate and reorganise the different components of the output sentence.

Features of relative clauses in Arabic

A relative clause is one of the subordinate adjective clauses underlying the complex sentence in Arabic .The relative clause (جملة الصلة [ʒɒmlələt əsilə]) follows the relative noun (الإسم الموصول [əl ism əl məwsu:l]) in order to clarify the meaning of the relative noun and its antecedent.

The relative noun is a noun which has no meaning without the relative clause. It is essential to have a referent pronoun (الرابط أو العائد [əl əid əw əl rəbit]) that refers to the relative noun. There are two types of adjective clauses in Arabic, defining and non-defining. The defining clause needs a relative noun, such a clause is syndetic (connected); while the non-defining clause does not need a relative noun, such a clause is asyndetic (unconnected).

As regards the relative noun, 'it is a noun used to refer to a specific entity by a sentence (clause) which is nominal, verbal, or sub-clause ' شبه

جملة' and comes after the relative pronoun. The relative clause should have a resumptive pronoun which refers to the relative noun. This referent pronoun can sometimes be omitted if it is implicitly understood.

Relative nouns are of two types in Arabic: nominal relative ' موصول إسمي' and particle relative 'موصول حرفي'. However, the particle relatives such as '**إن**'-in-, '**لو**'[ləw] (if), and '**كي**'[kəi] (in order to) are not commonly used as relativising elements. On the other hand, the nominal relatives are of two types; specific (مختص [mɒktəs]) and common (مشترك [mɒ□tərək]). The specific relative nouns are used with the following elements:

- (الذي [ələði]:) with singular masculine eg:

أحترم الرجل الذي يتقن عمله 'I respect the man who masters his job'

- (التي [ələti]:) with singular feminine eg:

أحترم المرأة الذي تتقن عملها 'I respect the woman who masters her job'

- (اللذان [ələða:ni]) with dual masculine eg:

أحترم الرجلان اللذان يتقنان عملهما 'I respect the two men who master their job'

- (اللتان [ələta:ni]) with dual feminine eg:

أحترم المرأتان اللتان تتقنان عملهما 'I respect the two women who master their job'

- (الذين [ələði:nə]) plural masculine:

أحترم الرجال اللذين يتقنون عملهم 'I respect the men who master their job'

- (اللائي– اللاتي [əla:ti]/[əla:i]) with plural feminine eg:

أحترم النساء اللاتي/ اللائي تتقنن عملهن 'I respect the women who respect their job'

The syntactic functions of the relative clause in Arabic

The relative clause in Arabic qualifies definite nouns that are treated as adjuncts and thus termed 'صلة' [silə] (attachment). The feature which determines the syntactic behaviour of the relative clause is determination (definiteness vs. indefiniteness) which combines a/syndesis to produce connected relative clauses or unconnected ones. In other words, the relative clause is used throughout in preference to the 'antecedent'. In this respect, they can be classified as follows,

- Definite head plus syndetic clause = relative structure

جلس الرجل اللذي يتحدث 'The man who is talking sat'

- Definite head plus asyndetic clause = circumstantial structure.

جلس الرجل يتحدث / متحدثا 'The man sat talking'

- Indefinite head NP plus asyndetic clause = adjectival clause.

جلس رجل يتحدث 'A man sat talking'

- Indefinite head plus syndetic clause is empty and there is no structure of this type in Arabic, like :

جلس رجل الذي يتحدث 'A man, the one who talked, sat'

This means that an agreement in case and definiteness is required between the head noun and the relative clause. Hence, a definite adjunct clause cannot modify an indefinite head.

On these grounds, the relativisation strategy in Arabic can be summed up as follows: relative clauses with indefinite heads are asyndetic (unconnected) and always adjectival, while those with definite heads are syndetic (connected) and always relative clauses.

The semantic functions of the relative clauses in Arabic

Generally, Arabic and English relative clauses have similar semantic functions since they shorten the sentence and connect its parts by using connective markers to avoid any redundancy which may result from the repetition of the head noun. Unlike English, movement of the antecedent in the defining relative clause/syndetic does not affect the meaning since the Arabic sentence can start with either a verb or a subject. This is clearly shown in the following instance:

تفوق الطالب الذي درس جيدا 'The student who studied hard succeeded'

الطالب الذي درس جيدا تفوق 'The student who studied hard succeeded'

Like in English, this type of relative clause has its pertinent impact on differentiating the meaning of the clause. In this respect, the Arabic defining clause (syndetic) identifies the NP antecedent. On the other hand, the non-defining clause (asyndetic), which stands as an adjective of the sentence, describes the NP antecedent but does not define it. To figure out the meaning assigned by the two clauses, let us have a look at the following sentences:

لا أثق بتاجر يكثر الحلف 'I don't trust a merchant who swears a lot'

لا أثق بالتاجراللذي يكثر الحلف 'I don't trust the merchant who swears a lot'

These two sentences have two different meanings due to their types. For instance, in the first sentence, the listener does not know the 'merchant', as it could be any merchant. Meanwhile, in the second sentence, the speaker means a definite merchant who is known for swearing a lot. Incidentally, determination as a syntactic feature is considered to be the distinguishing marker of these two types of clause, which in turn, as indicated above, imposes this semantic difference in meaning. On the contrary, punctuation and the position of the relative clause are the two main factors that determine the two types of clause in English.

In this paper, we focus on the study of the relative pronouns ‘that’ and ‘who’. For this reason, we propose a method based on dictionaries and translation rules. For the dictionaries, we add semantic information like animals, objects etc together with other grammatical aspects. We also build a morphological grammar to solve the agglutination problem and syntactic grammars to translate and reorganise the different components of the output sentence.

To start with, let us consider relative pronouns in English. A relative pronoun is a pronoun that marks a relative clause within a larger sentence. It is called a ‘relative’ pronoun because it ‘relates’ to the word that it modifies (Walid, 2010), as in the following example:

- The person who phoned me yesterday is my brother.

In the above example, ‘who’:

- relates to ‘person’, which it modifies.
-introduces the relative clause ‘who phoned me yesterday’.

✓ **Who**

This relative pronoun is used as a subject or object for persons. ‘Who’ is always used in relative clauses referring to human beings. It can be the subject of the relative clause, as in the following sentences:

- The student who came in the morning has left a letter for you.
- I saw the boy who is your friend.

✓ **That**

This relative pronoun is used as subject or object for people, animals, and things especially in defining relative clauses where ‘who’ or ‘which’ are possible.

- I don't like the table that stands in the kitchen.
- The house that I live in is nice.
- This is the book that I was reading loudly.

Rule-based method implemented with NooJ

Arabic is characterised by a rich morphology. In addition to being inflected to gender and number, words can be attached to various clitics for conjunction ‘و’ [wə] (and), the definite article ‘ال’ [əl] (the), prepositions, for example ‘ب’ [bi] (by/with), ‘ل ’ [li] (for), ‘ك ’ [kə] (as) and object pronouns (eg ‘هم ’ [hɒm] (their/them)). In our study of translating into English Arabic sentences containing relative clauses and having different structures, we applied morphological grammars to solve problems of agglutination, and syntactic grammars to translate and reorganise the different components of the output sentence.

Examples of applied morphological grammars

The following is an illustration of the morphological grammars that we added in order to solve the agglutination problems resulting from the translation of Arabic sentences into English (Fehri, Haddar and Ben Hamadou, 2011).

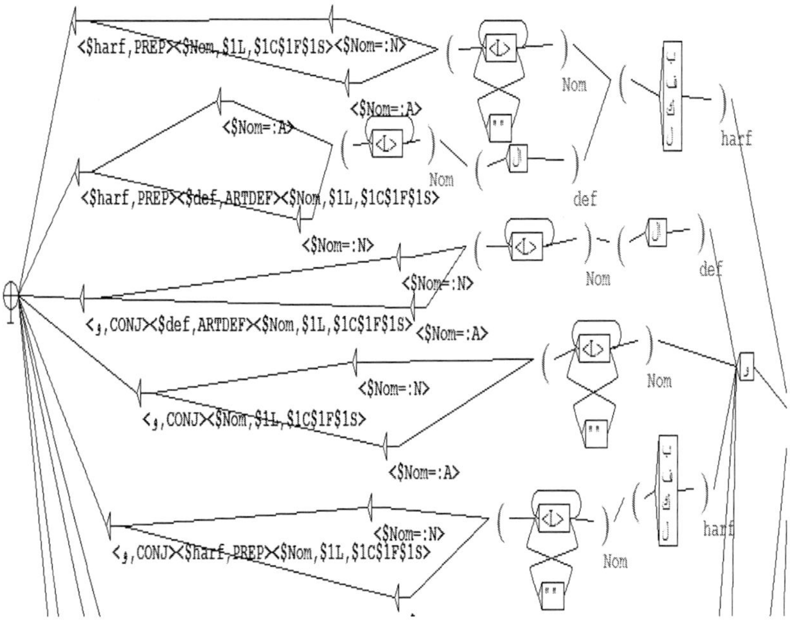

Figure 1 – Extract of morphological grammar

Examples of syntactic grammars

Below is an illustration of the added syntactic grammars that enabled us to translate relative clauses and to recognise the different components of the output sentence:

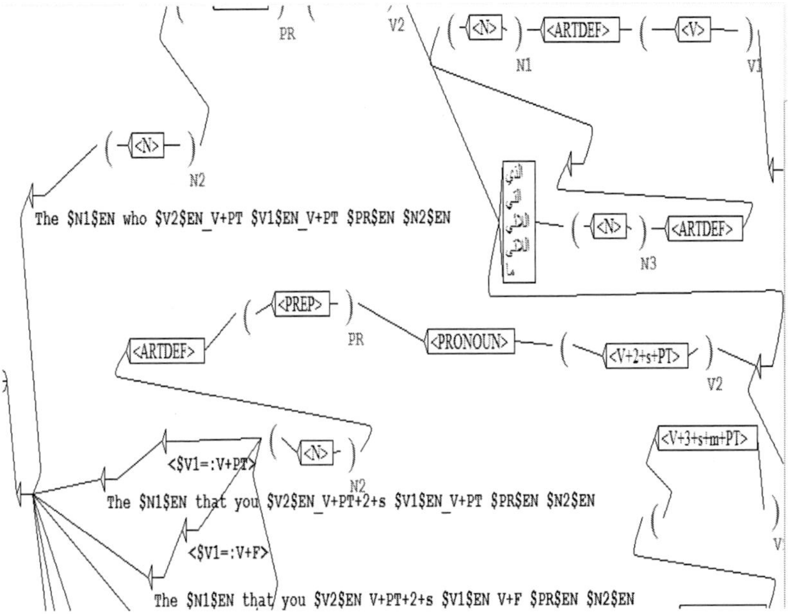

Figure 2 – Extract of syntactic grammar

Examples of structures studied

Below are some of the structures we dealt with in the translation of relative clauses from Arabic into English:

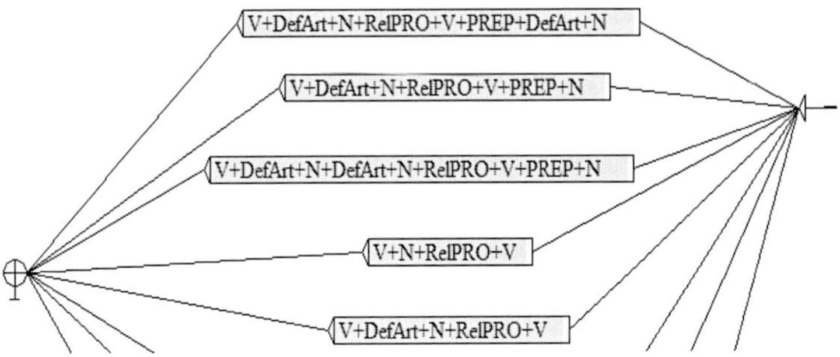

Figure 3 – Examples of structures studied

V+DefArt+N+RelPRO+V+PREP+DefArt+N

ذهب الرجل اللذي تراه إلى السوق ‘The man that you see went to the souk’
V+DefArt+RelPRO+V
غادرت الفتاة التي كانت تتكلم ‘The girl who was speaking left’

Experimentation and Evaluation

After studying a number of structures applying NooJ dictionaries and syntactic local grammars, we measured the concordance of our sentences to test the effectiveness of our approach and the method followed.
The concordance table below gives some examples of the sentences we studied and shows the results of the use of NooJ dictionaries and translation rules:

Figure 4 – Results obtained with NooJ platform

We can conclude that our method provided 80% of well-translated relative clauses. The results proved to be very promising despite still having some unsolved problems.

To better evaluate our work, we made a comparison between the NooJ translation and a Google translation. Some of the results we found are shown below:

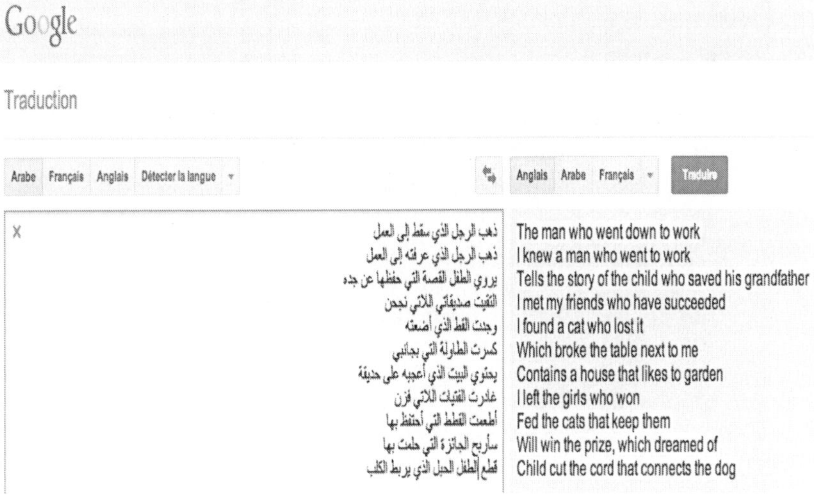

Figure 5 – Results obtained with Google translation

As we can see, the word order in all sentences is wrong. For example, the sentence 'ذهب الرجل الذي سقط إلى السوق' was translated into 'The man who went down to work'. The word order is completely incorrect. The exact translation is 'The man who fell went to the market'.

The choice of the suitable relative pronoun in some sentences is not correct. For example:

'وجدت القط اللذي أضعته' was translated into 'I found a cat who lost it'. Obviously the 'cat' is a non-human animal, which is why we should use the relative pronoun 'that' and not 'who' as given by the Google translation. Furthermore, the problem of agglutination was not solved in the sentence 'أضعته' (I lost it): the subject is implicit referring to 'I', the verb is 'أضاع' which is translated into 'lost' and the 'ه' is considered to be the direct object referring to the cat. The correct translation should be as follows: 'I found the cat that I lost'.

Conclusion

This method of translating relative clauses containing the relative pronouns 'who' and 'that' from Arabic into English was based on the use of NooJ morphological local grammars and syntactic local grammars. It showed how the use of these grammars can solve the problems resulting from the differences between the source language (Arabic) and the target language (English).

We aim to deal with other structures that may help to solve problems resulting from translating relative clauses from Arabic into English in order to develop a system for translating relative clauses from Arabic into English using NooJ. However, in order to do so, it is necessary to study other relative pronouns such as 'where' referring to places, 'when' referring to time, 'whose' referring to possession etc.

References

Fehri, Héla, Haddar Kais, and Ben Hamadou Abdelmajid. 2011. *Recognition and Translation of Arabic Named Entities with NooJ Using a New Representation Model*. FSMNLP 2011. France.

Silberztein, Max and Agnès Tutin. 2005. *NooJ, un outil TAL pour l'enseignement des langues. Application pour l'étude de la morphologie lexicale en FLE.* spécial Atala, 8(2), pp.123-34.

Walid, Mohammed Amer. 2010. *On the Syntactic and Semantic Structure of Relative clauses in English and Arabic: A Constrastive Study.* IUG journal, Published paper, 2010.

CONVERTING QUANTITATIVE EXPRESSIONS WITH MEASUREMENT UNITS INTO AN ORTHOGRAPHIC FORM, AND CONVENIENT MONITORING METHODS FOR BELARUSIAN

ALENA SKOPINAVA, YURY HETSEVICH, AND JULIA BORODINA

Abstract

This paper describes a NooJ syntactic grammar developed for recognising quantitative expressions with measurement units (QEMU) and converting them into the grammatically correct orthographic form in Belarusian. In addition to a general description of the grammar, the paper suggests methods for easy monitoring of the results received by means of the developed grammar. These methods involve the replacement of QEMUs in an initial document with their resulting orthographically-correct equivalents in an exported XML-document which can be used further in different applications.

Introduction

In order to make text interfaces more 'natural', systems of human-computer interaction should be able to voice electronic texts. High-quality text-to-speech synthesis cannot be achieved without solving various computer-linguistic problems. By 'computer-linguistic problem', we mean a task which refers to electronic texts, and concerns the identification, classification, and processing of sequences of letters, digits, and symbols. Solving the problem means developing a program for preliminary text processing.

At the international NooJ (Saarbrücken, 2013) and Dialogue (Bekasovo, 2013) conferences, we demonstrated solutions to several computer-linguistic problems which concern QEMUs. In particular, we gave a detailed overview of syntactic grammars and linguistic resources which identify, analyse, and classify QEMUs. All of these were built in the form of finite-state automata with the help of the linguistic processor NooJ and its built-in visual graphic editor. So far three complementary algorithmic blocks have been built for the Belarusian language. They allow:

- identification and classification of QEMUs according to the system of the International Bureau of Weights and Measures (expressions with SI-basic, SI-derived, and non-systemic measurement units)
- classification of QEMUs according to word formation peculiarities (full or shortened, with multiple or submultiple prefixes)
- expansion of QEMUs into orthographic words.

Although much has already been done, there is still room for further improvements. Problems concerning QEMUs are not so easy to solve due to the enormous variety of ways in which they are expressed in writing.

Moreover, many of the ways they are expressed differ within various language systems.

Difficulties in Belarusian

There are some difficulties which must be taken into consideration in order to develop an accurate grammar. Let us begin with the most difficult cases. The first difficulty arises in the linguistic category of case: there are six cases in Belarusian (nominative, genitive, dative, accusative, instrumental, and prepositional), while, in English, for example, there are only two cases, common and possessive. As a result, a context can influence how words agree within one expression. In addition, numerals also influence the case of the nouns which follow them. Thus, the quantitative expression *1 хв.* ‘1 min.’ has 6 forms in Belarusian: *1 хв. – адн**а** хвілін**а**; каля 1 хв. – каля адн**ой** хвілін**ы**; на 1 хв. – на адн**ой** хвілін**е**; больш за 1 хв. – больш за адн**у** хвілін**у**; жыць 1 хв. – жыць адн**ой** хвілін**ай**; аб 1 хв. – аб адн**ой** хвіліне*. In English, the equivalent expression ‘1 min. – 1 minute’ will always remain unchanged, regardless of the context.

Secondly, word endings in Belarusian depend not only on the category of case but also on the categories of number and gender. Table 1 illustrates the endings taken by the numeral *один* ‘one’ in the nominative case. In Belarusian this numeral takes different endings depending not only on the case but also on the gender of a noun which follows it (Table 1).

Belarusian	English
1 ст. = адно стагоддзе **(neuter)** 1 хв. = адна хвіліна **(feminine)** 1 м. = адзін_ метр **(masculine)** 1 сут. = адны суткі **(pluralia tantum)**	1 c. = one century 1 min. = one minute_ 1 m. = one meter_ 1 d. = one day_

Table 1 – Declension of QEMUs containing the numeral '1' in Belarusian and English

Thirdly, in addition to word declension, another difficulty is the variety within one language system. For example, the Belarusian language possesses a second system of spelling, which is called the *Taraškievica* or Belarusian classical orthography. Nowadays, the modern and classical systems co-exist, so it is important to take both of them into consideration. Thus, the full list of variants for the Belarusian word *секунда* 'second' (ie the SI-basic measurement unit of time) will be the following: *с, сек, сэк, секунда, секунды, секундзе, секунду, секундай, секундаю, секундзе, секунд, секундаў, секундам, секундамі, секундах, сэкунда, сэкунды, сэкундзе, сэкунду, сэкундай, сэкундаю, сэкундзе, сэкунд, сэкундаў, сэкундам, сэкундамі, сэкундах* – 27 variants. This phenomenon can be compared with lexical variants within American English and British English. Thus, according to the World English Dictionary, there are American forms (meter-meters), and British forms (metre-metres).

Finally, the problem of processing QEMUs is complicated by homonymy. For instance, the abbreviation *г* (in Belarusian) can stand for four different measurement units: *гадзіна, год, грам* 'hour, year, gram', and sometimes even *градус* 'degree'.

Construction of the Grammar

Last year an algorithm for the nominative case was created. As well as the improvement of the algorithm by the addition of more measurement units and more models which can be processed, the algorithm is now able to handle QEMU sequences and intervals. However, the most important achievement is the processing of two more cases: genitive and accusative. The analysis of the NooJ-corpus of scientific and technical texts has shown that these cases are the ones used most frequently.

The grammar is fully self-containable and works without any dictionaries applied. It contains 351 graphs; therefore, we had to come up with a convenient way of ordering the graphs (Figure 1). Traditionally in Belarusian, the six cases are listed in a certain order, in particular: 1st is nominative, 2nd genitive, 3rd dative, 4th accusative, 5th instrumental, and 6th prepositional. This is why we have put *1* before *Nom*, *2* before *Gen*, and *4* before *Acc*. The capital Latin letters in the names of graphs signify a model of QEMU described by the graph. The model is specified by abbreviations at the end of the names of the graphs. For instance, the letter *A* in the name '1A_Nom_WN_MU' stands for a QEMU with a numeral descriptor expressed by a whole number *WN_MU*. With such ordering, we receive an algorithmic tree which is clear and easy to work with.

Other graphs in the grammar describe mathematical signs which can be found in front of numeral quantifiers, as well as the most probable prepositions and other pieces of the remaining context. The latter are stored in the graphs 'Gen_Features' and 'Acc_Features'.

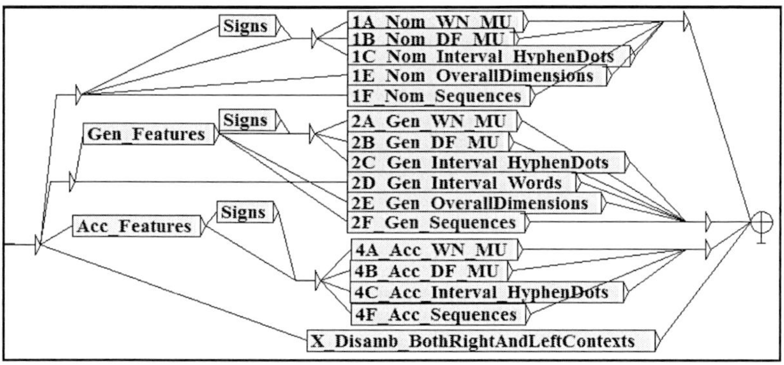

Figure 1 – General view of the grammar for QEMU processing

For a more detailed view of the work of the grammar, let us look at what is inside the graph '1A_Acc_WN_MU' (Figure 2). The graph has been created for QEMU which are used in the nominative case, and which contain a numeral quantifier expressed by a whole number. Graphs of the A-group (whose names start with *a_...*) process numeral quantifiers according to the required grammatical form: singular or plural; feminine or masculine; nominative, genitive, or accusative cases. Graphs of the B-group, in turn, describe measurement units of each grammatical form and class (basic SI, derived from SI, and out of SI).

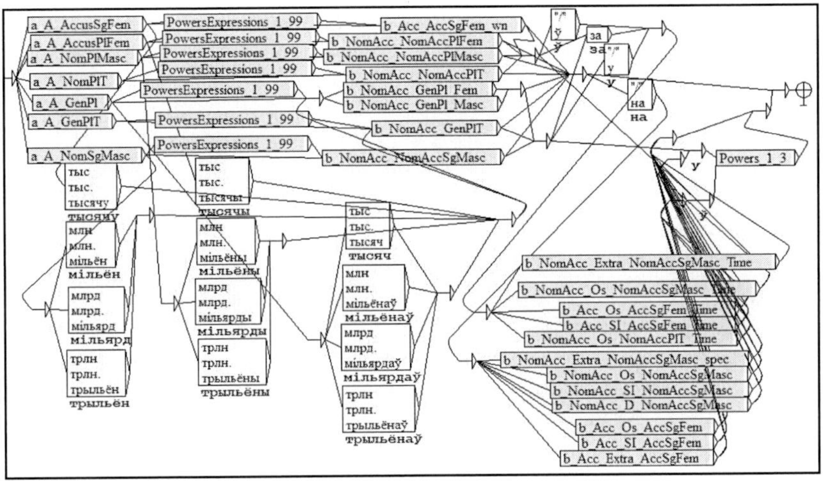

Figure 2 – Graph for QEMUs with a whole number in the nominative case

For example, the expression *74 градусы* '74 degrees' is processed within this graph. Since *74* is a whole number and the expression takes the nominative case, the grammar will use this exact graph. As a result of the processing, *74 градусы* '74 degrees' is converted into the orthographic form *семдзесят чатыры градусы* 'seventy-four degrees'.

This example can be represented as a common model: *WXY*, where *X* is any numeral quantifier, *Y* is a measurement unit and *W* is a context determining the grammatical case. This model of the formation suits the majority of QEMUs, but there are some other models which the grammar can process (Table 2).

Model	Example	English Translation
X Y	12 % | 40-50 тыс. м	12 % | 40-50 thousand m.
X Y/Y	0,5144444 м/с	0,5144444 m/s
X-[… ..]X Y	1-1,5 года | +13... +19 °C	1-1,5 years | +13... +19 °C
X-[… ..]X Y/Y	0,1-5,7·10^{-2} м/с	0,1-5,7·10^{-2} m/s
~[+-±><]X Y	±0,3° | > 6 Зв	±0,3° | > 6 Sv
~[+-±<>]X Y/Y	~107 К/с | ~9,8 м/с^2	~107 C/s | ~9,8 m/s^2

X,[i] X Y	2 і 4 метры	2 and 4 meters
X, X, X Y	5, 6, 7 шт	5, 6, 7 pc
X Y - X Y	0,1 Гц - 300 кГц	0,1 Hz - 300 kHz
X × X Y	1136×640 пікселяў	1136×640 pixels
X × X × XY	146,8 × 75,3 × 8,9 мм	146,8 × 75,3 × 8,9 mm

Table 2 – Models of QEMU formation which can be processed by the grammar

Apart from the models listed above, the grammar can process numeral quantifiers of various structures such as: whole numbers (*5,791*), decimal fractions (*0.5144*), intervals (*+13...+19*), positive and negative numbers, quantifiers with or without context determining the case of the whole expression (*~20*), exponents ($0.1\text{-}5.7 \cdot 10^{-2}$), etc.

The graphs starting with *b_...*, describe measurement units. The grammar can process about 120 measurement units belonging to various classes: SI-basic units (*кілаграм* 'kilogram', *ампер* 'ampere'), SI-derived units (джоуль 'joule', *радыян* 'radian'), units belonging to other systems (*гектар* 'hectare', *градус* 'degree'), and additional words which are not officially considered units but can still be used for measuring (*штука* 'piece'). These classes are illustrated by the names of the graphs: *SI*, *D*, *OS*, and *EXTRA* respectively. See Figure 3 for more examples of measurement units from Belarusian.

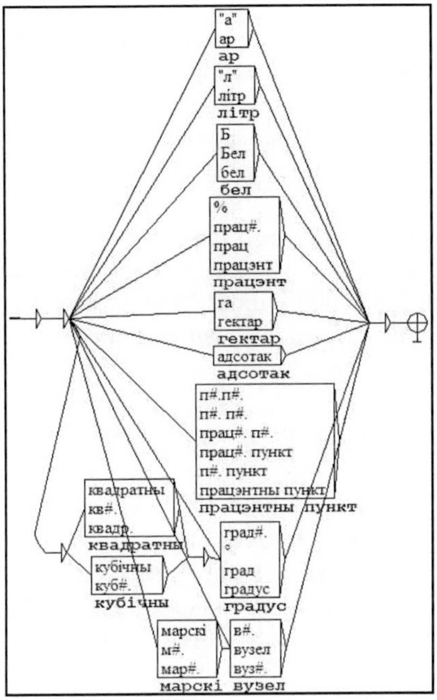

Figure 3 – Examples of measurement units belonging to other systems in Belarusian

Quality Evaluation

As we have already mentioned, the algorithm consists of 351 graphs. It can process a variety of numbers: up to 12-digit, whole and fractional, positive and negative, exponents, intervals, etc. Also, the algorithm is capable of recognising more than 120 measurement units, including an extra category containing units which can be used for measuring but are not officially considered units eg: *штука* 'a piece'; or units which are relatively seldom used eg *дыяптрыя* 'a diopter' etc.

The quality evaluation test has been performed on the material of a text corpus of over 100 thousand tokens containing 1,765 QEMU, and it has shown quite good results: precision 86%, recall 82%, and F-measure 84%. For now the grammar covers three linguistic cases out of six, but the performance of the grammar is quite accurate: QEMU tend to be most frequently used in the following cases: nominative, genitive and accusative – the ones which our grammar covers.

However, one of the difficulties mentioned above is homonymy, which affects the performance of the grammar. Due to full homonymy of some phrases, there is a small number of false-positive results (approx. 1%). The context of the following example *у пастанове ад 29.03.1996 г* 'in the resolution of 29.03.1996' clarifies that the last letter stands for the word *год* 'year' (but not *грам* 'gram'); however, the part *3.1996 г* is processed separately and converted into an orthographic form as *тры цэлыя адна тысяча дзевяцьсот дзевяноста шэсць дзесяцітысячных грама* 'three point one thousand nine hundred ninety nine grams'.

Thus, the grammar performance can be improved by adding the rest of the cases and solving the homonymy issues.

Replacer for QEMU

In the previous sections we have observed results with the help of the 'Outputs' checkbox in the NooJ concordance mode. This is extremely useful for the intermediate monitoring of performance at the development stage. However, different researchers have different goals and objectives concerning text extraction, recognition or processing. Therefore, we suggest a technology which turns the resulting outputs into a form which can be further handled by another application and can be understood by any user. A description of the process is as follows:

First, we need to add special markers to the main graph of the algorithm (Figure 4). With their addition, the correct grammatical forms which have been previously generated as comments become part of the XML tag. Later these markers will let us replace the initial quantitative expressions with their full equivalents.

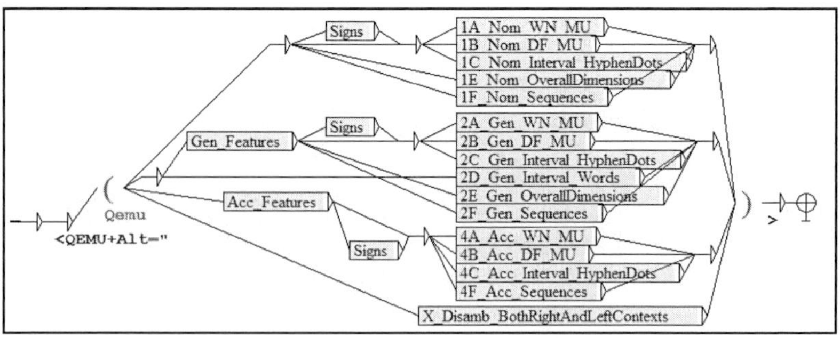

Figure 4 – General view of the grammar with XML markers added

Second, we must apply the grammar as a linguistic resource. At the stage of lexical analysis conducted on the corpus, QEMUs are identified and annotated with XML tags. Figure 5 shows the annotated text.

```
Amazon будзе дастаўляць заказы беспілотнікамі
Амерыканская інтэрнэт-крама Amazon плануе запусціць
дастаўку пасылак з дапамогай Дронаў.
Пра гэта гаворыцца ў паведамленні кампаніі.
Дроны змогуць дастаўляць пасылкі вагой <QEMU
Alt="да дзвюх цэлых трох дзясятых кілаграма ">да
2,3 кг</QEMU>, якія цяпер складаюць <QEMU Alt="каля
васьмідзесяці шасці працэнтаў ">каля 86%</QEMU>
усіх заказаў на Amazon, сказаў генеральны дырэктар
кампаніі Джэф Безас у інтэрв'ю тэлеканалу CBS.
Дастаўка будзе ажыццяўляцца <QEMU Alt="ў радыусе
дзесяці міль ">ў радыусе 10 міль</QEMU> (прыблізна
<QEMU Alt="шаснаццаць кіламетраў ">16 км</QEMU>) ад
складоў інтэрнэт-крамы, максімальны час ад
афармлення заказу да атрымання тавару <QEMU
Alt="складзе трыццаць хвілін ">складзе 30
хвілін</QEMU>. Авіядастаўка будзе ўключаная ў
```

Figure 5 – A piece of text with QEMU annotations in Belarusian

The third step is to export the annotated text in the XML format. We see in Figure 5 that QEMUs have received the markers and have been converted into their full forms, but the abbreviated form of the expression is still preserved. Annotated text can then be exported as an XML document.

In order to complete the replacement of the initial expression, we launch and apply a specially written script program in the PEARL language, which is called ‘Replacer for QEMU’.

An input file must be an annotated text in the txt–format. It is placed in the folder ‘in’ (Figure 6). After launching the ‘Start.bat’, the program starts to work. The output htm-file appears in the folder ‘out’. The final result can be seen in Figure 7. All the initial sequences of signs, digits, and letters are now transformed into linguistically correct word expressions. In addition, their font colour is automatically changed to red and underlined.

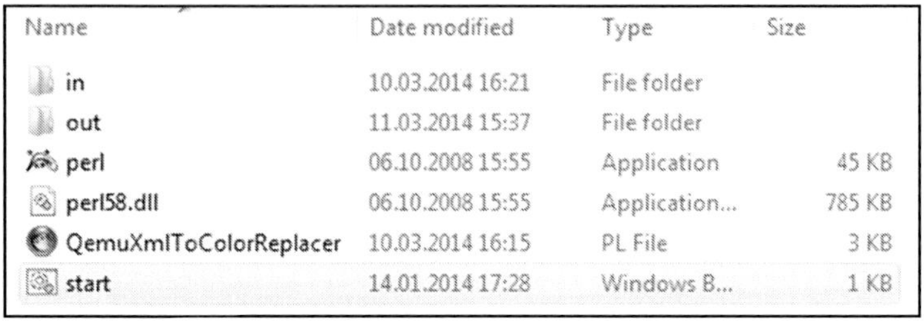

Figure 6 – Program 'Replacer for QEMU'

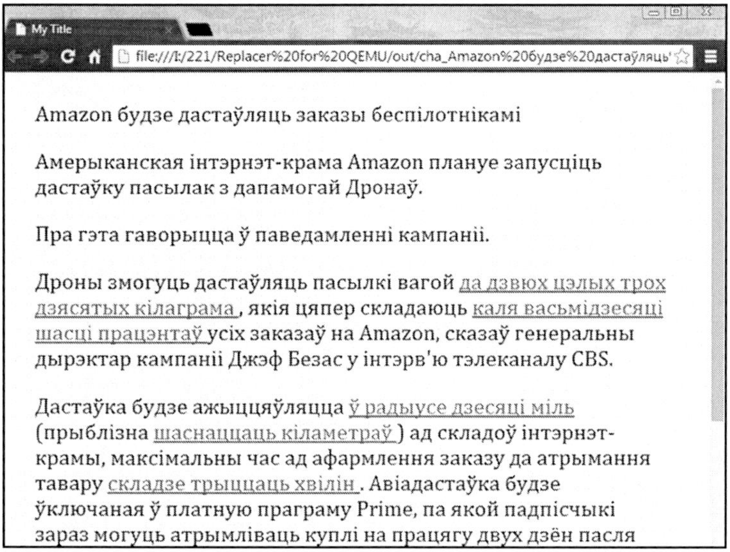

Figure 7 – Resulting text with underlined QEMUs

Anyone who knows the basics of programming or HTML can easily change the style of a replaced text to any other by editing the <FONT…> line in the PEARL code.

Conclusion and Future Work

Quantitative expressions with measurement units can be found in electronic texts of almost any thematic domain in various areas of everyday personal and professional life: culinary recipes; information about goods in online-shops or on labels; weather forecasts; transport schedules; commentaries on sport events; ticket prices; tourist guides; voiced transmission of scientific data from space satellites and probes; architectural descriptions; measurements of human body indicators, such as temperature, pressure, pulse, sugar, weight, cholesterol etc.

As a result, we have created an algorithm which transforms QEMUs into orthographical words in Belarusian. The grammar describes several particular models of QEMU formation, as well as an enormous variety of numeral quantifiers and measurement units. The grammar has been tested on a corpus containing 100,000 tokens, and it has shown relatively good performance, with precision and recall rates over 80 %. Nevertheless, the algorithm can be further improved. In order to reach the highest level of precision and recall, we plan to add the rest of the cases, more types of numeral quantifiers, measurement units, and structural models.

Acknowledgements

We would like to thank the linguist Adam Morrison for his help in revising the language of this paper.

References

Collins English Dictionary – Complete & Unabridged 10th Edition [Electronic resource]. – HarperCollins Publishers, 2011. – http://dictionary.reference.com/browse/sociology.

Hetsevich Yuras and Alena Skopinava. 2013. Identification of Expressions with Units of Measurement in Scientific, Technical & Legal Texts in Belarusian and Russian. In *Proceedings of the Workshop on Integrating IR technologies for Professional Search*, http://ceur-ws.org/Vol-968/irps_6.pdf (2013)

—. 2013. Transforming quantitative expressions with measurement units into orthographical words for text-to-speech synthesis to Belarusian and Russian. In *Вестник МГЛУ. Сер. 1, Филология*, pp. 133–144.

Skopinava Alena, Yuras Hetsevich, and Boris Lobanov. 2013. Processing of quantitative expressions with units of measurement in scientific texts as applied to Belarusian and Russian text-to-speech synthesis. In *Компьютерная лингвистика и интеллектуальные технологии: По материалам Международной конференции «Диалог»*, 29 мая – 2 июня 2013: Bekasovo, Russia, pp. 634–651.

The American Heritage Science Dictionary [Electronic resource]. – 2014. – Mode of access: http://dictionary.reference.com/browse/sociology. – Date of access: 03.03.2014.

Pedagogical Use of NooJ Dealing with French as a Foreign Language

Julia Frigière and Sandrine Fuentes

Abstract

In the context of higher education, the NooJ language engineering platform has proved its efficiency as a language reflection tool with French Philology students. By learning a new way of describing natural languages, students are able to test their knowledge regarding how the French language works and, at the same time, they can be aware of the richness and variety of human linguistic productions. The approach is therefore both bottom-up and top-down: on the one hand, learners have to use NooJ formalism with the aim of capturing some given sequences (bottom-up) and, on the other, they have to consider a linguistic phenomenon and attempt to encode it (top-down). As a result, this course will improve students' own competences in the French language as well as introducing them to the basic skills of language computer processing. In this contribution, we present a sample set of five activities carried out within the framework of this course.

Introduction

This paper reports a teaching experience with NooJ, undertaken at the *Universitat Autònoma de Barcelona* (Spain), between September 2013 and January 2014 with French Philology students in the *Introduction au traitement informatique de la langue française* course conducted by the authors of this contribution, both teachers in French as a Foreign Language as well as researchers in Natural Language Processing.

The target group has the following characteristics: it is a half-yearly course with six ECTS-credits[1]. The students are in the four-year degree programme and have already studied a total of approximately 4,650 hours

---

[1]In the Universitat Autònoma de Barcelona, one ECTS-credit amounts to twenty-five hours of student work (including homework).

of French language[2], thus they have reached an advanced level in French. Most of them are currently embarking on or planning their career in French as a Foreign Language (hereafter FLE) teaching.

The students may have just one first language or they may be native speakers of the Spanish, Catalan[3] and French languages. This heteroglossic context represents one more challenge for teaching since it has to manage this disparate linguistic command and to make it accessible for the formalisation of the language phenomenon.

The *Introduction au traitement informatique de la langue française* course aims to provide students with basic skills of Natural Language Processing (hereafter NLP), while at the same time seeking to improve the learners' French language skills. Using their existing competence in French and nascent skill in NLP, and enriching them both, we wish to enable the students to observe, identify, assimilate and formalise linguistic phenomena (at various levels of analysis: syntactic, morphological or semantic; and in a wide variety of texts and volumes: different typologies, registers, and clusters).

Once the NLP concept and its applications have been introduced, we focus on the problems that written and oral Natural Language Processing faces and present various kinds of solutions: resources such as types of linguistic formalisation, dictionaries and grammar.

In the final stage, the NooJ platform technology enables the students to effectively work on many and varied language phenomena, thus completing the previous formal framework.

Consequently, the five activities we submit are a representative selection[4] of all the activities carried out, including both training and evaluation exercises, and covering theoretical as well as applied notions. Different approaches are used: top-down and/or bottom-up, and different balancing combinations of the NLP or FLE objectives. In every activity, students can access the NooJ platform.

---

[2]The syllabus regarding French lessons sums a total of 186 ECTS-credits ie 4,650 hours which are divided into instrumental language, reflection on language classes, literature and culture classes.

[3]In Catalonia, Catalan and Spanish are both official languages.

[4]These exercises follow a non-presented series of introductory exercises and are thus destined to a not-totally NooJ neophyte public.

First activity (1E): evaluation exercise

In the first task, students have to predict the largest[5] result of the NooJ query application *<danser>* (to dance). Students are expected to remember the brackets inflection function and, as a consequence, to be able to predict that such a query retrieves each form which has for canonical form the ‘*danser*’ lemma. Another formulation, more intuitive from a linguistic point of view, is that such a query should be the NooJ formalisation for the ‘*danser*’ paradigm.

The second task which relates the abstract prediction with the effective application on a corpus asks why the sentence *J’adore la danse contemporaine* (I love contemporary dance) is recognised and questions whether such a match is desired. This ‘*danse*’ form does not belong to the sought ‘*danser*’ paradigm, the presence of the article ‘*la*’ and the adjective ‘*contemporaine*’ makes it clear that, in this context, ‘*danse*’ is a noun. With this apparent contradiction we wish to confront the students with the question: why is this noun recognised when applying a ‘verb’ query?

One way to solve this question is practical/instrumental: since NooJ is available, the students can work with real material. They have to use their formalism and platform command and build a NooJ text which contains *‘J’adore la danse contemporaine’*. After introducing the *<danser>* NooJ query in the ‘locate’ frame, they apply it to the text. Then, students may visualise the ‘text annotation structure’ of the studied match (by ticking the corresponding option box).

Decoding the appearing NooJ categories and inflection finally allows them to realise that ‘*danse*’, apart from admittedly being analysed as a noun, is also analysed as a verb[6]. This local ambiguous analysis is the cause of the query pattern recognition.

However, it is not necessary for the students to use this technological approach: thanks to their common background in French morphosyntax, they can easily notice that the first and third person of ‘*danser*’, in the present tense for example, have ‘*danse*’ as their verbal form.

In both approaches (NLP and linguistic), the students must detect the homography in the language; homography which explains the recognition of the noun and represents an ambiguity in computer language processing (at the morphosyntactic level).

---

[5]The exact wording is: ‘What are all the results that I can retrieve? Answer accurately with explanations and do not only give examples or matches.’

[6]The first and third persons singular in the present indicative and present subjunctive as well as the second person singular in the present imperative of the verb ‘*danser*’ are ‘*danse*’.

In this exercise, we have practised different NooJ tools such as: locate, concordance frames, text annotation structure option; and we have exploited students' basic linguistic abilities.

A clear extension could be refining the initial query in order to retrieve only the whole paradigm of '*danser*'.

Second activity example (2E): evaluation exercise

In the following evaluation activity, the global goal is to extract the sequences which contain pronominal verbs from a study corpus (composed by [texte_ok] and [texte_ko]) by using a NooJ query.

[texte_ok]
Je me suis douchée à 8 heures, après que tu t'es douché. (S1)
Nous nous promenons. (S2)
Il se souvient qu'elle se maquille beaucoup. (S3)
Pendant que vous vous amusez, elles se tuent à la tâche. (S4)

[texte_ko]
*Je l'ai donné à mon frère. (S'1)
*Il m'embrasse. (S'2)
*Il n'est pas allé à son rendez-vous. (S'3)
*Elle ne sait pas. (S'4)

One additional indication is that by applying[7] the correct query, the students should get seven matches on [texte_ok] and none on [texte_ko].

In order to prompt an analysis guiding the top-down abstract linguistic encoding task to a preliminary corpus, we ask '(1.) Which text ([texte_ok] or [texte_ko]) aims to verify the precision of the query? Justify your answer.' The complementary bottom-up approach permits using 'real'[8] language productions as initial patterns.

This question evaluates the students' theoretical NLP skills, particularly their ability to handle the 'precision' efficacy measure which quantifies how correct the retrieved set of items is: do all of the retrieved items correspond to the studied linguistic phenomenon? Are there any irrelevant items selected?

Thus, the next task is to identify the retrieved items. Using their syntactic and morphosyntactic knowledge of French, the students can

---

[7]We also indicate the query configuration settings: 'index' should be set to 'longest matches'.

[8]The corpus has been manually designed with a pedagogical aim, therefore it cannot be considered authentic.

detect in the corpus the pronominal verbal forms, of which there are seven in [texte_ok]. These seven sought sequences are continuous (subject-reflexive pronoun-verb, without insertions) so the query to generate them should be quite simple at a syntactic level. One of the corpus sentences obliges the student to consider and include the morphosyntactic phenomenon of elision (in S1, ‘*t’*’ replaces ‘*te*’ in front of a vowel).

On the other hand, the [texte_ko] sequence morphosyntactic analysis reveals four preverbal elements: ‘*n’*’ and ‘*ne*’, negation particle in its plain (S’4) and elided (S’3) forms; and ‘*m’*’ and ‘*l’*’ in respectively S’1 and S’2. Despite having the correct part-of-speech, these last two pronouns cannot be identified as reflexive pronouns. The preverbal ‘*l’*’ replaces ‘*le*’ or ‘*la*’, in the place of a direct complement. Nor can the ambiguous ‘*m’*’ (‘*me*’ elided) in this case be interpreted as a reflexive pronoun like in S1, since the verb subject is not ‘*je*’ but ‘*il*’. In other words, the preverbal pronoun and subject are not in agreement (first versus third person). In the end, [texte_ok] contains seven realisations of the sought linguistic phenomenon while there are none in [texte_ko], which is consistent with the statement. The [texte_ko] behaves as a catalyst to draw students’ attention to the importance of correctly distinguishing, in the subsequent query, the reflexive pronouns from the other preverbal elements, including other pronouns.

Knowing that [texte_ko] has four potential noisy matches, and since there is no match to make, in the first question the student is prompted to answer that [texte_ko] plays a control role to check query precision (while [texte_ok] represents a reduced set of the sequences that have to be retrieved). It is not necessary to design the adequate query following the wording features: ‘(2.) Write the NooJ query. The concision of the query and the use of NooJ categories are taken into account’. The ‘concision’ and ‘NooJ categories’ requirements are intended to prevent the student from making a simple list of the target sequences and to impel a real *formalisation* of the phenomenon.

Given that we seek, at the very least, sequences composed of a subject pronoun and its associated preverbal reflexive pronoun followed by a verb (in the affirmative or negative form, in the present or present perfect), one of the accepted queries is:

(<je> <me>| <tu> <te> | il <se> | elle <se> | nous nous | vous vous | ils <se> | elles <se>) ((<ne>* <être+PR> <pas>* <V+PP>)| (<ne>* <V+PR><pas>*))

Although this prototypical query is not exhaustive[9], it helps to retrieve all of the correct sequences from [texte_ok] and does not recognise any 'erroneous' sequence (zero matches in [texte_ko]). In this proposal, we have prioritised the encoding *process* rather than the work of enriching the grammar, a task that occupies the forefront of the next 3T and 4T activities.

Third activity example (3T): training exercise

For the third activity, set for homework, we used the corpus[10] 'Les Misérables' (by Victor Hugo) to retrieve the verbal periphrasis with inchoative value by using a NooJ query.

In the first task, the students' theoretical linguistic knowledge allows them to interpret the expression 'inchoative value' as the expression referring to the beginning of a state. Formalising this phenomenon implies a top-down approach while the second step allows them to exercise the NooJ platform command.

In Figure 1, we present a student's work for this activity. A first overview on the queries 'history' (old versions are chronologically ordered from a) to d)) demonstrates how, little by little, the student (hereafter, STU1) analyses the concordances found and how the description is improved in order to retrieve more relevant items and fewer irrelevant items. STU1 finally presents the definitive results: the query which responds to the question, and illustrates it with the list of its associated concordances.

On a linguistic point, STU1 chooses two verbal periphrases to express the inchoative value: '*commencer à*' and '*se mettre à*'. A first naive try (a) demonstrates to STU1, given that there is no ('*aucun*') sequence with '*se mettre*', that within the NooJ formalism the pronominal verbs are not encoded together with the pronoun in the entry but are separated. In order to cover more cases, STU1 introduces variations in the queries. In query (b), the structure for recognising compound tenses in verbal forms is

---

[9]We have not considered any construction other than the one contained in the study corpus: the subject description includes only pronominal units and drops for example nominal ('*la mère*') or verbal ('*manger*') phrases; the verbal syntagma may be generalised with more tenses, and at the sentence level, we may consider insertions (such as adverbial ones).

[10]The corpus under study has been chosen for several reasons: its size (vast, thus providing many examples for the studied structures), its availability (freely downloadable on the Gutenberg project website) and its writing quality (normalised French).

added. In query (c), the focus is on precision because of the added syntactical constraint: the verb has to be followed by a preposition followed by an infinitive verb. In the final and delivered query(d), admitting insertions yields twenty matches.

6. Toutes les périphrases verbales à valeur inchoative.

(((se|s')(<être>|<E>)<mettre>à)|(<commencer> à))(<WF>|<E>)<V+INF>

a. (<se mettre>|<commencer>) (87 matches dont aucun se mettre)

b. ((se|s')(<être>|<E>))<mettre>|<commencer> (147 matches)

c. (((se|s')(<être>|<E>)<mettre>à)|(<commencer> à))<V+INF> (75 matches)

d. (((se|s')(<être>|<E>)<mettre>à)|(<commencer> à))(<WF|<E>)<V+INF> (95 matches)

1. de la logique. Le conventionnel commençait à haleter ; l'asthme de l'agonie
2. frappe, nous la laissons faire. 1812 commence à nous désarmer . En 1813, la lâche rupture de
3. et pourtant hérissés; car ils commençaient à pousser un peu, et semblaient n
4. un oreiller tout trouvé, il se mit à déboucler une des courroies. En ce

Figure 1 – STU1 student's process of designing a query

To summarise, this mainly methodological exercise has trained the students to adopt a systematic approach: keeping track of their attempts and results until they reach a satisfactory conclusion.

Fourth activity example (4T): training exercise

The following activity combines autonomous and supervised work. Its wording (W) is: 'Retrieve in the text 'Les Misérables' through a NooJ query, all matches in which '*prier*' is not employed with its religious meaning'. The vast volume of this corpus permits us to observe that '*prier*' can mean either 'pray' or 'beg', depending on the syntactic structure of the sentence.

Following a systematic methodology, the students aim to list all the corpus sequences that contain '<prier>' (QI) in order to delimit a sub-corpus which includes the whole set of the required sequences. Once this recall control procedure is complete, they analyse the retrieved sequences in order to divide them into what does and what does not correspond to the semantic requirement (the 'beg' meaning).

In Figure 2, another student (hereafter, STU2) identifies three sets -originally distinguished by colours-: the sequences numbered {1, 12} constitute (a part of the) target set T; on the contrary, the noisy results are divided into two sets: N1 contains the particular cases of the '*prie-Dieu*' ({5, 6, 7} sequences); and N2 covers different structures for the 'pray' meaning ({2, 3, 4, 8, 9, 10, 11, 13} sequences).

a. <prier>

1.	La visite terminée, il fit	prier	le directeur de vouloir bien venir jusque chez
2.	de lui, oubliant la nourriture et le sommeil,	priant	Dieu pour l'âme du condamné et priant
3.	priant Dieu pour l'âme du condamné et	priant	le condamné pour la sienne propre. Il lui
4.	celui que les frères chassent retrouve le Père.	Priez	, croyez, entrez dans la vie! le Père est
5.	Dieu. Il avait dans son oratoire deux chaises	prie	-Dieu en paille, et un fauteuil à bras
6.	du salon d'hiver, dans l'oratoire les	prie	-Dieu, et le fauteuil dans la chambre à
7.	le fauteuil de paille. Devant le lit, un	prie	-Dieu, emprunté à l'oratoire. Deux portraits dans
8.	prochain fait, Dieu le permet. Bornons-nous à	prier	Dieu quand nous croyons qu'un
9.	nous croyons qu'un danger arrive sur nous.	Prions	-le, non pour nous, mais pour que notre
10.	madame Magloire, je rentre dans ma chambre, je	prie	pour lui, et je m'endors. Je suis
11.	Mais à présent le pli est pris. Nous	prions	toutes les deux, nous avons peur ensemble, et
12.	-Avant de vous répondre, dit-il, je vous	prie	de me pardonner. Je viens d'avoir un
13.	rentés, habiles, acceptés du monde, sachant	prier	, sans doute, mais sachant aussi solliciter,

Figure 2 – STU2's sub-corpus division into relevant and irrelevant items

STU2 analyses the seven final relevant sentences ({1, 12, 18, 23, 27, 32, 34} which he describes at a syntactic level (cf. Figure 3). These structures are finally unified in the last query (c), *<prier><WF>*(de|d')<WF>*<V>* which retrieves the eight sentences listed immediately below.

1. prier + det + nom + de + verbe
12. prier + de + pronCOD + verbe
18. pron COD + de + pron COI + verbe
23. pron COD + prier + de + verbe
27. prier + nom + det + nom + de + verbe
32. pron COD + prier + de + verbe
34. prier + det + nom + de + pron adv + verbe

b. <prier><WF>*de<WF>*<V>

c. <prier><WF>*(de|d')<WF>*<V>

1.	La visite terminée, il fit	prier le directeur de vouloir bien venir	jusque chez lui. --Monsieur le
2.	répondre, dit-il, je vous	prie de me pardonner	. Je viens d'avoir un
3.	de la distillerie et le	pria de le payer	. Le maître ne proféra pas
4.	le maire, je viens vous	prier de vouloir bien provoquer	près de l'autorité ma
5.	monsieur le président pour le	prier de vouloir bien assister	monsieur Madeleine et le reconduire
6.	dit-il. Elle lut.--«Je	prie monsieur le curé de veiller	sur tout ce que je
7.	Valjean l'aborda et la	pria d'aller lui changer	ce billet de mille francs
8.	au présent. Cela dit, nous	prions le lecteur d'en tenir note	, et nous continuons. Jean Valjean

Figure 3 – STU2's interpretation of relevant sequences retrieved and query design process

To sum up, this exercise deals with polysemy, the prepositional regime of verbs in French, and deals with the insertions diversity issue, and their unification in the NooJ formalisation (ex: <WF>*). From a methodological point of view, it also shows why the query is modified on the basis of the concordances retrieved and of their own knowledge.

Fifth activity example (5E): evaluation exercise

The following activity tests the student abilities to identify a linguistic phenomenon by 'decoding' a grammar which is its (partial) representation, and finally to analyse its deficiencies.

We present, in an evaluation work, a NooJ graphical grammar to the students and ask them to recognise firstly (1) 'which linguistic phenomenon this grammar is trying to describe'.
As we can see in Figure 4, the graph (hereafter, Gr) includes a sequence of one pronominal subject followed by one verbal form (any verb in the conditional mood or present tense) followed by 'if' in French (<si>) followed by one pronominal subject followed by another verbal form (any verb in the present tense, simple past or past perfect).

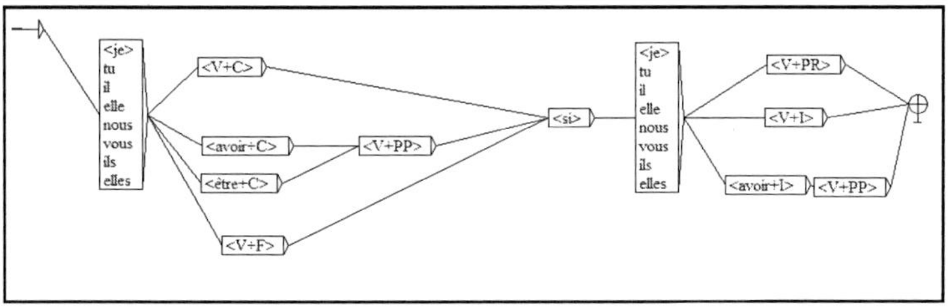

Figure 4 – Graphical NooJ grammar to 'decode'

Students should detect a basic intent to encode full hypothetical sentences (consequences with the associated condition introduced by <si>) basing their conclusion on the presence of the first, second and third conditionals in the graph. Thus, a (third conditional) sentence like '*J'aurais accepté si j'avais su*'[11] (S1) does match.

However, we also want to show the students (2) the incompletion and inaccuracy of its grammar for describing *any* hypothetical sentence in French. Thus we ask them (2a) to provide one example of an *incorrect* sentence which *can* be recognised by this grammar and (2b) two examples of *correct* sentences which *cannot* be recognised by this grammar.

[11] S1 could be translated by 'I would have accepted if I had known' and obeys the consequence-condition construction.

(2a) This part of the exercise serves as the evidence for the lack of precision[12] in Gr in relation to the intuitive achieved task (expressing hypothetical sentences). The grammar is unable to reject erroneous combinations in which the tense agreement between both consequence and condition phrases is not respected.

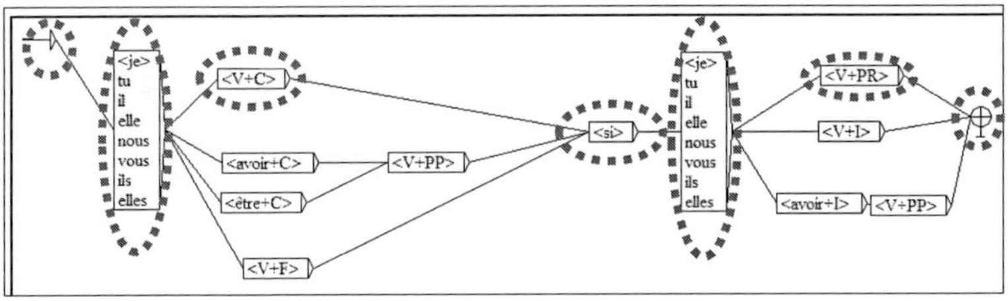

Figure 5 – Example of a wrong tenses sequence recognised by the grammar Gr

(2b) Through a detailed Gr analysis, students can uncover the syntactic recall defects for which we draw up a non-exhaustive list below.

- It only takes into account structures in which the consequence precedes the condition, so correct sentences constructed following the inverted *condition – consequence* order cannot be retrieved and turn to *silences*. S2 '<u>Si j'avais su j'aurais accepté</u>'[13] would not match.
- Gr is unable to capture structures like 'J'aurais accepté <u>la proposition/de venir (I1)</u> si je <u>l'(I2)</u> avais su' since it doesn't admit many variations: neither insertions between the consequence verb and the hypothetical phrase (for postponed complements, like I1) nor insertion within the verbal forms (for pre-verbal complements, like I2) nor negations/adverbs placed between the auxiliary and the past form of the verb in the condition phrase.
- Gr only accepts pronominal subjects and excludes, as a consequence, the sentences with nominal phrase subjects.

[12]In applications like corpus analysis, the precision of the rules has no such importance since texts are real human productions, so it is not necessary to check their correctness, but within our combined approach of NLP and FLE, this kind of exercise underlines the hypothesis specific syntax and morphosyntax in French and highlights the importance of agreement rules/conventions in a natural language.

[13]S2 could be translated by 'If I had known, I would have accepted' and obeys the condition-consequence construction.

- Gr ignores one verbal sequence type: only verbs which use the '*avoir*' auxiliary in the compound past forms[14] will be selected.

One obvious possible extension of this activity might be to effectively improve the grammar in order to catch a maximum of structures and to achieve a really natural sentence description.

We mention that such an activity would hardly be representative as an evaluation activity without adequate training. We have used in class a similar NooJ manual exercise (Silberztein, pp. 60-61) which presents a graphical grammar for the preverbal pronouns. It constitutes a base to lead the learner to reach the complete and correct local grammar. Step by step, the students train their graphical grammar command and are guided towards generalising the grammar by considering optional insertions (negation for example), while also taking into account morpho-syntactic transformations depending on the context (elisions) to reach completion. The use of a corpus as a validation resource for the formalised descriptions is also introduced.

Conclusions

In doing these activities with NooJ, students are encouraged to carry out an active use of their linguistic background while formalising, using NLP tools, a linguistic structure: going from simple intuitions to real languages, students become aware of the natural languages flexibility - thus FLE skills meet NLP skills.

A preliminary analysis of some classical NLP applications provides students with an awareness of the difficulties of a correct linguistic processing. Emulating NLP and linguistic researchers, students are able to grasp basic linguistic procedures and to value the relevance of well-established linguistic expertise, developing systematic methodological skills and testing the efficacy of measuring instruments. In this sense, our exercise makes it possible to highlight the skills (multilevel linguistic formalisation) and resources (grammars and dictionaries, including lexicon-grammars) implied in the task of language processing in order to overcome its obstacles (ambiguity, polysemy, etc.).

The language engineering platform NooJ, through its user-friendly, open-access and multilingual interface, provides a twofold epistemological goal: a methodological one (to be familiar with a NLP processing

[14]In the French past perfect, the auxiliary verb can be '*avoir*' or '*être*', depending on the lexical verb.

application) and a theoretical one (for a better understanding of linguistic structures). Putting the tools of NLP techniques at the service of theoretical linguistic knowledge further achieves a secondary objective of great practical relevance in the pedagogical sense: it counteracts the commonplace reluctance of students of Humanities and Social Sciences to use technology and computational techniques.

A further step would be to design activities (in collaboration between teachers and students) oriented to strengthen the synergy between technical learning and linguistic theoretical background in order to better discriminate more specific linguistic features (ie meanings, tenses, etc.), particularly in the French language.

References

Chevalier, Gisèle. 2005. 'Laboratoire de Syntaxe NooJ.' http://www.nooj4nlp.net/LaboSyntaxe.pdf.

Garrigues, Mylène. 1999. 'Nouvelles concordances pour l'enseignement des langues.' *Linguisticae Investigationes* XXII: 59–70. doi:10.1075/li.22.1-2.05gar.

Silberztein, Max. 2003. 'NooJ Manual.' http://www.nooj4nlp.net/NooJManual.pdf

Silberztein, Max, and Agnès Tutin. 2005. 'NooJ, un outil TAL pour l'enseignement des langues. Application pour l'étude de la morphologie lexicale en FLE' *Alsic* 8 (Vol. 8, n° 2) (December 15): 123–134.

BUILDING FAMILY TREES WITH NOOJ

KRISTINA KOCIJAN AND MARKO POŽEGA

Abstract

This paper proposes NooJ as a pre-processing tool for building an ontology based project ie building family trees from Croatian obituaries. The names of an ego (deceased) and his family members, extracted from the list of grieving family members, are mapped into specific family relationships and extracted in an XML-like format which is then sent to Python for hierarchical presentation.

Family relationships in Croatia

The words used to describe family relationships in Croatian language make quite a rich addition to Croatian kinship terminology since separate terms are used for family members (relationships created by birth) and in-laws (relationships created by marriage). The terminology also differs among different geographical areas of Croatia.

The main idea behind this project is to find which kinship terms are in use in Croatia today by using on-line obituaries, and to make a graphical representation of those terms for each deceased person.

Tanocki (1986) describes 1,699 distinct relationship terms. However, we found only 99 in the corpus we used. This is important information which implies that the 'old' kinship terminology is being replaced with a less detailed one, ie multiple terms are being replaced with one term. When comparing the list of terms used in contemporary obituaries to that of Tanocki's (1986) kinship terms, we conclude that this change in terminology is only occurring at more distant levels of relationship, while closer relationships (mother, father, son, daughter, sister, and brother) use the same terminology regardless of time or geographical region.

However, it is not the purpose of this paper to explain either the reason for this terminological shift or when and where it started. Jozić et al. (2010), Tikvica (2009) and Šokota (1998) have more to say on that subject. In this paper, the authors will merely try to define a list of kinship terms currently used in on-line obituaries in order to produce their hierarchical representation. NooJ is used for finding and annotating family relationships and Python for drawing family trees.

Both Pleše (1998) and Tanocki (1986) suggest that there is a difference between the normative and used terminology. This is also certainly the case of the modern Croatian language and it is very likely that the terms used in writing obituaries are not the ones used in everyday communication by those who write obituaries. This is the reason why we do not hold our list of kinship terms as the final list of family relationships in contemporary Croatian language.

In brief, our task is to extract information (personal names) from obituaries and fill the prepared slots (relation types) in order to present a system (family tree) that has an ontological nature (Biemann, 2005).

This is not the first use of NooJ as a pre-processing tool for an ontology-related project (Salza, 2014). Although our topics differ, we both recognized NooJ (Silberztein, 2003) as a powerful tool for NLP.

The process for building our ontological framework can be described with the following four steps: preparing a corpus from Croatian obituaries, applying NooJ's syntactic analysis to recognize the kinship terms, annotating the text with the xml notation within NooJ, drawing the tree from an xml file with Python. We proceed with a more detailed description of each step.

Preparing the corpus

For our preliminary research, we build a small corpus of 44 obituaries published on-line on the obituaries site (http://www.osmrtnice.hr/) during the month of November 2013. This corpus was used as our training corpus for the building of the initial syntactic grammars.

After we obtained 100% of both precision and recall on training corpus, we applied the grammar to two test corpora constructed from obituaries from the two separate web sites. The first test corpus (Text A) has 4,498 obituaries posted to the http://www.osmrtnice.hr/ web site during June and December of 2013 and January, February, March and April of 2014 and the second (Text B) has 312 obituaries posted to the web site http://www.osmrtnica.net/ during May, June, July, August, November and December of 2013 as well as February, March and April of 2014. The obituaries that had only the name of the deceased, without any family members, were removed from the test corpora.

Before we started to work on the grammars, it was important to recognise the structure of an obituary, which can be split into 5 sections.

The first section is (1) a notice of death, followed by (2) the list of relationships of the deceased to the other members of the family describing how that person was related to those who are left behind. This is a list of comma separated, gender dependant relationships like mother, sister, grandmother, great grandmother, mother-in-law, aunt. What follows is (3) the name of the person (Figure 3) and (4) the information about the funeral. At the end (5) the list of bereaved family members, with additional information about the relationship of that person to the deceased, is provided. The list contains two types of constructions. One is the nominative construction that holds a relationship followed by the first name and none or all of the following: last name, nickname, 'with a spouse', 'and children' as in the following examples[1]:

- *kći Ruža* 'daughter Ruža'
- *kći Ruža Matić* 'daughter Ruža Matić'
- *kći Ruža sa suprugom Markom* 'daughter Ruža with husband Marko'
- *kći Ruža sa suprugom Markom i djecom* 'daughter Ruža with husband Marko and children'
- *kći Ruža sa suprugom Markom i djecom Anom i Perom* 'daughter Ruža with husband Marko and children Ana and Pero'

The second construction is in the genitive and it holds expressions like 'family of (deceased)' followed by the first name and none or all of the following: last name, nickname, 'with a spouse', 'and children' as in the following examples:

- *obitelj sestre Ruže* 'family of sister Ruža
- *obitelj pokojne sestre Ruže* 'family of the deceased sister Ruža
- *obitelj sestre Ruže sa suprugom Markom i djecom Anom i Perom* 'family of sister Ruža with husband Marko and children Ana and Pero'

Building grammars

After applying the preliminary lexical analysis in NooJ, including only Croatian dictionaries, to both corpora we detected which kinship terms were not present in the main dictionary. This problem was solved with a two-step process. The first step was to add to the main dictionary the

---

[1]Out of respect for the deceased and his/her families, all the names in examples used in this paper will be scrambled and used only to show the patterns that are being described.

missing kinship terms found in NooJ's UNKNOWN list including only terms that describe blood relationships between grandparents and grandchildren. All kinship terms in the dictionary are further described with the new semantic feature *+obt* as an abbreviation of the Croatian word for family (*obitelj*).

With the second step we needed to cover all remaining blood relationships (those hierarchically above the grandparents and below grandchildren) and all of the half-relationships (obtained either by remarriage or adoption) where possible. We opted to build a lexical grammar that recognises a large number of relationships that are rarely found in texts.

The grammar checks if there is a noun in the dictionary that has *+obt* notation and recognizes any such word that has one prefix '*polu'* or 'po' as a half-relationship or one or more occurrences of the prefix '*pra'* or '*šukun'* for the distinct kinship relations. Thus, words like ***pra**baba* (great-grandmother), ***prapra**baka* (great-great grandma), ***praprapra**teta* (great-great-great aunt) or ***pra**unuk* (great-grandson), but also words like ***polu**brat* (half-brother) or ***po**majka* (stepmother) are recognised. However, the word *pastorak* (stepson) would not be recognised with our lexical grammar and was, among a few others that are not derived in the above described manner, added directly to the dictionary. The dictionary now consists of 143 kinship terms with the following distribution: 86 terms of blood relationships, 46 terms of marriage relationships, 5 terms used for blood or marriage relationships and 6 terms used for relationships obtained through adoption or remarriage.

After having defined all of the kinship terms, we constructed syntactic grammars for recognising relationships among the deceased and his/her family members. Four main syntactic grammars were built for this project: a) for disambiguating personal names; b) for annotating the deceased person (section 3 in the obituary); c) for annotating the irrelevant text (sections 1 and 4 in the obituary); d) for annotating the individual relationship (section 5 in the obituary). Grammars for sections a, b and d will be shown, described, explained and evaluated in the following sections.

Disambiguation of personal names

After the preliminary lexical analysis, we were surprised to discover a very high number of unknown first and last names even though the Croatian dictionary of personal nouns has 36,359 last names and 5,414 first names (2,809 female and 2,605 male) (Vučković, 2009; Bekavac,

2005). Since the recognition of personal names was important for the project we needed to find a solution that would work not only for the corpus we had but also for any future additions to that corpus. We were faced with two types of problems concerning: unknown words (words missing from the dictionary) and ambiguous words. Following further analysis we were able to recognise five categories of missing names:

- foreign names – not characteristic for Croatia: Max, Carmen, Ellie
- different spelling variants of the name that exists in our dictionary: Mihael (in the dictionary) – Mikael or Mihail (not in the dictionary)
- names used for both genders but found only as M or F in our dictionary: Nedjeljko (M) – Nedjeljka (F) (same genitive form that causes problem in construction *sa suprugom Nedjeljkom* 'with spouse Nedjeljkom')
- name used both as a first and last name: Vukman – last name (in the dictionary) – first name (not in the dictionary)
- misspelled names.

The second type of problem is related to ambiguity. We recognise two types of ambiguity: inner and outer homographs. It is very common for Croatian nouns to have the same forms in different cases (eg singular Nominative, Accusative and Vocative, or plural Dative, Locative and Instrumental). This type of ambiguity is marked as inner ambiguity and is disambiguated with the grammar in Figure 1. Consequently all nouns marked as proper nouns in Genitive or Nominative case that are found immediately after the common noun in the same case with the semantic tag **+obt** (+family) are disambiguated as proper nouns <N+vl>.

The list of bereaved family members is mainly populated with the Nominative phrases like: *brat Nikola* (brother Nikola), *sestra Nada* (sister Nada), but in the construction where the whole family is listed in the form 'family of (deceased) brother Nikola', the expression following the Nominative noun 'family' is in the Genitive. If the personal name in this expression is male with both first and last names given, both names are in the Genitive case (*obitelj brata Nikole Jurića* -> 'family of Nikola Jurić's brother'). However, if that person is female, than her first name is in the Genitive case, but the last name remains in the Nominative case (*obitelj sestre Nade Jurić* -> 'family of Nada Jurić's sister').

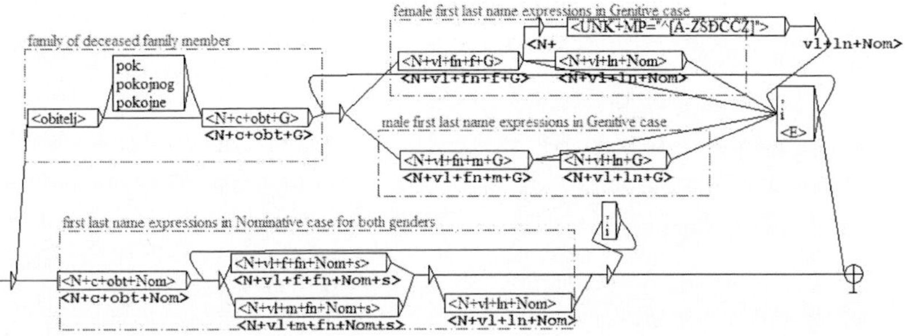

Figure 1 – Disambiguation of personal names

The next subset of proper names that are ambiguous in the Croatian language appears as common nouns (*Nada* -> *nada* <N> 'hope'), as well as adjectives (*Mila* -> *mila* <A> 'dear') or verbs (*Mare* -> *mare* <V> 'to care'). A new grammar (Figure 2) was built to solve the problem of unknown names and names marked as another word category. The logic behind this grammar is to annotate the unknown word depending on the kinship term that precedes it while taking into account the gender, number and case of that term. If a kinship term is given in the singular form, than the name that follows it inherits the gender in the following fashion: a female relationship in the singular is followed by a female first name, and male relationship in the singular is followed by a male first name. The same is true for the plural female relationship that is followed by a list of female comma-separated names in the singular form with the last two names connected with 'and'.

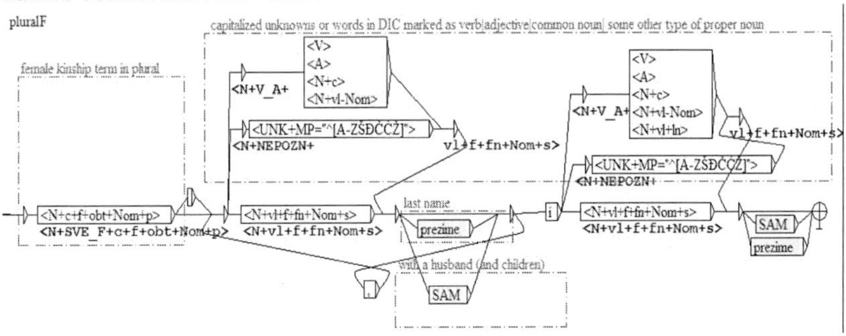

Figure 2 – Annotating unknown and wrong type names after the plural female kinship term

However, when some plural male or neuter term is used followed by a list of names, the problem arises. The list can hold both male and female names, known and unknown names or even words that belong to other word categories. Fortunately, this list of kinship terms is short and it includes the following: *djeca* (children), *nećaci* (nephews), *pastorci* (stepchildren), *praunučad* or *praunuci* (great-grandchildren), *rođaci* (cousins), *unučad* or *unuci* (grandchildren). We used some logical operators that helped us solve the following two possibilities:

a) IF only two names follow the plural male term AND known name is female THEN the one unknown name must be male
b) IF more than two names follow the plural male term AND only one is unknown AND all known are of female gender THEN the unknown must be male.

For all other combinations, a separate, more detailed study is needed.

Annotating the deceased person

The deceased person is written with capitalised (one or two) first and (one or two) last names in the Nominative case. Very often, the male names have their nicknames written immediately following their names, with or without brackets. In some cases, the name is preceeded with a title attached to the name by virtue of office, rank or as a mark of respect (see node <N+titula> in Figure 3).

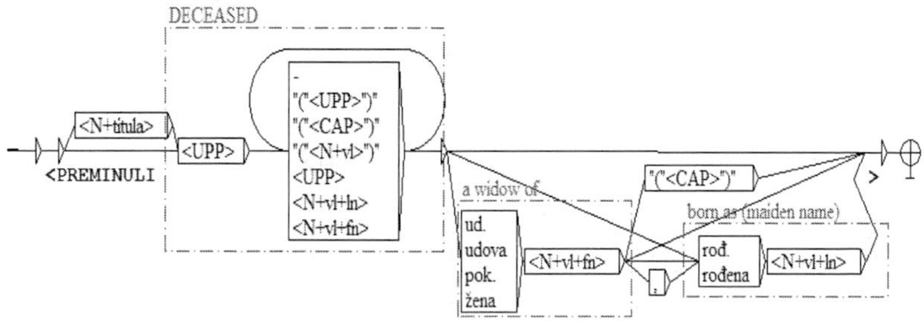

Figure 3 – Recognising the deceased person

After the male names, constructions that mark whose son he was, may be found. After the female names two additional constructions are found, either separate or in combination, marking whose wife or widow she was, and/or her maiden name (Figure 3) as in the following examples:

- *gđa. RUŽA MATIĆ rođ. Ružić* 'Mrs. Ruža Matić born Ružić'
- *gđa. RUŽA MATIĆ žena Markova rođ. Ružić* 'Mrs. Ruža Matić wife of Marko born Ružić'

The grammar in Figure 3 is a subgraph of a larger graph where its exact context is defined. The grammar has the following performance: Text A (P: 0.95; R: 0.82; f: 0.88) and Text B (P: 1; R: 0.99; f: 0.99). Some city names that are MWUs, like *Kaštel Lukšić* or New Jersey, are falsely recognised with this grammar, as well as other capitalised words found after the name of the person (due to the missing full stop after the name). These occurrences are the main cause of lower precision in Text A.

Recognising the individual relationships

The Croatian language offers kinship terms for all gender-dependant relationships like, for example :

- pašanac –wife's sister's husband — *svastika* –wife's sister
- šurjak –wife's brother — *šurjakinja* –wife's brother's wife
- djever –husband's brother — *zaova* –husband's sister
- *svak* –sister's husband — *jetrva* –husband's brother's wife

However, not all parts of Croatia use the same terminology. Sometimes, *šogor* or *kunjad* replace four different male relationships (*pašanac, šurjak, djever* and *svak*) and *šogorica* or *kunjada* four different female relationships (*svastika, šurjakinja, zaova, jetrva*). To get a more unified list of relationships, only one term was used where multiple possibilities exist, eg we used the term <MATI> for occurrences *mama, majka, mati* (mom, mother).

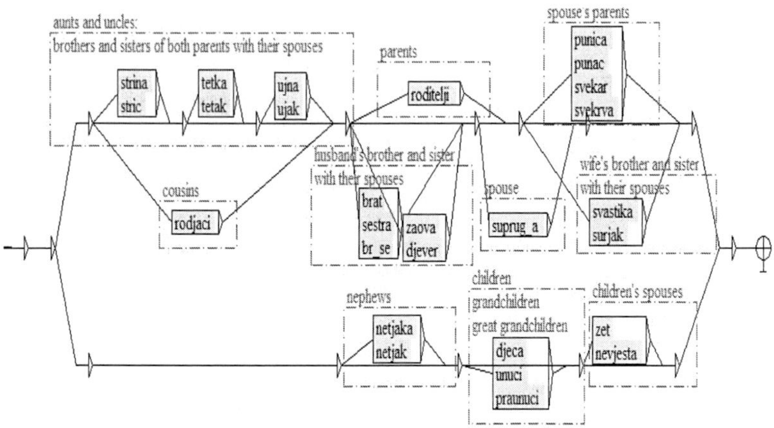

Figure 4 – Recognising each family member of the deceased

The more detailed subgraph, describing the relationship *sestra* (sister) is given in Figure 5. The main graph *sestra* is in the middle while its subgraph <obtPok> describing the constructions like 'the family of the deceased', is positioned above and the subgraph describing female name <nameF> below it. The graphs of other relationships are similar and are gender dependent, ie <nameF> is replaced with the subgraph describing male names <nameM> for the male-directed relationships.

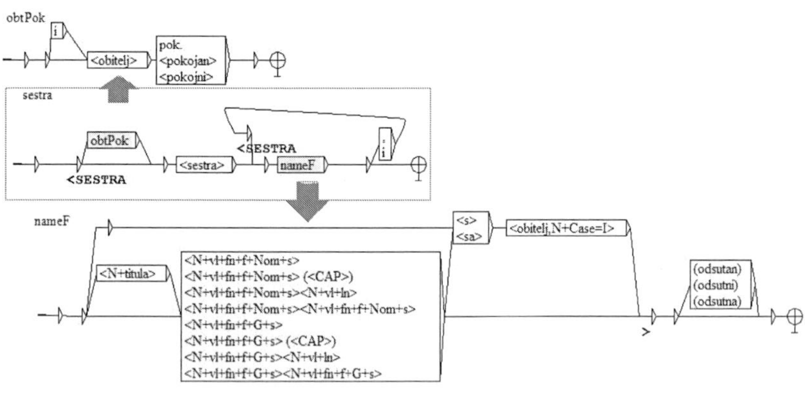

Figure 5 – Detailed description of the node '*sestra'* (sister)

Unlike Japanese, Chinese or Korean (Baik et al, 2010), there is no distinction between the older or younger siblings in Croatian kinship terminology. Figure 4 presents a main grammar with subgraphs describing each relationship found in the corpus. This grammar has a somewhat better performance on Text B (P: 0,98; R: 0,93; f: 0,95) than on Text A (P: 0,95; R: 0,85; f: 0,90).

Building the XML File

The last grammar that is applied to an obituary is the grammar that produces an XML notation for each family. The main node, marked <OBITELJ> (family), has a set of atribute-value pairs. The first pair is always the deceased and his/her name. In other pairs, an attribute is the name of the relationship and the value is a name. Thus, an example for the deceased person MARA KEVO and a list of the grieving family members 'daughter Ruža, son-in-law Marko and grandchildren Ana and Pero' is rewritten as:

<OBITELJ PREM='MARA KEVO' KĆER='Ruža' ZET='Marko' UNUKA='Ana' UNUK='Pero'>

Drawing the relationships with Python

We built an algorithm in Python to process the XML files with predefined family relations. The main purpose of this algorithm is to generate a graphic representation of the family relations and the family members (family trees). We used one of Python's modules, Pydot, not to draw graphs or visual representations of data, but to send commands and instructions to the software application called 'Graphviz'.

Following our first theoretical idea for the algorithm, we imagined a simple GUI which takes 1 argument as the input ("Name of XML file") and returns the graphic images of the family trees (family tree relations). After some time, we ran into a problem with large data processing and organisation of outputs, so we determined 2 inputs: 'Directory of multiple XML files' and 'Directory of output files'. This solution helps the algorithm to process multiple XML files in one loop and output the images to defined directories and subdirectories named after the XML filename. The name of each output file (.gif, .pdf, .png, .jpg) is defined by the name of the corresponding family it represents, thus making the outputs easier to search and organise.

There are three main steps in our Python algorithm. In the first part of the algorithm each line of the document is parsed and attribute-value pairs are extracted into lists and diagrams in form (TAG, Name). In the second step, the FOR loop iterates through all the diagrams in the family list and checks for values of TAG. From those values the algorithm coordinates and organises specific predefined clusters according to the Name variable. After organising all names to matching clusters, the algorithm checks the gender of the person and sends a command to Graphviz to create a cluster and write names within that cluster. The main part of the third step is setting relationships between clusters and adding empty clusters to make the graph look like a family tree. Finally, the graph is closed and the image is placed into a predefined directory.

Because of some limitations within Graphviz, we decided on a unique output solution (http://darhiv.ffzg.unizg.hr/4752/). The deceased person (ego) is highlighted and oriented in the centre of the graph and all other family members are placed in relation to him/her. Individuals are grouped into clusters (Children, Parents, Cousins etc). The edge of every cluster is colour-coded according to the relation (red → blood relatives, green→ spouse, brown → spouse's family) and the gender (blue → male, purple → female). However, only a spouse, parents and parents–in-law of an ego are known. Marital connections of other relatives are not marked since they were ambiguously stated in the text.

Unsolved Problems

There are still two main types of unsolved problems that will be hard to find the (unambiguous) solutions to. The first type makes building a family tree from all obituaries impossible and the second one makes it a challenge. The first list would include those occurrences from which a list of bereaved family members is built:

a) only names, without the type of relation (*njegova Maria, Ana, Ivo i Nikola* - his Maria, Ana, Ivo and Nikola);
b) only relationships, without the personal names (*sinovi i kćeri s obiteljima* - sons and daughters with their families);
c) only the last names (*obitelj Frankopan* - family Frankopan)-

The second type includes:

a) list of (mixed) names given after the plural relationship that appear both as male or female names (*unuci Matija i Saša* - grandchildren Matija and Saša);
b) two or more names after the relationship that can be either last name or second part of first name (*kći Ana Franka* - daughter Ana Franka);
c) ungrammatical constructions, eg - there is no comma before *i* (and) (*unučad Luka, Nina, Ivan, i Andrija.* - grandchildren Luka, Nina, Ivan, and Andrija).

Conclusion

In this paper, we described the process of information extraction with NooJ in order to fill an ontological framework dealing with Croatian family relationships.

Due to the problems described in the previous sections, it is not possible to build a family tree from all obituaries. However, those which have a list of bereaved family members in the form of relationship-personal name(s) easily fit into the prepared framework.

In a future work, in order to improve our recall and precision, we intend to further enhance our grammars describing additional contexts and to add more frequent personal names to NooJ dictionary.

References

Baik, Songiy and Hee-Rahk Chae. 2010. An Ontological Analysis of Japanese and Chinese Kinship Terms. In *PACLIC*, 349–56. http://www.aclweb.org/anthology-new/Y/Y10/Y10-1039.pdf.

Bekavac, Božo. 2005. *Strojno prepoznavanje naziva u suvremenim hrvatskim tekstovima*. (Machine Named Entity Recognition in Contemporary Croatian Texts.) PhD Thesis. Zagreb: Department of Linguistics, Faculty of Humanities and Social Sciences, University of Zagreb.

Biemann, Chris. 2005. Ontology Learning from Text: A Survey of Methods. In *LDV Forum*, 20 (2): 75–93.

Jozić, Željko, Perina Vukša, and Dijana Ćurković. 2012. *Nazivi za bratova sina u hrvatskome jeziku.* (Brother's son in the Croatian language.) *Rasprave: Časopis Instituta za hrvatski jezik i jezikoslovlje* 37 (2): 393–422.

Pleše, Iva. 1998. *Neki aspekti hrvatske terminologije srodstva.* (Some Aspects of the Croatian Kinship Terminology.) *Etnološka tribina: godišnjak Hrvatskog etnološkog društva* 0351-1944 (28): 59–78.

Salza, Edoardo. 2014. Using NooJ as a System for (Shallow) Ontology Population from Italian Texts. In *Formalising Natural Languages with NooJ 2013: Selected Papers from the NooJ 2013 International Conference,* S. Koeva, S. Mesfar, M. Silberztein Eds. 191–202. Newcastle Upon Tyne: Cambridge Scholars Publishing.

Silberztein, Max. 2003. *NooJ Manual*. (223 pages) http://www.nooj4nlp.net/NooJManual.pdf.

Šokota, Mirjana. 1999. *Rodbinsko-svojbinski i slični nazivi u Ždrelcu.* ('Family–in-laws' and similar names in Ždrelac.') *Čakavska Rič. Polugodišnjak za proučavanje čakavske riči* 26 (1-2): 33–44.

Tanocki, Franjo. 1986. *Rječnik Rodbinskih Naziva.* (Dictionary of kinship terms.) 2. izd. Osijek: Revija, Izdavački centar radničkog sveučilišta "*Božidar Maslarić.*"

Tikvica, Ljubica. 2009. *O hrvatskoj terminologiji srodstva -Neki aspekti obradbe u suvremenim rječnicima hrvatskoga jezika.* ('About Croatian Kinship Terminology – Some aspects in contemporary Croatian dictionaries'). *Hum*, no. 5: 106–24.

Vučković, Kristina. 2009. *Model parsera za hrvatski jezik.* ('Model of a Parser for Croatian Language.') PhD Thesis. Zagreb: Department of Information and Communication Sciences, Faculty of Humanities and Social Sciences, University of Zagreb.

KNOWLEDGE-BASED CLIR MODEL FOR SPECIFIC DOMAIN COLLECTIONS

JOHANNA MONTI, MARIO MONTELEONE AND MARIA PIA DI BUONO[1]

Abstract

The effectiveness of Cross-language Information Retrieval (CLIR) applications clearly depends on the quality of translation, thus inaccurate or incorrect translations may cause serious problems in retrieving relevant information. Indeed, a very frequent source of mistranslations in specific domain texts is represented by multiword units (MWUs), and particularly, terminological word compounds: Processing and translating these forms of compound words is not a straightforward task since their morpho-syntactic and linguistic behaviour is quite complex and varied according to the various types and their translations are practically unpredictable. Our contribution presents an outline of the knowledge-based resources (dictionary, ontology and rules), developed by means of NooJ and used in the development of a knowledge-based CLIR system.

Introduction

In Cross-language Information Retrieval (CLIR) applications information is searched for by means of a query expressed in the user's mother tongue. This query is translated into the desired foreign language (query translation) and the results are translated back into the user's mother tongue (document translation). Translation is usually based on bilingual or multilingual Machine Readable Dictionaries (MRD), Machine Translation (MT) and parallel corpora.

---

[1] Johanna Monti is author of the Abstract, the Introduction, the Related work and the Translation routines, Mario Monteleone is author of the Bilingual Machine Readable Dictionaries and Local Grammars, Maria Pia di Buono is author of the System workflow and the Conceptual Model and Semantic Annotation.

CLIR applications are often used in domain specific collections, such as the Europeana Connect[2], which is aimed at facilitating multilingual access to Europeana.eu, an internet portal that acts as an interface to millions of books, paintings, films, museum objects and archival records that have been digitised throughout Europe. In domain specific texts compound terms, mainly noun compounds, are very frequent: in some cases they account for 90% of the terms belonging to a domain specific language and they are a very frequent source of mistranslations (Monti, 2012).

CLIR success clearly depends on the quality of translation and therefore inaccurate or incorrect translations may cause serious problems in retrieving relevant information.

Contrary to generic simple words, terminological word compounds are mono-referential, ie they are unambiguous and refer only to one specific concept in one special language, even if they may occur in more than one domain. Their meaning, similar to all compound words, cannot be directly inferred by a non-expert from the different elements of the compounds, given that it depends on the specific area and the concept it refers to.

Processing and translating compound words is not an easy task since their morpho-syntactic and semantic behaviour is quite complex and varied according to the different types and their translations are practically unpredictable.

The main contribution of this paper is the design of an ontology-based CLIR system for specific domain collections, which properly addresses MWU processing and translation. This experiment has been set up for the Italian/English language pair in the archeological domain and can be easily extended to other language pairs as well as to other domains.

Related work

There are several approaches to CLIR: they are either based on bilingual or multilingual Machine Readable Dictionaries (MRD), Machine Translation (MT), parallel corpora and finally ontologies. For a description of the different approaches see Hull & Greffenstette (1996), Oard & Dorr (1996), Pirkola (1999) and more recently Oard (2009). Both MRD-based and MT-based CLIR are very popular but they present several shortcomings especially in relation to domain-specific contexts because of the lack of consideration for MWUs, a very frequent and productive linguistic phenomenon in Languages for Specific Purposes (LSPs).

[2]http://www.europeanaconnect.eu/

Various techniques have been proposed to reduce the errors due to the presence of MWUs introduced during query translation. Among these techniques, phrasal translation, co-occurrence analysis, and query expansion are the most popular.

Concerning MT-based CLIR, MWU identification and translation problems are far from being solved. Recently, several papers based on human assessment of the translation quality of specific multiwords have highlighted that current MT is still unable to correctly translate these complex linguistic phenomena. Ramisch et al. (2013) discovered that current SMT technology can only translate 27% of phrasal verbs correctly. Barreiro et al. (2013 and 2014) show that, for distinct reasons, multiwords remain a problematic area for MT independently of the approach, and require adequate linguistic quality evaluation metrics founded on a systematic categorisation of errors by MT expert linguists.

Increasing attention has been paid to MWU processing in MT and translation technologies in general since it has been acknowledged that MT cannot be effective without proper handling of MWUs of all kinds. One of the latest initiatives in this research area is the MTSUMMIT workshop series on 'Multiword Units in Machine Translation and Translation Technology' (Monti et al., 2013). MWU processing and translation in Statistical Machine Translation (SMT), the dominant paradigm in MT, has only very recently begun to be addressed and different solutions have been proposed so far. However, they are basically considered either as a problem of automatically learning and integrating translations or as a problem of word alignment.

Current approaches to MWU processing move towards the integration of phrase-based models with linguistic knowledge and scholars are starting to use linguistic resources, either hand-crafted dictionaries and grammars or data-driven ones, in order to identify and process MWUs as single units. Monti (2012) provides a thorough overview of the various research approaches in this field.

Ontologies are also used in CLIR and are considered by several scholars to be a promising research area for improving the effectiveness of Information Extraction (IE) techniques, particularly for technical-domain queries. Volk et al. (2003) use ontologies as *interlingua* in CLIR for the medical domain and show that semantic annotation outperforms machine translation of the queries, yet the best results are achieved by combining a similarity thesaurus with the semantic codes. Yapomo et al. (2012) perform ontology-based query expansion of the most relevant terms, exploiting the synonymy relation in WordNet.

The work described in this contribution is a knowledge-based approach to CLIR in the Cultural Heritage domain, in which we use (1) both domain-specific and general linguistic resources, (2) a domain-specific ontology and (3) a set of grammars. An accurate semantic annotation of relevant terms and relations in both queries and documents is the main feature of our approach.

Linguistically-Motivated Semantic Annotation

The essential part of our CLIR application is the identification of domain specific concepts and their mapping to a language-independent conceptual level. The main resources for a linguistically motivated semantic annotation are:

- the ICOM International Committee for Documentation (CIDOC) Conceptual Reference Model (CRM);
- bilingual and monolingual Machine Readable dictionaries;
- local grammars (FSA/FST)

The development and testing of these components are performed by means of NooJ[3] (Silberztein, 2003), which has been already used in previous experiments carried out to develop ontology-based lexical resources for MT (Barreiro, 2010).

System Workflow

The architecture of our CLIR application maps data and metadata exploiting the morpho-syntactic and semantic information stored both in electronic dictionaries and Finite State Automata/Finite State Transducers (FSA/FSTs). This architecture allows identification of MWUs as domain concepts, assigning them linguistic information (ie POS) and semantic annotations to analyse complex lexical and grammatical structures (ie sentences and discontinuous MWUs, among others) during the information retrieval process.

Figure 1 illustrates the workflow of our application. The first step is the linguistic analysis, a pre-processing phase which analyses, tokenises and indexes natural language texts, tags the meaning units with morpho-

[3]NooJ allows the user to automatically analyse texts to locate and retrieve linguistic patterns, and to parse ambiguities. For more information about NooJ refer to www.nooj4nlp.net.

grammatical, terminological and semantic information. During this first phase, the system also extracts information from free-form user queries, and matches this information with already available ontological domain conceptualisations. The subsequent steps concern the execution of transformation and translation routines, prior to running a query against a knowledge base.

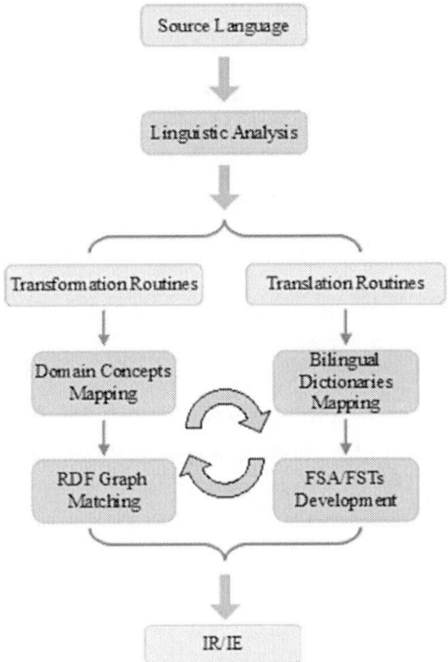

Figure 1 - System workflow

These routines are carried out simultaneously but with independent workflows.

The benefits of keeping these two workflows separate are:

1. the development of an architecture with a central multilingual formalisation of the lexicon, in which there is no specific target language, but each language can be, at the same time, target and source language.
2. the development of an Ontology-Based Information Extraction (OBIE) system in which SPARQL Protocol and RDF Query Language are integrated, a standard not only for our

multilingual electronic dictionaries, but also for any lexical and/or language database for which translation is required.

The transformation routines concern domain concept mapping and RDF graph matching, whereas the translation ones regard bilingual dictionary matching and FSA/FSTs development.

Conceptual Model and Semantic Annotation

In our CLIR application for the Archeological domain we refer to the CIDOC CRM, an ISO standard since 2006, which allows the exchange and integration of cultural heritage data from heterogeneous sources. This object-oriented semantic model and its terminology are compatible with the Resource Description Framework (RDF). The CRM is a formal ontology. (Crofts N., Doerr M., Gill T., Stead S., Stiff M. 2008), which provides definitions and a formal structure for describing the implicit and explicit concepts and relationships used in Cultural Heritage documentation. It is composed of 90 classes (which include subclasses and superclasses) and 148 unique properties (which include subproperties and superproperties).

The use of this ontological model allows for creation of a semantic annotation describing terms both formally, using the Resource Description Framework (RDF) prescriptions, and ontologically.

CIDOC CRM classes and properties, encoded in this form, can be translated into any language, preserving semantic annotation.

Bilingual Machine Readable dictionary

Our dictionary is compiled according to the Lexicon-Grammar (LG) theoretical framework LG, set up by the French linguist Maurice Gross in the 1960s and subsequently applied to Italian by Annibale Elia, Maurizio Martinelli and Emilio D'Agostino.

It provides lexical information: a listing of word forms and their lemmas, part-of-speech and morphological, semantic and syntactic information.

To date, the Archaeological Italian Electronic Dictionary, based on the Thesauri and Guidelines of the Italian Central Institute for the Catalogue and Documentation (ICCD)[4] has been developed (di Buono et al., 2014).

The following example represents an excerpt from the Italian-English dictionary of Archaeological Artifacts:

[4]http://www.iccd.beniculturali.it/index.php?it/240/vocabolari.

fregio dorico,N+NA+FLX=C523+DOM=RA1+CLS=E26+EN=doric frieze, N + AN + FLX=EC3
fusto a spirale,N+NPN+FLX=C7+DOM=RA1+CLS=E19+EN=spiral stem, N + AN + FLX=EC3

For each entry, a formal and morphological description is given with (1) the Part of Speech (POS) information; (2) if the entry is a word compound, the internal structure, as in *fregio dorico* (doric frieze), where the tag «NA» indicates that the given compound is formed by a noun (N), followed by an adjective (A); (3) the inflectional class, for which the tag «+FLX=C523» (associated to a local grammar) indicates the gender and the number of the compound *fregio dorico*, together with its plural form, ie that it is masculine singular, does not have any feminine correspondent form, and its plural form is *fregi dorici*; (4) the domain tag «DOM=RA1», which stands for «Archaeological Artifacts»; (5) the conceptual label «CLS=E26», which refers to the corresponding CIDOC CRM class, (6) the English translation *doric frieze*, followed by its POS, internal structure and inflection tags.

Local Grammars

Local grammars are used to deal with specific characteristics of natural languages and their design is based on syntactic descriptions, which encompass transformational rules and distributional behaviours. We develop local grammars in the form of Finite State Transducers/Automata (FST/FSA).

RDF graph matching

RDF graph matching is obtained by means of an FSA, which is typically used to locate morpho-syntactic patterns inside corpora, and to extract matching sequences in order to build indices, concordances, etc.

In our system, FSAs allow us to identify the three parts of an RDF graph in a natural language statement and to assign to each of them ontological classes and properties.

The development of a syntactic FSA is the result of the analysis of domain sentence structures, in which dependence and co-occurrence rules are identified. Our syntactic analysis relies essentially on a proper recognition of both verb and noun groups. Thus, the verb group predicates the ontology properties and the noun group indicates the ontology classes.

Matching linguistic raw data to RDF triples and their translation into SPARQL/SeRQL path expressions allows the use of specific meaning units to process natural language queries.

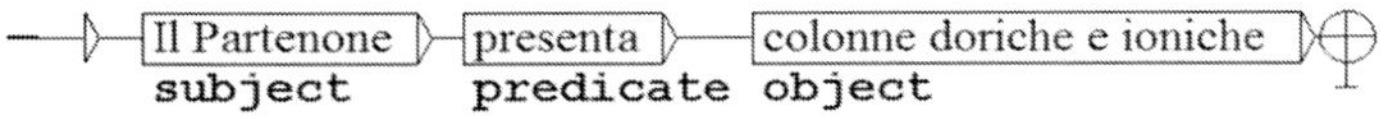

Figure 2 - Simple FSA with RDF Graph.

Figure 2 shows an FSA which associates an RDF graph to the following sentence:

Il Partenone (subject) *presenta* (predicate) *colonne doriche e ioniche*(object)[En: The Parthenon presents Doric and Ionic columns]

Figure 3 presents an FSA with variables used for POS and properties annotation. In the upper part of the FSA we identify the Part of Speech (POS) for the different constituents of the sentence. ie: *Il Partenone* (DETerminer + Noun), the verb *presenta* (V) and *colonne doriche e ioniche* (Noun+Adjective+Conjuntion+Adjective). In the lower part of the FSA, we annotate the two noun phrases and the verb phrase with the CIDOC CRM ontology classes, respectively as (1) E19 for the "Physical Object" class and (2) P56 for the "Bears Feature" property and, finally, (3) E26 for the "Physical Feature".

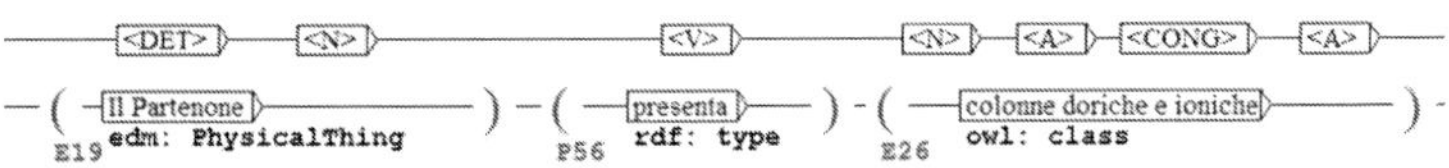

Figure 3 – Sample of the use of the FSA variables for identifying classes and property.

The role pairs Physical Object/name and Physical Feature/type are triggered by the RDF predicate *presenta* (presents).

In Figure 3 we use variables to apply a tag which indicates classes for the compound words; when the FSA recognises the text string, it applies a text annotation.

By applying the automaton in Figure 3 we can recognise all instances included in classes E19 and E26, the property of which is P56. In fact, Parts Of Speech (POS) present two levels of representation, which are separate but interlinked: a conceptual-semantic level, pertaining to ontologies, and a syntactic-semantic level, pertaining to sentence production (di Buono et al., 2014).

This feature:

1. grants a coherent identification and extraction of ontological constraints;
2. simplifies the process of the information extraction procedure, because it is based on a consistent reusable repository of pre-constituted sentence descriptions.

Translation routines

In our model, the Translation Routines are applied independently of the mapping process of the pivot language. This allows preservation of the semantic representation in both languages. The translation routines are based, on one side, on the bilingual dictionary mapping and, on the other, on the development of FSTs specifically aimed at automatic translation.

Bilingual dictionary mapping

The first step of this process is the bilingual dictionary mapping, which allows identification of the Atomic Linguistic Units (ALUs)[5] of a sentence and their annotation with the morpho-syntactic, semantic and translation information stored for the corresponding entry in the bilingual dictionary, ie for *fusto a spirale*:

fusto a spirale,N+NPN+FLX=C7+DOM=RA1+CLS=E19+EN=spiral stem, N + AN + FLX=EC3

This information is used during the Lexical analysis to obtain the Text Annotation Structure (TAS) of the text, in which all Atomic Linguistic Units (ALUs), whether simple words or multi-words, are associated with one or more annotations. These annotations are then used during the syntactic and semantic analysis performed by means of local grammars in the form of FSA/FSTs. Each piece of information stored in the dictionary is relevant for the translation process: the morphological information allows the identification of the inflected forms of the simple words and multi-words and the annotation of this information for the corresponding ALU in the text, the semantic information and in particular the +CLS information allows us to preserve the semantic information in the target

[5]Atomic Linguistic Units (ALUs) are the smallest elements that make up the sentence (Silberztein 2003).

language and, lastly, +EN information allows us to assign the corresponding English translation and the correct morphological information during the translation process.

Development of Translation FSTs

The second step in the translation routines is based on the development of specific translation FSTs. On the basis of the Text Annotation Structure obtained during the Lexical analysis, it is possible to use translation FSTs to perform syntactic analysis and translation in the target language. Figure 4 shows an FST which performs a translation process from Italian to English.

This FST identifies and annotates the different linguistic elements of declarative sentences such as '*Il Partenone presenta fregi dorici*', '*I templi romani hanno fusti a spirale*', etc, with the morpho-syntactic, semantic and translation information stored in the dictionary.

For instance, if a variable, say \$E26, holds the value "fusti a spirale", the output \$E26\$EN will produce the correct translation "spiral stems", on the basis of the value associated to the +EN feature in the bilingual entry "fusto a spirale, N+NPN+FLX=C7+DOM=RA1EDEAES+EN= spiral stem,N+AN+FLX= EC3" and the morpho-syntactic analysis performed by the graph in Figure 4, which identifies and produces the plural form of the compound noun "fusto a spirale".

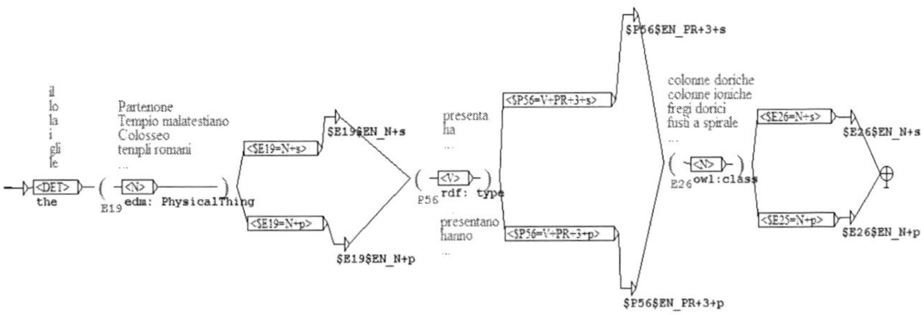

Figure 4 – Example of a translation FST

Conclusions

In this paper, we described a knowledge-based CLIR model for specific domain collections which takes into account a proper processing and translation of MWUs using NooJ.

A future work aims to further develop the Linguistic Resources, both MRDs and local grammars, with the objective of improving the accuracy of cross-language information retrieval, information extraction and semantic search. In order to test and validate this methodological framework we plan to use the MiBac datasets, which are freely downloadable and reusable under different kinds of Creative Commons licences.

References

Barreiro Anabela, Johanna Monti, Brigitte Orliac, Susan Preuß, Kutz Arrieta, Wang Ling, Fernando Batista, and Isabela Trancoso. 2014. Linguistic Evaluation of Support Verb Construction Translations by OpenLogos and Google Translate. In *Proceedings LREC 2014, Ninth International Conference on Language Resources and Evaluation*, Nicoletta Calzolari, Khalid Choukri, Thierry Declerck, Hrafn Loftsson, Bente Maegaard, Joseph Mariani, Asuncion Moreno, Jan Odijk, Stelios Piperidis Eds, Reykjavik, 26- 31 May 2014

Barreiro, Anabela, Johanna Monti, Brigitte Orliac, and Fernando Batista. 2013. When Multiwords Go Bad in Machine Translation. In *Workshop Proceedings for: Multi-word Units in Machine Translation and Translation Technologies* (Organised at the 14th Machine Translation Summit). Monti Johanna, Mitkov Ruslan, Corpas Pastor Gloria, Seretan Violeta Eds), CH-4123 Allschwil: The European Association for Machine Translation, Nice - France , 2-6 September 2013, pp. 26-33,

Barreiro, Anabela. 2010. Linguistic Resources and Applications for Portuguese Processing and Machine Translation. In *Applications of Finite-State Language Processing. Selected Papers from the NooJ 2008 International Conference (Budapest, Hungaria)*. Kuti Judit, Silberztein Max, Varadi Tamas Eds. Cambridge Scholars Publishing, Newcastle, UK.

Crofts, Nick, Martin Doerr, Tony Gill, Stephen Stead, and Matthew Stiff Eds. 2008. *Definition of the CIDOC Conceptual Reference Model, Version 5.0*.

di Buono, Maria Pia, Mario Monteleone, and Annibale Elia. 2014. Terminology and Knowledge Representation Italian Linguistic Resources for the Archaeological Domain. In *Proceedings of 25th International Conference on Computational Linguistics (COLING 2014)* - Workshop on Lexical and Grammatical Resources for Language Processing (LG-LP 2014).

Hull, David A. and Gregory Grefenstette. 1996. Querying across languages: a dictionary-based approach to multilingual information retrieval, *Proceedings of the 19th annual international ACM SIGIR conference on Research and development in information retrieval*, pp. 49-57.

Monti, Johanna, Ruslan Mitkov, Gloria Corpas Pastor, and Violeta Seretan. 2013. *Workshop Proceedings for Multi-word Units in Machine Translation and Translation Technologies* (Organised at the 14th Machine Translation Summit). CH-4123 Allschwil: The European Association for Machine Translation, Nice - France , 2-6 September 2013.

Monti, Johanna. 2012. *Multi-word Unit Processing in Machine Translation. Developing and using language resources for multi-word unit processing in Machine Translation* – PhD dissertation in Computational Linguistics - University of Salerno.

Oard, Doug W. 2009. Multilingual Information Access. In *Encyclopedia of Library and Information Sciences*, 3rd Ed., edited by Marcia J. Bates, Editor, and Mary Niles Maack, Associate Editor, Taylor & Francis.

Oard, Doug W. and Bonnie J. Dorr. 1996. A survey of multilingual text retrieval. Technical Report UMIACSTR- 96-19, University of Maryland, Institute for Advanced Computer Studies.

Pirkola, Ari. 1998. The Effects of Query Structure and Dictionary Setups in Dictionary-Based Crosslanguage Information Retrieval. In *21st Annual ACM SIGIR Conference on Research and Development in Information Retrieval (SIGIR 2008)*, Croft, W. *et al.* Eds, Melbourne, Australia, August 24-28, pp.55-63.

Ramisch, Carlos, Laurent Besacier, and Oleksandr Kobzar. 2013. How Hard is it to Automatically Translate Phrasal Verbs from English to French? In *Workshop Proceedings for: Multi-word Units in Machine Translation and Translation Technologies* (Organised at the 14th Machine Translation Summit). Monti Johanna, Mitkov Ruslan, Corpas Pastor Gloria, Seretan Violeta Eds., CH-4123 Allschwil: The European Association for Machine Translation, Nice - France , 2-6 September 2013.

Silberztein, Max. 2003. *NooJ Manual*. Available at www.nooj4nlp.net.

Volk, Martin, Spela Vintar and Paul Buitelaar. 2003. Ontologies in Cross-Language Information Retrieval. In *Proceedings of WOW2003 (Workshop Ontologie-basiertes Wissensmanagement)*, Luzern, Switzerland.

Yapomo Manuela, Gloria Corpas Pastor and Mitkov Ruslan. 2012. CLIR and ontology-based approach for bilingual extraction of comparable documents. *The 5th Workshop on Building and Using Comparable Corpora.* Istanbul, Turkey, pp. 121-125.

KNOWLEDGE MANAGEMENT AND EXTRACTION FROM CULTURAL HERITAGE REPOSITORIES

MARIA PIA DI BUONO AND MARIO MONTELEONE[1]

Abstract

In this paper we present our methodology for structuring ontology-based Linguistic Resources. The approach aims to improve tasks of Knowledge Management and Extraction, specifically in the Cultural Heritage domain. In order to achieve our goals, we develop the Archaeological Italian Electronic Dictionary and a set of local grammars, which use CIDOC Conceptual Reference Model (CRM) prescriptions. Our LRs, updated through CIDOC CRM and LLOD URIs, are the starting point for structuring SPARQL queries. Future works include implementing an environment to query online repositories and so creating a Question-Answering system.

Introduction

Cultural Heritage repositories store a wide range of content, variable by type and properties, and semantically interlinked with other domains. Due to these features, the specific domain represents a critical challenge for NLP tasks ie Knowledge Management (KM) and Extraction (KE).

According to the definition of Davenport (1994), by KM we mean 'the process of capturing, distributing, and effectively using knowledge'. In order to achieve those aims, it seems necessary to use an integrated approach to content management of online repositories. In fact, knowledge bases are heavily linked to capabilities of optimising the information flow. Therefore, managing linguistic and language resources is a crucial step towards improving the KE task.

In this paper we present our methodology, based on a Lexicon-Grammar framework, aimed at improving KM. In order to achieve our goal, we developed NooJ Italian Linguistic Resources (LRs) for the Archaeological domain, in which, through formal grammars, we integrate formal ontology classes and properties into electronic dictionary entries, using a standardised conceptual reference model. Indeed, our idea also springs from Bachimont (2000) who states that 'defining an ontology for knowledge representation tasks means defining, for a given domain and a given problem, the functional and relational signature of a formal language and its associated semantics'.

Linguistic Resources: The Italian Archaeological Electronic Dictionary

Our LRs have been developed according to the theoretical and practical Lexicon-Grammar (LG) framework. LG was set up by the French linguist Maurice Gross during the 1960s, and subsequently applied to Italian by Annibale Elia, Maurizio Martinelli and Emilio D'Agostino. This approach describes the mechanisms of word combinations and gives an exhaustive description of natural language lexical and syntactic structures.

All electronic dictionaries, built according to the LG descriptive method, form the DELA System which works as a linguistic engine embedded in automatic textual analysis software systems and parsers.

The Archaeological Italian Electronic Dictionary (AIED) is composed of approximately 11,000 entries, with both simple and compound words, including spelling variants and synonyms. It includes information taken from the Thesauri and Guidelines of the Italian Central Institute for Catalogue and Documentation (ICCD). AIED also reports the low-level taxonomy, used by ICCD to indicate univocally the relationship among archaeological artifacts and between those and the specific lemma.

ICCD resources are organised in:

- Object definition dictionary
- Marble sculptures
- Marble sculptures – Sarcophagi and reliefs
- Metal containers
- Vocabulary of Coroplastics
- Vocabulary of Glasses
- Vocabulary of Materials
- Vocabulary of Metals
- Vocabulary of Mosaics
- Vocabulary of Mosaic Pavement Works
- Vocabulary of non-figurative mosaics

In our dictionary, for each entry we indicate:

- its POS (Cat), internal structure and inflectional code1 (FLX)[1];
- its variants (VAR) and synonyms (SYN), if any;
- the reference to an FSA to generate a link (RDF and/or HTML) (LINK);
- with reference to our taxonomy, the pertaining knowledge domain (DOM)[2];
- the pertaining ontological class, extracted from the CIDOC Conceptual Reference Model (CCL)[3].

Entry	Cat	Internal Structure	FLX	VAR	SYN	LINK	DOM	CCL
dinos con anse ad anello	N	NPNPN	C610	dynos /déinos		LLOD_S	RA1SUOCR	E22
kylix a labbro risparmiato	N	NPNA	C611		lip cup	LLOD_S	RA1SUOCR	E22

Table 1 – Excerpt from AIED

The main formal structures recorded in AIED are:

- Noun+Preposition+Noun+Preposition+Noun (NPNPN), ie *fibula ad arco a coste* (ribbed-arch fibula);
- Noun+Preposition+Noun+Adjective (NPNA), ie *anello a capi ritorti* (twisted-heads ring);
- Noun+Preposition+Noun+Adjective+Adjective (NPNAA), ie *punta a foglia larga ovale* (oval broadleaf point).

LRs Updating

Due to specific formal and lexical features of archaeological domain terminological entries, we could use an FSA in order to identify new entries of AIED.

In fact, we noticed the presence of MWUs in which one or more fixed elements co-occurred with one or more variable ones. Those ALUs are defined as open series compounds.

---

[1]All inflectional codes refer to Italian local grammars for simple and compound words.

[2]The taxonomy we use is structured on the basis of the indications given by the ICCD guidelines. Therefore, the tags RA1SUORC stands for Archaeological Remains/Tools/Receptacles and Containers.

[3]For more information see Ontology Integration in Local Grammars paragraph.

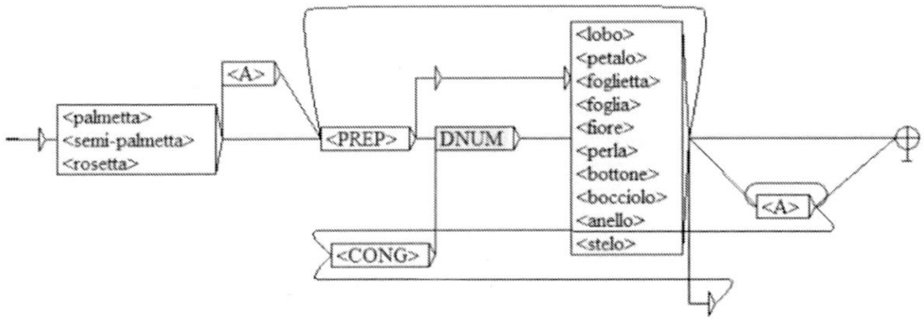

Figure 1 – Sample of FSA to recognise open series compounds

Figure 1 shows an automaton which recognises open series compounds describing a type of decorative feature used in architecture, sculpture, and for earthenware and arms. In this automaton, the fixed element is represented by *(<palmetta>+<semi palmetta>+<rosetta>)* (<little palm>+<semi little palm>+<rosette>), the variable sequence is composed of both a numerical determiner (<DNUM>) and a set of elements *(<petalo>+<foglia>+<lobo>+...)* (<petal>+<leaf>+<lobe>) with its denotative features (<A>). Due to the use of this open series in different subsectors, the inclusion in a certain class of ontology is evinced from the context of the sentence and from the co-occurrences taking place with the verb and all other elements of the sentence. Therefore, in the dictionary we label entries with a generic tag +DOM=RA1OT[4], while the +CCL tag is assigned using specific syntactic analysis[5].

As far as semantic peculiarities are concerned, we also observe the presence of compounds in which the head does not occur in the first position; for instance, the open series *frammenti di (terracotta+ anfora+laterizi),* places the heads at the end of the compounds, being *frammenti* (fragments) used to explicate the notion 'N0 is a part of N1'.

As far as syntactic aspects are concerned, we observe that some open series compounds, especially those referring to a coroplastic description, are sentence reductions in which a present participle construction is used.

This is observable for instance in *statua raffigurante Sileno* (Silenus statue), a reduction of the sentence

[4]RA1OT stands for Archaeological Remains/Overall Terms.

[5]For more information see Ontology Integration in the paragraph on Local Grammars.

Questa statua raffigura Sileno (This statue represents Silenus)

[relative] → *Questa è una statua che raffigura Sileno* (This is a statue which represents Silenus)

[pr. part.] → *Questa è una statua raffigurante Sileno* (This is a statue representing Silenus).

In order to recognise these ALUs we use an FSA (Figure 2) in which Noun Group (NG) represents the fixed part, extracted from a specific set (ie statue, profile, figure etc), the Verb Group (VG) is formed by a sub-graph containing sentence reductions and paraphrases, and the Adjective Group (AG) is the variable part.

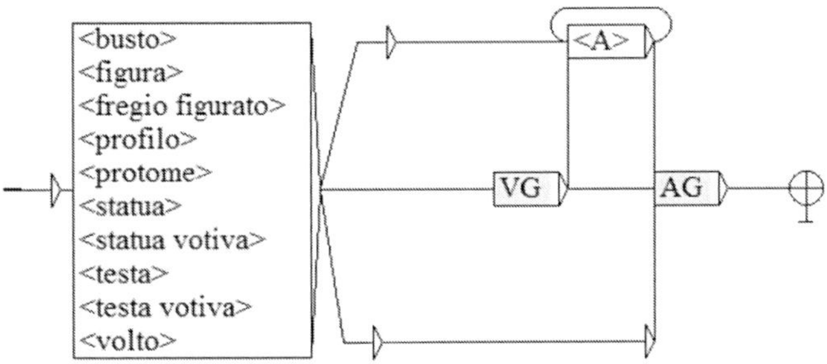

Figure 2 – FSA for coroplastic description.

In compounds containing present participle forms, semantic features can be identified using local grammars built on specific verb classes (semantic predicate sets); in such cases, co-occurrence restrictions can be described in terms of lexical forms and syntactic structures.

Figure 3 shows the sub-graph for the VG in coroplastic descriptions; within it, we did not use the specific semantic set or descriptive predicates, in order to emphasise elements extracted from the verbal classes (20A and 47B[6]).

[6]Classes refer to Italian Lexicon-Grammar Tables, available at http://dsc.unisa.it/composti/tavole/combo/tavole.asp.

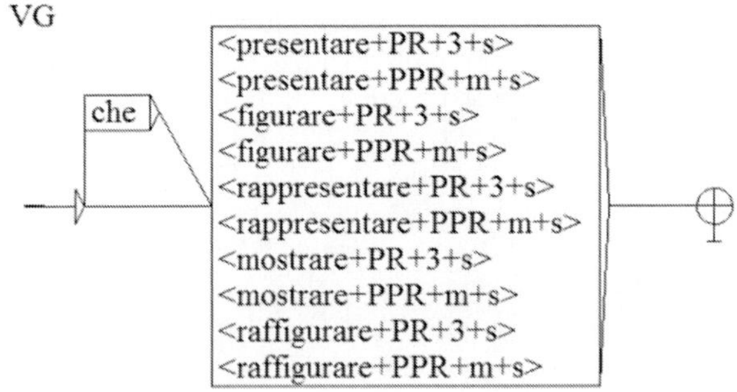

Figure 3 – Verb Group in coroplastic description.

The AG is useful for recognising the variable part in this open series. Due to the complexity of coroplastic descriptions, the sub-graph presents many recursive nodes, especially <N>. The structure allows us to retrieve a very large amount of expressions and MWUs among those present in the corpus analysed.

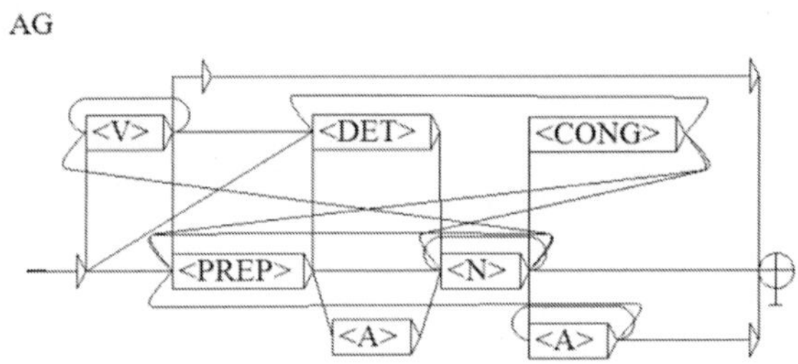

Figure 4 – Adjective group in coroplastic description

Linguistic Linked Open Data Cloud

Linking LRs with other resources can be seen as a crucial step in order to combine information from different knowledge sources. According to Chiarcos et al. (2013a), 'linking to central terminology repositories facilitates conceptual interoperability'.

To achieve this goal, the Open Linguistics Working Group (OLWG) developed the Linguistic Linked Open Data (LLOD) project. The initiative intends to link LRs, represented according to the Resource Description Framework (RDF) format, with the resources available in the Linked Open Data (LOD) cloud. According to the LOD paradigm (Berners-Lee, 2006),

Web resources must present a Uniform Resource Identifier (URI) for entities to which they refer, and include links to other resources.

The LLOD project aims to create a representation formalism for corpora in Resource Description Framework/Web Ontology Language (RDF/OWL). The goal of the LLOD is not only to provide LRs in an interoperability way, but also to use an open licence. Benefits of LLOD are also identified in linking through URIs, federation and dynamic linking between resources (Chiarcos et al., 2013b).

According to Linked Data prescriptions, URI schema is structured as

http://it.dbpedia.org/resource/ordine_dorico	Resource URI
http://it.dbpedia.org/page/ordine_dorico	HTML representation
http://it.dbpedia.org/data/ordine_dorico.{ rdf | n3 | json | ntriples }	Machine-readable resource representation

Table 2 – URI schema structure

The most relevant LLOD resources are stored in and presented by DBPedia (www.dbpedia.org). DBPedia is a sample of large Linked Datasets, which offers Wikipedia information in RDF format and incorporates other Web datasets. We refer to DBPedia Italian datasets[7] to integrate our LRs with LLOD. In order to reuse such prescriptions, we adopt a Finite State Automaton system which merges specific URIs with electronic dictionary entries.

We use an inflectional grammar in order to add the dbpedia/resource link to AIED entries (Figure 5).

Figure 5 – Sample of inflectional grammar used for URIs

The transducer generates a new string in which the resource URI is placed before the original entry. In this way, the transducer enriches all entries of our electronic dictionary with DBPedia resources. For instance, the result given by the transducer for the compound *Ordine dorico* (Doric order) is the following string:

[7]DBPedia Italian is an open project developed and maintained by the Web of Data research unit of Fondazione Bruno Kessler.

```
# This dictionary was automatically built from archaeology.dic
#
#use rdf.nof
#
<http://it.dbpedia.org/resource/Ordine_dorico>,Ordine dorico,N+FLX=LLOD_C+URI
```

Figure 6 – Sample of inflected dictionary

In order to apply also the standard inflectional grammar to entries (for singular and plural forms), we use a Python routine. It also allows us to invert the order in dictionary strings and so to have the lemma and not the link in the first position.

Resulting strings may be used to automatically read text by means of Web browsers and/or RDF environments/routines. When the generated string is processed by a Web Browser, it will generate a link to the HTML representation. Otherwise, when the header 'HTTP Accept:' of the query is produced by a RDF-based application, it will produce a link to the machine-readable representation.

Ontology Integration in Local Grammars

The use of an ontology in the upgrading of LG LRs may ensure knowledge sharing, maintenance of semantic constraints, solving of semantic ambiguities, and inferencing on the basis of concept networks.

This stems from the fact that ontology-based LRs are likely to incorporate more information than thesauri. In fact, compared to a thesaurus, an ontology also stores language-independent information and semantic relations.

We refer to the CIDOC Conceptual Reference Model (CRM), an ISO standard since 2006. This ontology schema provides definitions and a formal structure for describing the implicit and explicit concepts and relationships used in cultural heritage documentation.

CIDOC CRM is composed of 90 classes (which include sub-classes and super-classes) and 148 unique properties (and sub-properties). It is compatible with the Resource Description Framework (RDF).

We use FSA to identify entities for triple RDF (subject, object and predicate) associating CIDOC CRM classes and properties to those.

In order to develop an ontology FSA, we analyse domain sentence structures recognising rules of dependence and co-occurrence. Syntactic analysis relies essentially on a proper recognition of both verb and noun groups. In fact, 'verbs typically denote events and states, nouns typically denote entities' (Hanks, 2013). In other words, the verb group predicates the ontology properties and the noun group indicates the ontology classes. We use semantic role sets, established on the basis of CIDOC CRM constraints (properties), matched with grammatical and syntactic rules.

Figure 7 shows the FSA for the P56 property which stands for 'Bears Feature'. This property presents the E19 class ('Physical Object') as Entity - Domain and the E26 ('Physical Feature') class as Entity – Range.

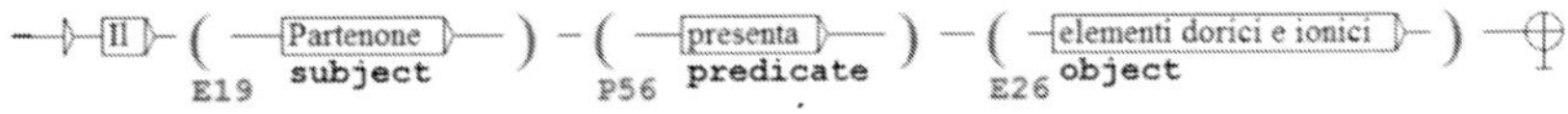

Figure 7 – Sample of ontology integration in local grammars

We develop FSA with variables which apply the ontology classes and property to a given sentence ie *Il Partenone presenta elementi dorici e ionici* (The Parthenon combines Doric and Ionic elements). The role pairs Physical Object/name and Physical Feature/type are triggered by the RDF predicate *presenta* (combines).

Knowledge Extraction

In our proposal, KE from online repositories is achieved using SPARQL, a query language for RDF data.

In addition, data structured in RDF format can be queried by means of the SPARQL language. Indeed, if RDF triples represent a set of relationships among resources, than SPARQL queries are the patterns for these relationships.

Linked data sources usually provide a SPARQL endpoint for their datasets. SPARQL endpoint is a SPARQL query processing service that supports the SPARQL protocol[8].

SPARQL endpoints usually support different result formats:

- XML, JSON, plain text (for ASK and SELECT queries)
- RDF/XML, Ntriples, Turtle, N3 (for DESCRIBE and CONSTRUCT queries).

Our LRs, updated through CIDOC CRM and LLOD URIs, are the starting point for structuring queries.

A sample of SPARQL query to display the results for *Tutti i templi di ordine dorico* (all Doric order temples)

[8]For DBPedia data source, the endpoint address is http://dbpedia.org/sparql.

```
SELECT * WHERE
{
?Physical_Object a
        <http://dbpedia.org/ontology/tempio>
 . ?Physical_Feature
        <http://dbpedia.org/ontology/stile>
        <http://it.dbpedia.org/resource/ordine_dorico> .
        }
```

We can see that in this query sample, the same string that comes from our dictionary may be used. CIDOC classes are also used to indicate the set of classes in the dataset we refer to.

Conclusions and Future Work

We have seen that the LRs here outlined could be used to generate SPARQL queries:

- ontology classes and properties inserted in grammars will be the reference for the dataset,
- dictionary entries will be the reference for URIs.

As a further step we will develop an automatic routine which:

1. processes a query in natural language by means of NooJ
2. retrieves from it all of the atomic linguistic units (ie ordine dorico – doric order) which corresponds to ontology classes and properties
3. uses the URIs stored in our inflected electronic dictionary to build the SPARQL query
4. runs the SPARQL query against a given knowledge base
5. displays results in different formats (XML, JSON, plain text, RDF/XML etc)

Our future goal is also to develop an application useful for both retrieving and processing RDF data from LLOD resources. We intend to implement an environment structured into two workflows: the first one (based on SPARQL language) to query online repositories and create a Question-Answering system, the second one to retrieve natural language strings, in particular those contained in the fields ‘rdfs: comment’ and ‘dbpedia-owl: abstract’. Such data will constitute the basis for the development of a supervised machine-learning algorithm that, by matching with existing dictionaries and local grammars, will further upgrade the LRs.

References

Bender,Edward A. 1996. *Mathematical methods in artificial intelligence.* Los Alamitos, CA: IEEE Press.

Berners-Lee, Tim. 2006. *Design issues: Linked Data.*

Brewster, Christopher, Kieron O'Hara, Steve Fuller, Yorick Wilks, Enrico Franconi, Mark A. Musen, Jeremy Ellman, and Simon Buckingham Shum. 2004. Knowledge representation with ontologies: The present and future. *IEEE Intelligent Systems*, 19(1):72–81.

Chiarcos, Christian, John McCrae, Phillip Cimiano, and Christiane Fellbaum. 2013b. Towards Open data for Linguistica: Linguistic linked data. In Oltramari A., Vossen P., Quin L., Hovy E. (eds.). *New Trends of Research in Ontologies and Lexical Resources.* Springer, Heidelberg.

Chiarcos, Christian, Phillip Cimiano, Thierry Declerck, and John Mc Crae. 2013a. Linguistic Linked Open Data (LLOD). Introduction and Overview. *Proceedings of LDL 2013*, Pisa, Italy.

Cocchiarella, Nino. 1996. Conceptual realism as a formal ontology. In Poli, R., & Simons, P. (Eds.). *Formal ontology.* Kluwer Academic, London, UK:27-60.

Crofts, Nick, Martin Doerr, Tony Gill, Stephen Stead, and Matthew Stiff. 2010. *Definition of the CIDOC Conceptual Reference Model.* ICOM/CIDOC Documentation Standards Group. CIDOC CRM Special Interest Group. 5.02 ed.

Elia, Annibale, Maurizio Martinelli, and Emilio D'Agostino. 1981. *Lessico e strutture sintattiche. Introduzione alla sintassi del verbo italiano.* Liguori Editore, Napoli.

Gillam, Lee, Mariam Tariq, and Khurshid Ahmad. 2007. *Terminology and the construction of ontology.* 11 (1):55-81.

Gross, Maurice. 1968. *Grammaire transformationnelle du français: syntaxe du verbe.* Larousse, Paris.

Gruber, Tom. 1993. *A translation approach to portable ontology specifications. Knowledge Acquisition*, 5(2):199–220.

Hanks, Patrick. 2013. *Lexical Analysis. Norms and Exploitations.* MIT Press. Cambridge.

Harris, Zellig S. 1970. *Papers in Structural and Transformational Linguistics.* Reidel, Dordrecht.

Harris, Zellig S. 1976. (translation by Maurice Gross), *Notes du Cours de Syntaxe*, Éditions du Seuil, Paris.
http://www.w3.org/DesignIssues/LinkedData.html.

Liang, Hao. 2010. Ontology based automatic attributes extracting and queries translating for deep web. *Journal of Software*, 5:713–720.

Martin, Philippe. 2003. Correction and Extension of WordNet 1.7. *ICCS 2003, 11th International Conference on Conceptual Structures.* Springer, Verlag, LNAI 2746:160-173.

Sanchez, David. 2010. A methodology to learn ontological attributes from the web. *Data & Knowledge Engineering*, 69(6), 573–597.

Sowa, John Florian. 2000. *Knowledge Representation: Logical, Philosophical, and Computational Foundations.* Brooks Cole Publishing Co., Pacific Grove, CA.

Surmann, Hartmut. 2000. Learning a fuzzy rule based knowledge representation. In *Proceedings of the ICSC Symposium on Neural Computation*, Berlin, Germany:349-355.

Tijerino, Yuri A., David W. Embley, Deryle Lonsdale, Yihong Ding, and George Nagy. 2005. Towards ontology generation from tables. *WWW: Internet and Information Systems*, 8(3):261–285.

Vaquero, Antonio, Francisco Álvarez, and Fernando Sáenz. 2006. Control and Verification of Relations in the Creation of Ontology- Based Electronic Dictionaries for Language Learning. In *Proceedings of the SIIE 2006 8th International Symposium on Computers in Education*, Vol. 1:166-173

Wang, Yingxu, Yousheng Tian, and Kendal Hu. 2011. Semantic manipulations and formal ontology for machine learning based on concept algebra. *International Journal of Cognitive Informatics and Natural Intelligence*, 5(3):1–29.

Zadeh, Lotfi A. 2004. Precisiated Natural Language (PNL). *AI Magazine*, 25(3):74–91.

AUTOMATIC DOCUMENT CLASSIFICATION AND EVENT EXTRACTION IN STANDARD ARABIC

ESSIA BESSAIES AND SLIM MESFAR

Abstract

This work deals with the extraction of economic and financial events from journalistic articles automatically collected from Arabic newspaper websites. First, we were faced with the problem of classifying the documents in order to retain only economic and financial articles. A hybrid approach was used to solve this issue since we merged the use of the linguistic engine NooJ with some additional statistical scores to determine whether the processed articles should be selected for the next step. Then, we processed the selected texts to prepare economic and financial monitoring tasks. These tasks use a rule-based approach. The written rules use some lexical markers (triggers) as well as a list of patterns formalised as NooJ syntactic grammars. Finally, the developed set of grammars was tested on the set of automatically collected journalistic articles. The precision and recall show that the results are encouraging and could be integrated into a more general monitoring system.

Introduction

Selecting a text classification system for Arabic documents is a challenging task due to the complex and rich lexical and morphological structure of the Arabic language. Text classification is used for various purposes including email routing and filtering, news monitoring and spam filtering. The main objective is to simplify the information extraction task, especially as regards classifying and indexing newspaper websites. Arabic information retrieval faces many challenges. Within a highly competitive business environment, financial institutions require regular monitoring in order to tackle the challenges of the market. As today's financial markets are sensitive to breaking news about economic events, accurate and timely automatic identification of events in news items is crucial. Nowadays, the financial and economic events in the Arab world represent an important business opportunity to European and American investors. Information related to these events could be extracted from large numbers of digital documents and can result in serious processing problems; to help to overcome these obstacles, we make use of automatic event extraction in order to identify economic and financial events using NooJ. The direct application of this kind of automatic extraction on collected documents could result in quite a lot of noise. This explains the need for document classification.

In the next section, a brief overview of the state of the art describes related works on approaches to automatic document classification as well as the extraction of economic and financial events in our proposed approach. The second section introduces our approach to automatic document classification and event extraction in standard Arabic. In section 3, we describe the automatic classification while in section 4 we describe the extraction of economic and financial events in Arabic. The results of experiments are described in section 5.

Related Work

The research in this article is based on two complementary axes: the first involves automatic document classification while the second concerns the extraction of economic and financial events. The table below shows some works on automatic classification and event extraction.

Automatic document classification	Event extraction
- (Khreisat, 2006) used Manhattan distance and Dice measures to compare the N-gram frequency statistical technique against Arabic data sets articles automatically collected from journalistic articles. - (El-Kourdi et al., 2004) used Naïve Bayes algorithm to automatically classify Arabic documents into five classes. The average accuracy reported was approx 68.78% and the best achieved result was approx 92.8%.	- (Alexander Hogenboom et al., 2012) proposed the Semantics-Based Pipeline for Economic Event Detection (SPEED), which aims to extract financial events from news articles (announced through RSS feeds) and to annotate these with meta-data, while maintaining a speed that is high enough to enable real-time use. - (Ludovic et al., 2013) used a two-step approach for template filling: first, an event-based segmentation is performed to select the parts of the text

- (Sawaf et al.) used a statistical approach based on the maximum entropy technique to classify the Arabic NEWSWIRE corpus and Reuters documents into four classes. The basic purpose was to simplify Arabic classification difficulties using subword units (character N-grams). - (Syiam et al., 2006) used a hybrid method of statistics and light stemmers, which is the most suitable stemming algorithm for the Arabic language and gives a general accuracy of about 98%. - (Sanan. M et al., 2008) evaluated a number of similarity measures for the classification of Arabic documents. Their experimental results showed that N-gram text classification using cosine coefficient measure classification outperforms TF-ICF and Dice measure.	related to the target event; then, a graph-based method is applied to choose the most relevant entities in these parts for characterising the event. An evaluation of this model based on an annotated corpus for earthquake events shows a 77% F1-measure for the template-filling task.

Table 1 – Work of automatic classification and event extraction

Following this investigation, in order to solve the problem of classification we combine the use of the linguistic engine of NooJ with some additional statistical scores such as the measure of TF-ICF; the category to which a document belongs is the one which has the biggest Weight value. Named Entities recognition is a potentially important pretreatment for financial and economic field extraction. For this purpose, we have adopted a rules-based approach to recognising Arabic named entities and economic organisations, using different grammars and gazetteers.

Our approach

In our approach, we will solve the problem of classifying documents to retain only those relating to economics and finance using a hybrid approach, combining the use of the linguistic engine NooJ with additional statistical scores to determine whether items processed should be selected for the next step. Next, we treat the texts chosen in order to prepare economic and financial monitoring tasks. These tasks are based on syntactic rule-based grammars. In order to automatically classify documents, we use an extended version of the TF-ICF score. In addition to the Term Frequency (TF) and the Inverse Class Frequency (ICF), the new score introduces the use of the recognised sequence length to compute the weight of a document on each class. Furthermore, we adapted a rule-based approach to recognise Arabic named entities and economic and financial extraction, using different grammars and gazetteers. Using the platform of development, NooJ can create terminological dictionaries for six classes: Economics, Finance, Computer Science, Law, Medicine, and Politics. We also use the el-DicAr dictionary (Mesfar, 2008) as the basis for our system.

For the construction of our training corpus, we used a collection of journalistic texts collected from newspaper websites. These collections of texts can help users determine how tokens are commonly used or combined. NooJ allows us to extract plain text from these items and to eliminate anything that is superfluous eg HTML tags, advertising, images and other automatically-added elements. We built a dynamic corpus collected automatically from newspaper websites in Arabic using our own web crawler.

Automatic document classification

A hybrid approach is used to solve the problem of classification: we merge the use of the linguistic engine of NooJ with additional statistical scores to decide to which class the document belongs. NooJ development platform allows us to build dictionaries as well as permitting linguistic corpus analysis. This platform uses (syntactic and morphological) local grammars built for this purpose. Table 1 gives an idea about dictionaries which we added to the resources of NooJ. We used others dictionaries existing in NooJ, such as the dictionary of adjectives, nouns and first names el-DicAr (Mesfar, 2008).

Dictionaries	**Number of lexical entries**	**Annotation in the dictionary**
Economics	2,350	N+Economie
Finance	1,500	N+Finance
Computer science	1,453	N+Info
Law	868	N+Juridique
Medicine	2,109	N+Medical
Politics	573	N+Politique

Table 2 – Added dictionaries

The class weighting measure

$$Weight = TF \times ICF \times Length$$

- **TF**: Term Frequency is the number of occurrences of the term in the document concerned. The term frequency in the given class is simply the number of times a given term appears in that class. This count is usually normalised to prevent a bias towards longer classes (which may have a higher term frequency regardless of the actual importance of the term within the class). To give a measure of the importance of Ti within the particular class:

$$\boldsymbol{TFi = \frac{Ni}{\sum_K Nk}}$$

where Ni = the number of occurrences of the considered term. The denominator is the number of occurrences of all terms.

- **ICF:** Inverse class frequency is a measure that gives an idea of the value of the general importance of the term. It is obtained by dividing the total number of classes by the number of classes containing the term, and then taking the logarithm of that quotient.

$$\boldsymbol{ICF = \log_{Nbclasstotal}\left(\frac{TotalNb\ Class}{Nbclass\ of\ term}\right)}$$

where:
TotalNb class: Total number of classes.
Nbclass of term: Number of classes where the term occurs

- **Length:** Number of lexical units (in simple or compound entries).

$$\boldsymbol{Length = length(lexical\ units\ )}$$

By using the measure of TF*ICF*Length, which allows us to calculate the weight of each term that belongs to the class in the document

Example and evaluation

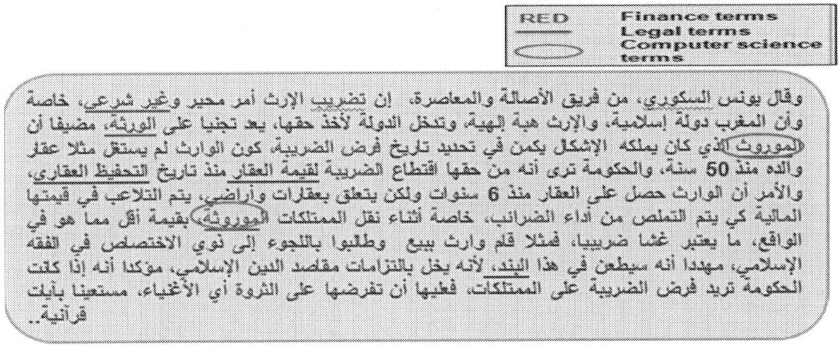

Figure 1 – Example

In the example given above, we see that the polysemic word form مَوْرُوث (Heritage) belongs to three classes:

- Computer science: a concept of object oriented programming.
- Law: a property received from a decedent, either by will or through state laws of succession.
- Finance: Any form of property received from a decedent. In most countries, heritage is taxed when valued over a certain amount.

```
عَقد مُحَدد المُدة,N+CMPD+Struct=N_N_N+Juridique+Finance+NBClass=2+Taille=3
عَقد مُقاوَلة من الباطِن,N+CMPD+Struct=N_N_PREP_N+Finance+NBClass=1+Taille=4
عَقد,N+CMPD+Struct=N+Juridique+Finance+NBClass=2+Taille=1
مَوْرُوث,N+CMPD+Struct=N+Info+Juridique+Finance+NBClass=3+Taille=1
عقوبة مالية,N+CMPD+Struct=N_ADJ+Finance+NBClass=1+Taille=2
عُقود المُسْتَقبَلِيات,N+CMPD+Struct=N_N+Finance+Juridique+NBClass=2+Taille=2
عَلامَة الإشْهار,N+CMPD+Struct=N_N+Finance+Economie+NBClass=2+Taille=2
عَلامَة تجارِيَة,N+CMPD+Struct=N_ADJ+Finance+Economie+NBClass=2+Taille=2
عُمْلَة مُزَوَّرَة,N+CMPD+Struct=N_N+Finance+NBClass=1+Taille=2
عَلامَة,N+CMPD+Struct=N+Finance+NBClass=1+Taille=1
عَمَلِيَة الصَّرْف,N+CMPD+Struct=N_N+Finance+NBClass=1+Taille=2
```

Figure 2 – Terminological dictionary

In order to compute the document weight in a given class, we need 4 steps:

Step 1: Linguistic analysis using the terminological added dictionaries (Text > Linguistic Analysis)
Step 2: Applying a NooJ regular expression to the annotated text (Text > Locate)
$(Seq <DIC+Finance> $) <E>/$Seq_#,SeqTaille#,SeqNBClass

The related concordance table shows the extracted financial terms and sequences in the text as well as their length and the number of classes in which they could occur.

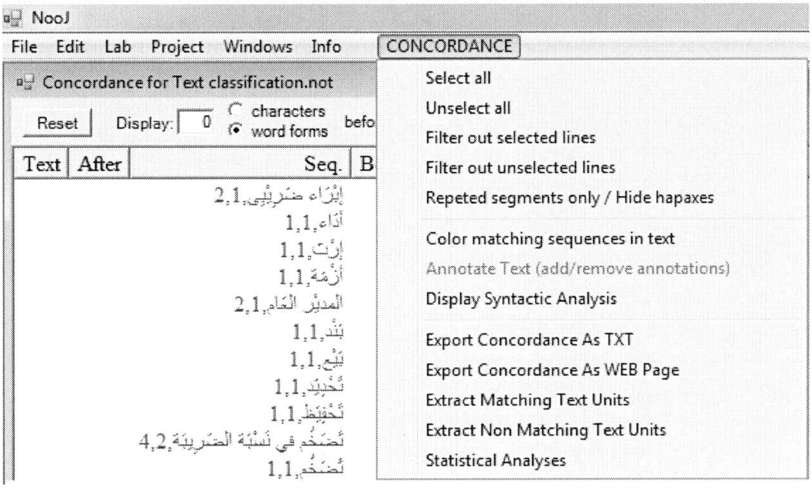

Figure 3 – Concordance Finance class

Step 3: Export Concordance as a text in CSV format (Concordance> Export concordance As txt)

First, the CSV file is imported in Excel. Then, we added the formula that uses the values extracted automatically to compute the document weight in the given class

LOG =LOG(6/D51;6)*C51*1

	B	C	D	E	F	G	H
51	سُنَّة	1	1		2309	4	=LOG(6/D51;6)*C51*1
52	تَخْطِيط	1	1		2389	5	1
53	عَقَار	1	1		2395	6	1
54	قَبُول	1	1		2467	4	1
55	ضَرِيبَة	1	1		2494	7	1
56	إِبْرَاء ضَرِيبِي	2	1		652	11	2
57	عَقَار	1	1		2592	6	1
58	سُنَّة	1	1		2793	3	1
59	وَارِث	1	3		230	6	0,386852807
60	دَعْم	1	1		3097	3	1
61	نُمُو	1	1		3101	5	1
62	مِيزَان	1	1		3234	5	1
63	حِسَاب	1	1		3260	6	1
64	قِيمَة	1	1		3277	4	1
65	مُعَامَلَات	1	1		3360	9	1
66	سُنَّة	1	1		3453	3	1
67	مِيزَان	1	1		3459	6	1
68	تَحْدِيد	1	1		3571	5	1
69	مَال	1	1		3583	6	1
70	مَوْرُوث	1	3		256	7	0,386852807
71	مِيزَان	1	1		3714	7	1
72	حُكْم	1	1		3745	5	1
73	مِيزَان	1	1		3861	5	1
74	مِيزَان	1	1		3963	6	1
75	TOTAL						72,93426404

Figure 4 – Concordance Finance class

The table above gives the document weight for the financial class (weight = 72.93). In order to get the complete list of weight values, we need to repeat these three steps for the different remaining classes.

Step 4: Collecting the different weight values

Classes	Weight
Finance	72,93426404
Law	26,2262944
Computer science	20,3394403

Table 3 – Automatic classification results given

The category to which a document belongs is the one which has the biggest value of Weight. This text could be considered a financial document. For the classification task, we use a sample corpus of 100 documents to be processed manually, split as follows: 10 political, 15 legal, 15 computer science, 35 economic, 20 medical, 35 financial. We repeat the same thing for the 100 documents using the same approach as in the example above. The result is as follows: 8 political, 13 legal, 15 computer science, 37 economic, 19 medical, 39 financial.

Event extraction in standard Arabic

Our event extraction system is a based on the definition of recognition rules represented as NooJ grammar rules.

Grammars

The event extraction module is based on the application the NooJ syntactic grammars to annotated texts. It takes into account all the specifities of the Arabic language to identify references to people, places and organisations (Mesfar, 2008). The recognition rules use some manually collected lists of trigger words which indicate that the surrounding tokens are probably known constituents of the entity, and can be used to reliably identify the type of entity named, determining that it is an economic term (director, manager, etc). These grammars recognise matching patterns and produce some distributional information such as economic meetings or seminars.

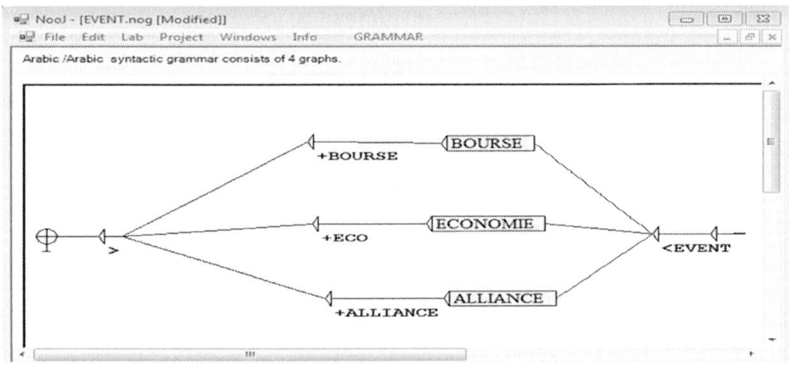

Figure 5 – EVENT NooJ syntactic grammar

Evaluation

Data are collected using a program for extracting regular journalistic texts online. Then the corpus is analysed using the NooJ linguistic engine. All downloaded items are filtered by automatically removing HTML tags, advertisements, images and other added elements to extract plain text. These texts are then analysed using the linguistic NooJ engine. In addition to using our linguistic resources such as electronic dictionaries with large coverage and local grammars, we use some other filtering dictionaries to resolve the most frequent ambiguous cases. To evaluate our NER local grammars, we analyse our corpus to manually extract all named entities. Then, we compare the results of our system with those obtained by manual extraction. The application of our local grammar gives the following result:

Precision	Recall	F-Measure
0.901	0.8729	0.88

Table 4 – EVENT grammar experiments on our corpus

According to these results, we have obtained an acceptable identification of economic event. Our evaluation shows an F-measure of 0.88. We note that the rate of silence in the corpus is low, as represented by the recall value 0.8729, because the journalistic texts of our corpus are heterogeneous and extracted from different sources.

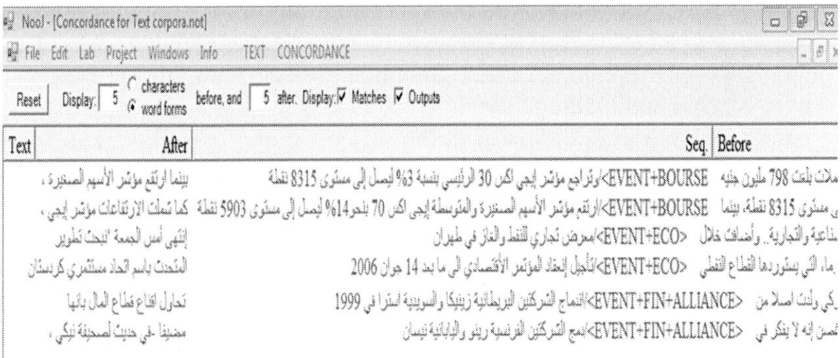

Figure 6 – Result of EVENT NooJ syntactic grammar

- Decline of 3% in main EGX 30 Index to reach the level of 8,315.
- تراجع مؤشر إيجي إكس 30 الرئيسي بنسبة 3% ليصل إلى مستوي 8315. - High, small and medium-sized stock index EGX 70 of approx 14% to reach the level of 5,903 points.
-ارتفاع مؤشر الأسهم الصغيرة و المتوسطة إيجي إكس 70 بنحو 14% ليصل إلى مستوى 5903.
-Oil and gas trade fair in Tehran.
- معرض تجاري للنفط والغاز في طهران .
-Delay of the Economic Conference until after 14 June 2016.
-تأجيل انعقاد المؤتمر الاقتصادي ما بعد 14 جوان2006 إلي .

-The merger of the two companies British Zeneca and Swedish Astra in 1999.

-اندماج الشركتين البريطانية زينيكا والسويدية استرا في1999 .

-The merger of the two companies French Renault and Japanese Nissan.

-دمج الشركتين الفرنسية رينو و اليابانية نيسان .

Conclusion and Future Work

In this article, we present an approach to automatic document classification and the extraction of economic and financial events. Automatic document classification uses a hybrid approach based on a linguistic analysis and statistical scores. This classification allows us to limit the application of event extraction to pertinent documents only. The preliminary experiments reveal encouraging results that could be integrated into a more general monitoring system. The proposed system could be enhanced by carrying out more tests on larger and more ambiguous texts, enhancing terminological dictionaries to cover more domains and also building generic event extraction grammars to deal with all domains, not only economic and financial ones.

References

Hogenboom, Alexander, Frederik Hogenboom, Flavius Frasincar, Kim Schouten, and Otto van der Meer. 2012. *Semantics-based information extraction for detecting economic events.* Open access at SpringerLink.com 2012.

Boujelben, Ines, Slim Mesfar, and Abdelmajid Ben Hamadou. 2010. Lexicalization of Arabic named entities: a methodological approach. *Finite-State Language Engineering with NooJ : Selected Papers from the NooJ 2009 International Conference* (Tozeur, Tunisia). Edited by Abdelmajid Ben Hamadou, Slim Mesfar and Max Silberztein. Centre de publication Universitaire : Sfax., Tunisia

Elkourdi, Mohamed, Amine Bensaid, and Tajje-eddine Rachidi. 2004. Automatic Arabic Document Categorization Based on the Naïve Bayes Algorithm. In *Proc. of COLING 20th Workshop on Computational Approaches to Arabic Script-based Languages*, Geneva, 2004.

Khreisat, Laila .2006. *Arabic text classification using N-Gram frequency statistics a comparative study.*DMIN2006, pp.78-82.

Ludovic, Jean-Louis, Romaric Besançon, and Olivier Ferret. 2013 *Une méthode d'extraction d'information fondée sur les graphes pour le remplissage de formulaires*, Laboratoire Vision et Ingénierie des Contenus F-91191 Gif-sur-Yvette, France.

Mesfar, S. 2008. *Analyse morpho-syntaxique et reconnaissance des entités nommées en arabe standard.* Thèse,Université de Franche-Comté, France.

Meslah, A.A, 2008.*Support Vector Machine Text Classifier for Arabic Arctices: Ant Colony Optimization based feature subset selection*, June 2008.

Najar Dhekra, Mesfar Slim, 2014. Political Monitoring and Opinion Mining for Standard Arabic Texts. *Formalising Natural Languages with NooJ 2013: Selected Papers from the NooJ 2013 International Conference (Saarbrucken, Germany)*. Edited by Svetla Koeva, Slim Mesfar and Max Silberztein. Cambridge Scholars Publishing, Newcastle, UK.

Sawaf H., Zaplo J. and Ney H. 2001. *Statistical classification methods for Arabic news articles.*, Natural Language Processing in ACL2001, Toulouse, France.

Syiam M., Fayed Z., Habib M. 2006, An Intelligent System for Arabic Text Categorization, In *IJICIS*, 6(1), pp. 1-19, 2006.

Sanan.M. and Rammal.M. and Khaldoun.Z.2008. Arabic documents classification using N-gram. Interactive Technology and Smart Education.

Silberztein, Max. 2003. *NooJ manual.* available at the WEB site http://www.nooj4nlp.net

Silberztein .M. 2015. *La formalisation des langues: l'approche NooJ.* ISTE edition Janvier 2015.

CONTRIBUTORS (IN ALPHABETICAL ORDER)

Mourad Aouini,
Université Paris 1 – France
aouini.mourad@gmail.com

Božo Bekavac
Faculty of Humanities and Social Sciences – Croatia
bbekavac@ffzg.hr

Hayet Ben Ali
Monastir University – Tunisia
hayetbenali344@yahoo.com

Abdelmajid Ben Hamadou
MIRACL – Tunisia
abdelmajid.benhamadou@isimsf.rnu.tn

Essia Bessaies
University of Carthage – Tunisia
essiabessaies@gmail.com

Julia Borodina
National Academy of Sciences of Belarus – Belarus
julia.baradzina@gmail.com

Elina Chatjipapa
Democritus University of Thrace – Greece
elinaxp@hotmail.com

Hajer Cheikhrouhou
University of Sfax – Tunisia
cheihkrouhou.hager@gmail.com

Valerie Collec-Clerc
Laboratoire informatique fondamentale Marseille – France
valerie.clerccollec@yahoo.fr

Maria Pia di Buono
University of Salerno – Italy
mdibuono@unisa.it

Maximiliano Duran
University of Franche-Comte – France
duran_maximiliano@yahoo.fr

Annibale Elia
University of Salerno – Italy
elia@unisa.it

Hela Fehri
MIRACL – Tunisia
hela.fehri@yahoo.fr

Julia Frigière
Universitat Autònoma de Barcelona – Spain
frigierejulia@yahoo.fr

Sandrine Fuentes
Universitat Autònoma de Barcelona – Spain
sandrine.fuentes@uab.cat

Zoe Gavriilidou
Democritus University of Thrace – Greece
zoegab@otenet.gr

Yuras Hetsevich
National Academy of Sciences of Belarus – Belarus
yury.hetsevich@gmail.com

Kristina Kocijan
University of Zagreb – Croatia
krkocijan@ffzg.hr

Alberto Maria Langella
University of Salerno – Italy
albertomarialangella@yahoo.it

Boris Lobanov
National Academy of Sciences of Belarus – Belarus
lobanov@newman.bas-net.by

Alessandro Maisto
University of Salerno – Italy
maisto.ale@gmail.com

Slim Mesfar
University of Manouba – Tunisia
mesfarslim@yahoo.fr

Simona Messina
University of Salerno – Italy
smessina@unisa.it

Mario Monteleone
University of Salerno – Italy
mmonteleone@unisa.it

Johanna Monti
University of Sassari – Italy
jmonti@uniss.it

Tatsiana Okrut
National Academy of Sciences of Belarus – Belarus
tatberrie@gmail.com

Lena Papadopoulou
Hellenic Open University – Greece
papadopoulou.lena@gmail.com

Serena Pelosi
University of Salerno – Italy
serenapelosi@gmail.com

Marko Požega
University of Zagreb – Croatia
mpozega1@ffzg.hr

Azeddine Rhazi
INPMA-USMBA-FES – Morocco
azeddin.rhazi@usmba.ac.ma

Max Silberztein
University of Franche-Comte – France
max.silberztein@univ-fcomte.fr

Alena Skopinava
National Academy of Sciences of Belarus – Belarus
skelena777@gmail.com

Matea Srebacic
University of Zagreb – Croatia
matea.srebacic@gmail.com

Marko Tadić
Faculty of Humanities and Social Sciences – Croatia
mtadic@ffzg.hr

Yauheniya Yakubovich
Universitat Autònoma de Barcelona – Spain
Yauheniya.Yakubovich@uab.cat

Krešimir Šojat
Faculty of Humanities and Social Sciences, Zagreb – Croatia
ksojat@ffzg.hr